D1500096

Books by Jess Stearn

THE SEEKERS

THE SEARCH FOR THE GIRL WITH THE BLUE EYES

EDGAR CAYCE—THE SLEEPING PROPHET

YOGA, YOUTH, AND REINCARNATION

THE GRAPEVINE

THE DOOR TO THE FUTURE

THE SIXTH MAN

THE WASTED YEARS

SISTERS OF THE NIGHT

The Seekers

JESS STEARN

The Seekers

DOUBLEDAY & COMPANY, INC.
GARDEN CITY, NEW YORK
1969

VILLA JULIE COLLEGE LIBRARY
STEVENSON, MARYLAND 21153

HV
5825
S7

LIBRARY OF CONGRESS CATALOG CARD NUMBER 69–10942
COPYRIGHT © 1968, 1969 BY JESS STEARN
ALL RIGHTS RESERVED
PRINTED IN THE UNITED STATES OF AMERICA
FIRST EDITION

30710

For Melodie:

Without whom this book would
never have been the same

CONTENTS

The Seekers

1

MARIJUANA—FAMILY STYLE

"Students who use marijuana often believe they are thereby increasing their sensitivity. Actually, the drug tends to distort their perception, carrying them further and further from the truth they seek through its use."

—Professor Donald J. Wolk
University of Bridgeport

Florrie was smiling over her typewriter. She was obviously enjoying her own thoughts.

"You should have seen his face when he got his Father's Day present," she said cheerfully.

"And what did you give your father?"

"Grass," said my pretty young secretary, dangling her slim, shapely legs.

"Grass?" I was frankly puzzled.

"Exactly," she said, "three tightly rolled cigarettes, in zigzag paper."

I suddenly felt uncomfortable. "Why would you do that?"

She swung her legs around. "It's time he knew what his kids were up to."

"That's a great Father's Day present," I said, shrinking a little inside.

"I'm just trying to shake him up a little," she acknowledged. "He's a good dad, but he's not with it."

"Why pick Father's Day for your little bomb?" I asked.

"Rather symbolic, don't you think? If I were in his position I'd want to know what all this new strange atmosphere around my kids was all about." She frowned. "Even all the kidding about marijuana hasn't evoked any inquiry on his part."

"Maybe he didn't want to know."

She smiled. "Exactly, and that's why I gave him the bomb."

I looked at her curiously. She was a highly attractive girl, a graduate of good schools abroad, and a good art school at home, and here she was at twenty-three, obviously intelligent, obviously well-schooled, doing routine stenography, when she was so eminently qualified for creative work.

"I don't see what grass has done for you," I said.

She flipped her shoulders carelessly. "We weren't talking about me."

"It's all interwoven."

"Perhaps," she agreed. "But people like my father just won't face up that their kids are different than they are, and so they bury their heads in the . . ."

"Grass," I finished up.

"Sand." She frowned again. "I don't want him downing grass, or anything else, without trying it himself."

She regarded me slyly.

"Have you?"

I shook my head. "If nothing else," I said, "it's a felony."

"How can you write about something you haven't tried?"

I thought the answer perfectly obvious. "I am writing about people like you, not me."

"But how do you know how it affects people?" she persisted.

"I still would only know how it affected me."

She was stumped only a moment.

"I resent people telling me something is bad, when they don't know about it themselves."

"If it's good for you," I said, "detached reporting should bring that out."

"Look at the articles on drugs these days. Everyone gets it pushed down their throats constantly. Drugs are even subversive. Everything else stinks in this system, but drugs are subversive. What a joke."

"And heroin?"

She grimaced. "Grass is not dope, it's a psychedelic drug. Actually, grass has a bad reputation, only because of association, not cause and effect."

And so she had wanted to open her father's eyes to the fact that all was not subversive that seemed so. She had planned the gift for a month, using her skills as an artist to hand paint a box which would suitably contain her offering. She worked over it zealously. It was painted inside and out, bright colors, Aztec designs. The interior was of royal blue with black incense cones glued to a bottom scattered with orange dots. The top of the box was psychedelically busy, painted many colors with *Happy Day* scrawled in white, a bottle cap pasted upside down serving as a handle. It was all very elaborate, a small flap opening into a smaller box, holding the three precious cigarettes.

She felt she had prepared him for his gift. "I often would say to my father jokingly, as he was going to the country club, 'If your friends were hippier, I'd give you a little grass.'" He had reacted with a wan smile.

"Other times with my brothers sitting around, I would mention that one of them [the straight arrow] looked rather sick to which the other would reply, 'No wonder you should see the tracks [needle marks] on his arms.' Everyone would laugh, my father a bit hollowly, though none of us, of course, had ever used a needle or any kind of drug like heroin."

The presentation itself was neat, groovy, hip. It could not have been more effective, she thought. He was an architect and he had been busy working at home that weekend, completing the plans for a vast new shopping center. He had a large household to support, four children to educate, and numerous other responsibilities. But it was Father's Day, and he cut himself off early to relax with his family. That was Florrie's moment. Sitting on the living-room couch, she reached back to the table behind and brought forth two boxes, the oblong container with the three cigarettes, and a long, thin red box, with incense. He was pleasantly surprised, and made quite a ceremony of it.

"Well, what do we have here? An artsy-craftsy what? Oh, this opens up. And what is this, these flowers?"

"There is something underneath," she smiled in anticipation.

"Cigarettes? But you know I don't smoke. Now what's inside this?" Her eyes danced, as he took the lid off the second box. "Now what are these?"

"The black pyramids are incense cones to burn when you smoke the cigarettes, they mask the odor."

He was impressed by the artistry of the box. "The whole thing looks like the magnification of the inside of a poppy. Quite ominous but beautiful." He kissed her lightly.

He turned back to the contents. "Now, what are these cigarettes?"

She regarded him with secret amusement. "It's grass."

He was still baffled.

"Marijuana, pot, Mary Jane, reefer, gange. The incense is for your privacy."

He held it uncertainly.

"If you don't want it, just throw it away. It's my gift to you, Daddy dear."

His face was a mask, but his voice kind and fatherly as he said, "Is this what you have been learning at all these schools?"

She smiled warmly, for she really "dug"—loved—her groovy, youthful dad, with his barely graying temples and lean handsome features. "I learned seven years ago," she said, "and thought maybe you'd want to."

He put the cigarettes in his pocket, and lit one of the incense cones. Nothing more was said about grass.

As I listened to Florrie, my sympathy went out to her father. "Do you think he'll try it?" I asked perfunctorily.

She shrugged. "Who knows? But it'll give him something to think about."

I wondered whether she had done much of the proselyting so characteristic of habitual users of marijuana and LSD.

"Only when they ask for it, or happen to be around. Why waste the stuff on ingrates?" Her brow knit reflectively. "Seven years ago, I was hanging around with a lot of artists who smoked all the time. They never did anything else, although they were artists supposedly. And so when you were with them, it was considered rude not to smoke." At first, she had been rather indifferent. "I had a preconceived idea that grass was the whole reason they never did anything, never worked, or cared about their appearance."

"And you were wrong?"

She gave me a tolerant glance. "You see, you're prejudging, too."

She had been only sixteen, and afraid of sex, which seemed rather logical at that tender age. "When I turned on, my fears left me." And so did her virginity.

As she kept turning on, she could see that her integrity lay not in such abstracts as chastity, but in savoring life to the fullest, in tasting, experimenting, accepting, rejecting. That was it, the name of the game. The sex interlude ended, with her partner moving on to where the grass was presumably greener. She felt terribly hurt and rejected, but she lit up and relaxed. It did wonders for her. But her memories were so painful she couldn't remain where they were constantly invoked. She moved on, and became involved with another artist community, convincing her family this was the best way of developing her artistry. Again, little got done, outside of pot. "I really started getting into grass. It was a social custom, almost a daily ritual with this group, and this time I didn't have a virginal approach to anything new." She laughed reminiscently. "Every day high, twenty-four hours a day. Painting all the time. It was great."

She went to one school after another, taking her habit with her. But her output, in sober reflection, was never quite as good as she had thought. Eventually, she became more the party smoker, smoking only three or four times a week. "I found I just couldn't work as well. I was no De Quincey or Baudelaire."

But where she had once attributed lack of productivity to immersion with pot, she now blamed her own laziness. Yet, she had not always been lazy.

She tried painting for a while in Paris, then came home and took a job as a commercial artist, telling herself she would paint seriously on the side. But there were so many other things to do, even her nine-to-five job got in the way.

She enjoyed being with people who enjoyed pot. They liked to talk about the things she liked talking about—life, sex, philosophy, religion. It was the easy unreality of the campus all over again.

There were good trips and bad trips, but she took them all in stride.

I mentioned the prevailing feeling among so many intellectuals that marijuana was harmless.

She made a face. "How do they know what they're smoking? If you're looking for an experience, you take your chances. But one thing balances off another." She frowned. "But anybody who turns anybody on is taking a lot on themselves."

I smiled. "How about your father?"

She grinned. "I was just trying to let him know there was another world. But Dad would never get it on. He's too cool."

But hadn't she felt everybody should try it?

"Oh, sure, but I don't want to feel responsible." She became smilingly reminiscent. "Poor Dick, I can see him now. He was studying to be a psychiatrist, and so naturally he had to get with it. You know, the whole mind-expanding bit."

Dick had dropped by while she was getting ready to roll a cigarette. She didn't stop. Casually, she pressed the grass she had gone down to a cellar hiding place to get and having poured it on to the zigzag paper, began to roll the paper as tightly as possible. She was amused by Dick's wide-eyed interest. "You really should smoke some of this experimentally," she said, "since you're to be a psychiatrist one day, right?"

Dick pondered her remark. "You know, Florrie, it may be time that I found out what you and a lot of others have been doing right along."

He frowned indecisively. "Will I be able to drive home?"

Florrie's roommate, Suzie, regarded him scornfully. "Of course, you'll be able to drive home. What are you, a baby?"

His eyes had brightened with excitement. "But how about tomorrow, will I be all right tomorrow?"

Florrie dabbed the rolled cigarette with her tongue. "Suit yourself," she said with a shrug, turning away.

"Come on, Florrie, I have to visit with my parents tomorrow, and I wouldn't want them to know. Will they be able to tell?"

"Not unless they're detectives," Suzie said scornfully.

Dick kept his eyes on Florrie. "Is there any chance of hurting myself? I've heard of that happening."

Florrie assumed a motherly tone. "Don't worry," she said. "It's relatively harmless." She handed him a cigarette. "Now, don't smoke this like a regular cigarette. Take the smoke all the way down into your lungs and keep it there as long as you can. It might hurt your throat at first, but you'll get used to that."

He was nervous but curious. "Okay, Florrie," he said, "but what happens if I flip out?"

Suzie chortled disdainfully.

"I guess it's all right," he reasoned doubtfully, "since I am doing this basically as a scientific experiment."

He had finally rationalized his own curiosity. He took the cigarette and gingerly placed it between his lips.

Florrie immediately lit a match.

"Now remember, right down to your lungs. Don't let the smoke linger in your mouth as you do with tobacco."

The first draw was too much for him and he coughed spasmodically.

"Easy does it," Florrie said, "there's no hurry."

Both she and Suzie took long, educated drags, as Dick watched intently. Dick joined in and all three finished their cigarettes without further conversation. Then Dick, with some disappointment, announced, "I don't feel a thing, Florrie; it's not affecting me at all."

Watching his eyes closely, they smiled knowingly; his pupils were glassy looking, his face pale, and his tongue thick.

"I don't feel a thing," he repeated heavily, and then slowly, he dropped to the floor, and with a sigh, stretched out on his back.

For two hours he lay there, alternately sighing and giggling, constantly repeating, "I'm not stoned, just tired."

The girls paid little attention to him, going on with their own smoking and chatter.

They hardly noticed as he suddenly got up and made for the bathroom. He proceeded to have the "dry heaves," nothing much coming up. In a few minutes he returned to the living room and slumped in a chair, closing his eyes. Abruptly, he stood up again, a frightened look on his face, "The top of my head is raising." He turned to Florrie, with a look of entreaty. "It is raising, Florrie, it really is." He clenched his hands to his head. "What the hell, it's coming off."

The girls were smiling.

"I don't like this feeling, Florrie," he said. "Is it going to stay?" He regarded her suspiciously. "Florrie, are you pulling on my head? I feel the top of it going."

Neither girl was alarmed. Suzie was suggestively darting her tongue in and out, crossing and uncrossing her bare legs.

Dick's eyes traveled the room as if he had never seen it

before, and stopped on Suzie. She gave him a melting glance, but he was too involved with his own reactions to react to her. He suddenly became weary, and slipped off a chair, again rolling over on his back. He was still preoccupied with his hallucinations.

"Someone is lifting me by my feet and by the top of my head." He rose on an elbow, and looked at Florrie accusingly. "Are you doing this to me?" His voice became a shrill, frightened scream. "Why doesn't everybody leave me alone? It's your fault, Florrie, my feet are lifting and I can't stop them. You're doing it."

Suzie, hopelessly stoned, stuck out her tongue again.

Dick's face twisted in panic. "Suzie," he cried, "don't look at me like that." He turned to Florrie with a mute appeal in his eyes. "Come, Florrie," he said, "let's go into your bedroom and lie down."

High herself, she regarded him playfully. "No, Dick," she teased, "you're unsafe at this point."

He shook his head in fresh bewilderment. "Florrie, stop pulling me, please."

Suzie laughed boisterously. "He's really hallucinating now. She isn't even touching you."

Dick's mood suddenly changed. "You know," he said musingly, "I did very badly in school, I mean in this one course on psychiatry, because my teacher had a grudge against me." His voice was now a whisper for Florrie's ear alone.

But she wasn't listening. She got up and went into the bathroom. She was gone quite a while, or so it seemed to the anxious Dick, before finally sauntering out in sheer bell-bottom pajamas. Walking over to Dick, who was still on his back, she dabbed some perfume on his nose, saying, "Smell this."

Dick's hand apprehensively went to his nose. "What's this?" he cried. "What did you put on my nose? What the hell is on my nose?" His voice spiraled ever higher. "You're burning my nose away, Florrie. My nose, it's burning." He reached out an imploring hand, "Take it off, please, get some water and take it off. I've got to get this stuff off my nose."

Florrie promptly got a bucket of cold water and poured it over Dick's head, laughing as it ran down his face.

Dick gave a sigh of relief. "Thank God," he said, clicking his fingers as if he were a camera. "Florrie," he said, "let me take a picture of you taking those pajamas off. You really saved me, you know. It was burning my nose, and I couldn't stand it."

His thoughts were obviously disconnected, though there was an undertone of prurience she had never noted before.

"Nothing was hurting your nose," she said flatly.

He was not listening, preoccupied with clicking his fingers at an opening in the fold of her pajamas.

The girls laughed uproariously. "To think, he was such a prude," Suzie giggled.

The room seemed to be getting unbearably warm. A ride in the fresh air was suggested, and Dick heartily approved, as he had soon tired of taking his pictures.

They climbed into Florrie's sports car, quickly revved up to top speed. As they screechingly took a bend, Dick decided he was a high-flier from Texas. "This is a mighty nice airplane you've got here, Florrie baby," he said with a simulated drawl. "Don't put on the brakes so hard, you all."

Finally, the car stopped at a friend of Florrie's, an artist named Jane. They proceeded into the living room where there were paintings all over the walls. Dick sidled over to a large painting above the fireplace, assuming the solemn posture of an art expert. "Now, Florrie," he said authoritatively, "look at all the things in this painting. Look at the red line over there, it's moving, it's a spider." His eyes suddenly boggled in disbelief. "No, by God, it's a crotch, a girl's."

Enraged, he turned on Jane, accusing her of having done a dirty painting, grabbing at her lewdly at the same time. She pushed him aside, and he jammed against the wall, pounding it furiously with his fists.

"God, Florrie," he cried, "I can see things moving into that red crotch. It's awful, just awful."

Florrie patted his head gently. "Down boy," she said. "Everything will be all right in the morning."

His eyes were glazed. "Do you know that Jane's blouse is open, and her breasts are showing? She's dirty."

Florrie giggled. "So what, haven't you ever seen anything like that before?"

Dick's mood again swiftly changed. "Let's go out and fly the airplane," he shouted. "Let me drive, all right?"

Florrie decided she would pilot her own plane, and Dick went off in a dudgeon, running like mad down the street. She did not see him for a couple of days, and he was properly chastened by this time. "I don't think I'll ever take it again," he said ruefully, "I had a bad trip."

She shrugged. "That's because you were afraid."

"Are you sure that was it?" His face expressed doubt.

"Sure, I'm sure, look at me, I'm stoned and you don't even know it." She was busy making a collage, and it was upside down. She quickly righted it. "You see," she said, "I know what I'm doing."

Even as she talked, I found it amazing that Florrie had not profited from her experience to the extent, at least, of suspecting that her preoccupation with "grass" might be holding her back.

"Only the other day," she argued in rebuttal, "I was listening to some professor say they should legalize marijuana since it was harmless, and the law was unfairly making criminals out of a lot of good, clean-cut college kids."

In its incongruity, I was reminded of the police enjoinder to motorists: "Don't leave the keys in your car; don't turn a good boy bad."

Obviously, marijuana was everywhere. A coed at Stanford University, whose face frequently adorned the San Francisco

social pages, told me that every student she knew on campus
had tried it. In some high schools, as far apart as Westchester
County, New York, and Los Angeles, California, the marijuana
habit was a membership requirement in the most elite undergraduate circles. Even the U. S. Naval Academy at Annapolis
was no longer sacrosanct, and many, characteristically, were
more critical of the midshipmen who turned in the offending
potheads than of the potheads themselves. Christina Kirk, a
prize-winning reporter for the New York *Daily News,* estimated
that twenty million Americans, risking arrest and ruin, had
smoked marijuana. The undergraduate newspaper at Yale jubi-
lantly called on young Elis to bring out the best "grass" for
their dates at Wellesley and Smith, pointing out on their own
dubious authority that marijuana was harmless.

In Naugatuck, Connecticut, a truly middle-class community,
police raided a birthday party for a seventeen-year-old high
school girl and found that a hundred well-scrubbed boys and
girls from "good families" had filled the house with clouds of
marijuana smoke. A contingent of reefered upper-crust youngsters from the Hun School, a preparatory school for Princeton,
were expelled from an institution where even tobacco and beer
were prohibited, and it was revealed that half the student body
felt marijuana should be properly legalized.

With marijuana as the catalyst, the recreational habits of
young America appeared to be changing. "Kids don't meet in
bars anymore because they don't drink, and besides it's too
expensive," pronounced the underground paper, *The East Village Other.* "They meet in someone's house and smoke pot and
talk or take their own trip. Ten people can chip in a buck
apiece and buy a bag of twenty sticks and that's enough for a
party." Like Florrie and her friends, the editor had no use for
alcohol, which dulled the senses, even as "pot heightens awareness and makes you available to do what you want."

Pot has become almost a staple in Vietnam. John Steinbeck
the Fourth, twenty-one-year-old GI son of the rebel chronicler

of another generation, reported that three-fourths of the fighting men in Vietnam were on "grass." Rather appropriately, he was arrested on marijuana charges after a tour in the war theater. A returning veteran reported that seven out of ten in his company smoked it, trading menthol-cooled Salem cigarettes, purchased for eleven cents at the Army PX, for the best quality grass. "If you sat in a rice paddy till your feet turned blue, you'd smoke grass too," he explained wryly.

To some, the penalties for marijuana seemed disproportionately high. To others, it was significant that, despite stringent penalties, smokers were sufficiently smitten by the habit to abandon normal prudence for something they rabidly defended as innocuous. By federal statute, enacted in 1937, punishment for use or possession carried a mandatory two to ten years in prison for the first offense, five to twenty years for the second, and ten to forty subsequently. The crime seemed hardly worth the punishment, and yet in a climate of permissiveness, millions dared it openly; talking about it, writing about it, keeping it at home, in a remarkable display of outstanding courage or bad judgment.

For a drug rated harmless by its advocates, marijuana strangely affected the human system.

"When smoked," reported Dr. Dana Farnsworth, chief of student medical services at pot-happy Harvard, "its effects are noted in a few minutes and usually last three to five hours. The drug causes a combination of excitation and depression. There may be an increase in the pulse rate, a slight rise in blood pressure and small increases in blood sugar and appetite for sweets.

"Psychologically, it produces a dreamy state of altered consciousness; ideas are rapid, disconnected and uncontrollable. There are often feelings of extreme well-being, exaltation, and excitement—that is, being high. At other times there is a 'down' with moodiness, fear of death and panic. Ideas may occur in disrupted sequences. Seconds may seem like minutes, minutes may seem like hours. Distance and sound may be magnified. Space may seem expanded, the head may feel swollen and extremities heavy."

Unlike those on alcohol, marijuana users seemed loath to acknowledge the mind-altering processes of the drug and insisted dangerously at times on doing business as usual. "A very dangerous effect produced by marijuana is the slowing of reflexes," Farnsworth observed. "Since the drug also causes a distortion of reality, particularly on the sense of time, serious automobile accidents may occur. Recently, one person barely missed running into the abutment of an overpass, while another destroyed her car (and nearly killed herself) by crashing into a vehicle ahead of her."

Without regard for marijuana's "harmlessness," Farnsworth cited a few characteristic results of marijuana usage by unstable personalities:

"A twenty-one-year-old woman was involved in a conflict with her mother regarding choice of serious dating partners, following which she renounced her religion, drank to excess and became promiscuous. When she became fearful of the effects of drinking, she began smoking marijuana regularly. She then became depressed. To combat her depression, she used more and more marijuana, and on one occasion, after smoking an unusual amount, slashed her wrists and was admitted to a hospital. Under psychotherapy, she improved, stopped using drugs and resumed effective academic work."

Suicide attempts were not unusual:

"A nineteen-year-old man with high moral standards became depressed, used marijuana to combat an acute depressive episode, experienced 'black despair,' and then obtained sedative pills from a friend which he took in an attempt at suicide. After admission to a hospital and subsequent treatment for his depression, he improved and has resumed his studies."

"A twenty-year-old woman with a long history of emotional conflict became socially irresponsible, intermittently depressed and occasionally overactive and irritable. She tried marijuana to combat her symptoms but found that it was not giving her the 'kick' she had sought. On the advice of friends, she began taking LSD with the hope that it would enable her to gain insight and become more aware of herself. Her potentially disastrous behavior continues and psychotherapy is refused."

It was not unusual for pot smokers to swing from one drug to another: "A nineteen-year-old man with dirty clothes, unkempt hair and beard, in conflict with his parents, hopeless about society, has been taking benzedrine, dexedrine, marijuana, and LSD 'to find out about himself.' He views those who encourage him to avoid drugs as part of the hostile Establishment who are infringing on his rights. His use of drugs serves as a barrier against development of the kind of satisfying interpersonal relations he desires."

While many smokers had no immediate reaction, marijuana, depending on its strength and quality, also affected the stable:

"A senior premedical student with an excellent academic record, already admitted to a medical school, suddenly began to do failing work in one course. He said his energy had been diverted into trying to stop using marijuana, which he had begun using extensively during his senior year. When faced with the necessity of studying, he found it easier to 'take pot.' Under its influence he was convinced that studying for examinations was not as important as other things. He wanted help, stating explicitly that he considered the use of marijuana harmful because it encouraged him as well as his friends who used it to 'evade reality and pursue illusory goals.' "

For everyone who recognized it as harmful, others held it blameless while acknowledging their own deterioration. "Another student denied that his extensive use of marijuana adversely affected his academic performance, but said that while under its influence he lost both the desire and the ability to study. At the end of the semester his grades dropped precipitously. He refused psychiatric help, saying that although he knew he had an emotional problem, drugs had nothing to do with his academic difficulties."

Far from being the harmless drug that its followers insisted it was, marijuana has been scientifically established as dangerous to body, mind and spirit.

Its intoxicating ingredient [tetrahydrocannabinol—THC], only recently isolated, was the same as that in hashish, and had a similar if less potent impact. "Among the more prominent subjective effects of Cannabis," reported the World Health Organization [WHO] Expert Committee on Addiction-Producing Drugs, in 1965, "were distortion of sensation and perception, especially of space and time, impairment of judgment and memory, hallucinations, illusions and delusions."

That much for the immediate effect on mind.

The body was equally affected. "Among somatic effects, often persistent, were oropharyngitis [inflammation of throat and mouth], chronic bronchitis, and asthma." Other experts reported damage to liver, kidneys, brain, and even to the chromosomes, impairing as LSD may have, the genetic health of future generations. Used over a long period, it made many slovenly, inert, passive to a point where they could neither wash, keep appointments or work productively.

Dr. Constandinos J. Miras, chairman of the department of biological chemistry at the University of Athens School of Medicine, saw little difference between hashish and its sister, marijuana. In his studies of chronic smokers for twenty years, implemented at the University of California at Los Angeles, he revealed that many of his subjects gradually drifted out of society because of their habit. "A degree of responsibility remained in some of them to the extent of finding the minimum money required to cover their living and hashish purchasing expenses." It was doubly dangerous, he asserted, because the first experience generally fascinated the beginner with a feeling of well-being, self-confidence, and the illusion of increased ability. "No other narcotic or alcohol," he stated flatly, "produced the same effect so rapidly."

It was a tricky drug, affecting different people differently, and the same people differently at different times. It even crossed some up sexually, apparently releasing inhibitions at the outset, but then with continued use "this increased sexual activity was altered to complete sexual apathy even at the age of forty."

"Sexual drive was reported increased among beginners," Miras pointed out, "and this was the reason why hashish and marijuana were usually recommended and introduced between sexual mates. However, experiments with animals as well as reports from chronic hashish smokers, revealed a loss of up to eighty percent of this activity occurring after chronic use, leading to a complete insufficiency."

In this country, Dr. Harris Isbell, eminent drug authority and WHO expert, was one of the first, in 1967, to experiment scientifically with THC, and reported drastic personality changes in his subjects. In a report to the Committee on Problems of Drug Dependence of the National Academy of Sciences, he mentioned "psychotomimetic effects" (imitative of insanity), described a musician, addicted to marijuana, who after smoking THC became "catatonic, mute and unresponsive for a period of several hours." During this period, the musician saw himself detached from his own body, "shriveled down to the size of a doll and witnessed his own funeral."

In the great marijuana debate, it seemed as if sanity had deserted many who should have had a special interest in objectively evaluating the drug. In their desire to take the onus off swarms of new upper-class smokers, educators and psychologists arbitrarily presented marijuana as a harmless drug, blandly ignoring mounting evidence that marijuana transcended alcohol, with all its alcoholics, as an unpredictably pernicious influence on contemporary living.

With the same permissiveness that contributed to the unbridled violence of the streets and campuses, the pseudo-intellec-

tuals in their ivory towers pressured for the legalizing of marijuana. They argued that, in its infraction, an unjust law was
now needlessly contributing a fresh breed of "criminal."

Even shown marijuana's hazards, they sneered at such as
Dr. David Gottlieb of the College of Human Development of
Penn State University, who told a council of the American
Medical Association: "The linkage between social and psycho-
logical disorders, drug abuse, and subsequent dangerous behav-
ior is too strong to be denied."

At times, it almost seemed as though there was a plot afoot
to exonerate marijuana. For just as deadly heroin was once
sold over drugstore counters without a prescription and LSD
passed out freely on college campuses, so were proponents of
marijuana now pushing a drug they knew little or nothing about.

"It was only since the recent discovery that LSD caused
genetic damage—this more than twenty years after the synthesis
of the drug," pertinently observed Dr. Julius Rice, narcotics
expert at Kings Park State Hospital, Long Island, "that the
accolades for the drug have ceased . . . How many youths
climbed on the LSD bandwagon and ingested the drug precisely
because they responded to the premature pronouncements of
mentors who jumped the gun?"

There was certainly no lack of authorized warning. In April
1968, the American Medical Association and the National Research Council bluntly described marijuana as a "dangerous
drug," which could cause psychological dependence and lead to
psychosis. Sixteen scientists spent two years reviewing evidence
and claims before making their report. They found that arguments
that alcohol was less harmful than marijuana were scientifically
unwarranted.

Even without being a scientist, it was obvious that the effects
of alcohol, its contents stabilized, were considerably more predictable than a drug whose potency could only be determined
through consumer reaction.

But however strong arguments against marijuana, they had

little impact on youthful users. And the more they used it, the more confident they were of its unmixed blessings. Adults were turning to it, too, some ironically in a valiant attempt to arrive at some understanding of their children. The intellectual pot-smoking fraternity, now comfortable about themselves for perhaps the first time, were its strongest proponents, deriding anybody who questioned its value.

Since marijuana was presumptively the drug of youthful alienation and rebellion, it was difficult for parents to understand its attraction, even in trying it, as their reason for taking it was entirely different.

Columnist Robert Sylvester of the New York *Daily News,* an acute if middle-aged reporter, noted a purely physiological reaction, with no mystical overtones. "The effect of the marijuana apparently varies with each smoker," he observed.

"First, a sensation of well-being and lassitude. No stimulant effect, rather the opposite. After smoking two reefers, I experienced a peculiar but not unpleasant change of perspective and tempo. The floor seemed a long distance away. All movement seemed much more leisurely. An observer said that the conversation of the smokers involved slowed down to a languid tempo which was almost a monotone. Also every attempt at humor sounded much funnier than it would have out in the fresh air.

"The effects of five reefers lasted a full evening and were evident when I went to sleep. Sleep came even more easily than usual and there were no remembered dreams. Even the expected hangover was something of a disappointment. The most noticeable feature of the next day's hangover was an extreme dryness of the throat and a slight aching at the corners of the eyes. The throat discomfort, my doctor explained, was the result of the marijuana drying out the secretions of the glands and membranes. The writer's throat was so dry for two days that the condition amounted to laryngitis."

Sylvester's conclusion: "It is not worthwhile. It has no potentialities for sharpening the thoughts or the imagination. It has nowhere near the lift to be derived from a similar expenditure in whiskey. It's a very silly thing for which to risk arrest and jail."

Still, parents, confronted with pot-smoking teen-agers, were often willing to try almost anything to understand Mary Jane's attractions. The social worker sitting across from me, picking at her lunch, was manifestly the epitome of respectability, and yet she had tried smoking pot with her children.

"I'm not a drug addict," she said with a smile, "just a mother trying to keep up with her teen-agers."

Her smile quickly faded.

"They're all taking something," she explained, "not just in the slums. My pair were in good private schools." She shrugged. "It's all part of the youthful searching today, mind expansion they call it—so they sniff glue, chew benzedrine, smoke marijuana, while their elders don't even know what's going on."

She was no soft-headed, permissive faddist, but a stringent disciplinarian who felt that parents knew more about bringing up children than the children did. But she was divorced, and like so many working mothers, necessarily away from home a lot.

One day she found a battered cardboard container in the living room, a wisp of a cigarette in it. It was not like other cigarettes but crudely rolled, the filling coarse and rough-grained, more green than brown. She held it to her nose. It smelled like burned tea.

The packet had been left by her older daughter, Linda, seventeen. "I think she wanted me to find it," the mother said. "She was apparently beginning to feel she might be getting out of her depth." The younger girl, Maude, fifteen, generally followed her sister.

The mother immediately surmised that she was sniffing marijuana. As a social worker she knew enough not to be surprised by anything.

Many would have criticized her next step, but having worked objectively with teen-agers, she realized that one of the lures of marijuana was its verboten status.

She boldly made ready for Linda.

"I found that little packet on the table," she said casually one evening.

"Yes, Mother," the girl replied evenly.

"It contained marijuana, didn't it?"

"Yes, Mother," the girl said, looking at her matter-of-factly.

"Have you smoked it?" She tried to make her voice as blandly impersonal as possible.

"Why, yes, Mother, all the girls do." She smiled, almost mockingly, "All the nice girls, Mother, all of them."

"Do their mothers know?" the sociologist asked.

The girl shrugged. "I suppose not, Mother. They wouldn't believe it anyway. They're such squares."

"And I suppose I'm a square, too?"

The daughter smiled faintly. "That's up to you, Mother."

"Well, I'll tell you how square I am," she said with a coolness she didn't feel. "I'd like to see what I'm missing. So have some of your friends over tomorrow right after school and we'll have a good old tea party right in the living room."

Linda's jaw dropped. "Mother, you don't mean it?"

"Why not, if it's doing something for you, maybe it'll do something for me. I'm never too old to learn." She looked up. "You won't have any trouble getting the . . . weed?"

Linda shook her head. "No, Mother, the kids sell it around the school."

Only two of Linda's hardier girlfriends turned up. Her younger sister was invited to observe but not partake. Linda, two years older, considered her too young and unsophisticated for pot.

The three girls uncertainly lit up their cigarettes. Mother took an experimental drag. "Show me how," she said. "I want to do it right."

"Inhale down to the diaphragm," one of Linda's friends

volunteered. "It doesn't do any good unless you get it way down."

Try as she might, the social worker couldn't turn on. "I found myself getting giddy," she recalled, "and the room seemed to fade out. I don't know whether it was nervousness or the weed or both, but I was very unhappy with my experience. I had no great illuminating visions and I didn't even relax."

She looked around and saw the girls self-consciously pulling on their cigarettes. They looked guiltily like a bunch of youngsters caught in the act of chewing plug tobacco behind the family barn.

Linda finally flung down her cigarette. "I don't know what's wrong with me," she said. "I guess I'm just not in the mood."

The other girls also viewed their cigarettes with distaste and butted them in the ashtrays. The party was over.

As far as she knew, her daughter never smoked another marijuana cigarette. The thrill seemed to have gone out of it. Nevertheless, she took her out of her school, and moved out of the neighborhood. But every neighborhood was the same. So she decided on the only safe course. "I sent both kids out of the country to school."

As a sociologist, she had a special interest in the over-all problem. Linda had argued that marijuana was neither addictable nor habit-forming. She seemed to know all about medical reports stating that marijuana was no more harmful than alcohol or tobacco, but nothing about reports showing how harmful it was. Youth, actually, didn't want to know.

Obviously, something was happening in the younger generation. In her teen generation, getting high had no reference to drugs. But so many teen-agers now felt alcohol was only for boobs or degenerates.

She kept searching around for reasons and picked up enough to know that her daughters' peers were in general rebellion. But every generation had rebelled against the one before it, hers in the late '30s and '40s; her parents before her were of the

disillusioned Lost Generation so vividly portrayed by Scott Fitz-
gerald and Ernest Hemingway.

But this rebellion of the young was unique. The widespread
use of drugs, she sensed, was indicative of something far deeper
than an apparent craving for thrills or escape—or idle curiosity.
It was symptomatic of the sweeping nature of youth's rejection
of a society it found tasteless and hypocritical. Today's young
rebels were like no other rebels in history. The current protest,
exemplified by drugs, demonstrations and violence, reached into
every social strata, spurning the most sacred institutions of two
thousand years, and rocking the very pillars on which our Western
culture uneasily rested—marriage, country, religion, work, education. The rejection was so complete it embraced dress, style,
speech, even at times cleanliness, on the ground that cleanliness,
traditionally, was next to Godliness, and God was out. It
attacked every form of materialism, ignoring the fact that without the basic products of materialism even the young could not
function. It went with the long hair, blue jeans, an attitude of
remoteness. It was part of the fight at Berkeley—and Florida
State—to use four-letter words, and of the crusade against the
Vietnam War (the Imperialist War). It even brought some into
the psychological fold of Communism because Communism was
theoretically opposed to the self-serving materialism "corrupting"
America.

Only *they* were pure, and *they* remained pure by withdrawing, by holding aloof, by not washing in a sham society that
spent millions on TV and in the newspapers stressing soaps and
suds. The long hair for boys, which made them hardly distinguishable from girls, was not only a bid for naturalness, but
part of an adolescent striving to stay out of the mainstream of
society.

Often, underneath all this bravado, especially among hippies,
was an undercurrent of uneasiness, a fear of testing themselves
in competition. "With long hair," the social worker observed,
"they know nobody will consider them for a job. They can

teeter on the sidelines, telling themselves how superior they are, since they have never really tried—and thus never failed."

With drugs, they told themselves, they were gloriously exploring their minds and souls, venturing into unseen frontiers where their smug elders had never dared, gaining revolutionary insights into themselves and the world about them.

What did they do with these insights?

Some stayed on drugs, and accomplished little or nothing, as the drugs appeared only to perpetuate their alienation from family and society. Others went on from drugs to form militant protest movements sweeping the streets and campuses.

And all too frequently the habituates of drugs threw up their hands and turned their backs, losing themselves in like-minded communities, colonies and sundry centers where they could flounder comfortably in their "idealistic" rejection of a crassly commercial world.

Their thinking so often barely scratched the philosophical surface. With almost regal contempt, for instance, a nineteen-year-old beauty, with a precocious figure and a three-year marijuana habit, announced: "The only accepted value today is money, and people with ideals can't participate in a quagmire of greed and cupidity."

And so why drugs?

"With marijuana and LSD, we see certain truths."

And these truths?

She was currently off marijuana—and aggressive. "We are able to see what our own course should be. I had given up school, but after an LSD experience, I found it necessary to be part of the system, long enough to prepare myself to lead the fight against it one day."

On drugs, they clung to one another in their emptiness—a marijuana experience was nearly always shared, providing the support, the "in" feeling needed to shore up fragile egos.

While the connection of drugs with the youthful rebellion was obvious, it still wasn't clearly delineated.

"I find it difficult," I told the sociologist, "to see cause and effect between immaterialism and drugs, or even between the drugs and the wish not to participate. Couldn't it all be done without drugs?"

She nodded understandingly. "You should meet Dirke," she said, "he's only seventeen, but he knows all about drug motivation. Besides," she smiled, "he's retired, he beat the habit."

Dirke had a commonplace enough background these days. His mother was an alcoholic, his father had deserted when he was an infant. His mother had spoiled him, fostering compensating delusions of grandeur as he was growing up.

Early in high school, Dirke had snipped the maternal apron strings. He had a small independent income, from a grandparent, and he lived alone. He was interested in music and the arts, and he sculpted a bit. He also wrote poetry and painted. Like many afficionados of drugs, he was a dabbler.

He was not terribly impressive at first sight. He was thin-faced, sandy-haired, with narrow shoulders, a concave chest, bony arms, and a thin, reedy voice. He had grudgingly accepted the sociologist's invitation to talk about drugs generally, yielding to unmitigated flattery on her part. "You have such insight into the motivations of people your own age," she had ingratiatingly suggested.

He had not come alone. His companion was a rather stocky, high-complexioned girl of the same age. There were other guests; a business executive of thirty-five or so, and a recent graduate of twenty-three from Berkeley.

Dirke seemed taken aback by the presence of the others, shifting about uneasily before he turned his gaze on me.

I had the obvious preliminary question.

"How did you get on drugs?"

He threw a pained look at the sociologist, as though he had been cruelly betrayed.

"I'd rather not talk about myself," he said sullenly.

"I'm only interested in you personally as it throws some light on the problem generally," I said. "In knowing what motivated you, I may find out what motivated others."

He shook his head. "Not necessarily," he said in an almost inaudible voice. "Everybody has a different hangup."

He studied his fingernails, while his girlfriend watched him with a fondly proprietary air. As he looked up, she nodded encouragingly, and he responded by talking hesitatingly about himself. He had begun at fourteen, a rather mature fourteen as he put it. He was already on his own, doing odd jobs; he cut school whenever he liked, there was no discipline in his life on any front. His introduction to marijuana was quite casual and normal. It had been offered by some older boys. He was flattered by their attention, but as he looked back, he didn't feel this had anything to do with his taking it. "Life seemed so confused and aimless, I thought the marijuana might give me a better glimpse of things around me and myself, like it had for others."

I didn't see how any drug could induce a short cut to enlightenment.

He gave me a pitying glance.

"Have you tried marijuana?"

It was a question I was to hear countless times.

I shook my head.

"Then how can you write about the way it makes people feel?" There was a faint disdain in his voice. "How can you report on something and not experience it?"

"I share the experience of people who've had the experience." I smiled. "I've written about smallpox without ever having it."

He was unimpressed.

"How do you know we're steering you right?" His lips curled into a mirthless smile.

"After a while, the stories follow a certain pattern."

"Maybe they're all putting you on," he said.

It was my turn to smile. "The average drug user, like the

average homosexual, is too intent on justifying himself to distort what he feels."

"Why do you bracket drugs and homosexuality?" There was a challenge in his voice.

Drug users, I had found, were not the most virile types.

"Some researchers have theorized young people take drugs so they can give themselves an excuse for not following a natural sexual inclination."

He snorted. "That's how much they know about it. That may be true of heroin but not pot. Not everybody reacts the same to marijuana. It may remove certain inhibitions and make some sexy as a matter of fact."

"How did it affect you?" I asked, with a secret glance at the girl.

His jaw set stubbornly. "I prefer not to get into anything personal."

"All right," I said, "why did kids start taking it?"

"It had glamour," he said. "Alcohol wasn't hep. That's for squares. It fuzzes you up. But with drugs you see clearly. Drinking, you may think the world's all right, but later you're more depressed than ever. Not with grass, there's no hangover, except for a little listlessness the next day."

"But what did it do for you?" I persisted.

He scowled. "I find it hard to explain to somebody who doesn't know how it works." He closed his eyes a moment, as though savoring a past experience. "My mind became cool, all doubts about myself disappeared. Things that had bothered me, like my feelings about my mother, vanished, and worrisome situations became funny. I became aware of a cool clubbiness sitting around with my friends who were also taking pot. The whole ritual of smoking together made me feel close to them. There was a delicious intimacy in just getting the stuff ready, rolling the joints and then passing along the same cigarette, so as not to waste any of it."

They had "turned on" in an empty loft where the police broke in and marched them all off to jail.

"Didn't it occur to you," I asked at the risk of appearing naïve, "that what you were doing was against the law?"

Before his sallow face had a chance to form a smile, there was a snicker from his girlfriend. "That's what makes it glamorous," she said bleakly, "the extra thrill and kicks." She shrugged. "They were just bored kids with nothing better to do."

He was about to protest, but instead, made an allusion to a young ill-starred actor who seemed to epitomize the restlessness of this generation. "Like Jimmy Dean," he said, "we are rebels without causes. We don't like the world we live in and the adults who fouled it up, but we have nothing positive to offer."

"Where has the world failed you?" I asked.

He laughed harshly, his eyes meeting mine evenly for the first time. "You're kidding, aren't you?"

"It's the same world for both of us," I said.

He shook his head. "You didn't have youth's private war in Vietnam and total destruction staring you in the face." His voice became harshly strident. "We're being asked to die before we've lived by crooked politicians and people not caring how rotten anything is as long as they get theirs."

The sociologist contemplated the boy thoughtfully. "It has always seemed that kind of a world to young, idealistic people, Dirke," she said gently, "but we try to find our own niche and then we do what we can to right the scales."

The business executive also came to life. "You kids want everything on a platter," he snapped. "We had to struggle for everything we got, work through school, work to get a job, and work to keep it. All some of you do is sit around for your unemployment insurance. We've made it too easy for you."

Dirke wasn't the least fazed. "If that's true, that's something else you've done that's bad." He thought a moment. "Look," he said, "I've an uncle who's a big success. He makes a hundred thousand dollars a year, runs a big office, and has a big house in Connecticut. He's got a good-looking wife, three cars, dogs, horses, cats, a swimming pool. And, still he drinks so many martinis after he leaves the job that his wife meets him at the station so he won't crack up the car."

There was a glint of defiance in his dull gray eyes. "Now tell me, where's he so much better than people on marijuana and other drugs?"

"I'd have to know more about him," I said, "just as I would about you."

His voice grated harshly. "They say we can't compete, so we deaden our minds and bodies with drugs to give ourselves excuses for not making it."

"That's one theory," I conceded.

The girl from Berkeley, sitting quietly until now, could hardly contain herself at this point. Her blonde good looks were distorted by rising impatience. "I've taken marijuana dozens of times," she said authoritatively, "it can't harm you. All the groovy kids do it at Berkeley. You're really out if you're not with it. It's cool sitting around in a group, talking about life, and smoking grass. You see things in new perspective."

Dirke frowned, then said quite unexpectedly, "I haven't touched marijuana for six months, I don't think it's good for you."

The girl charged full-tilt into the breach of this surprising defection.

"Why, I'd smoke marijuana right now if I had it," she snapped. "Out West, everybody smokes it." She looked disdainfully at Dirke, whose jaw had set stubbornly. "Not just a bunch of sniveling little boys and girls."

She regarded him almost accusingly. "You must have taken something else besides marijuana," she said. "Why, it's not even habit-forming like tobacco."

"You go to other things," Dirke said stolidly.

"You do if you're weak," she said testily. "I never took anything else, though I'd like to try LSD."

Dirke shrugged indifferently. "You can get LSD anywhere, that's no problem."

She was still eying him coldly. "You must have taken more than marijuana, or you wouldn't make such a big deal out of quitting drugs. You can stop taking marijuana any time, just like candy."

I had followed the exchange curiously. "Were you on anything else?"

Dirke hesitated briefly. "Originally," he said, "I smoked marijuana mixed with arregano. But after a while, the kicks wore off. I just couldn't get a high as quick. So I did what the older kids did, mixed marijuana with tincture of opium. It gave me a dreamier feeling, and all my problems disappeared."

The blonde gave a triumphant cry. "What did I tell you—it had to be more; marijuana never harmed anybody."

Dirke remained unconvinced. "If it gets you on opium, that's harm enough."

It occurred to me that Dirke must have had an expensive habit.

He shook his head. "I never paid for any of the stuff. I had friends with connections."

"But why give it to you when they had to pay?"

He smiled enigmatically. "Oh, they'd get a half-pound of Mexican marijuana for sixty dollars, and sell it in five-dollar bags mixed. And for every five a guy sold, he'd have one left over as commission. So I'd just share a commission bag most of the time."

Opium, more expensive and harder to acquire, was also a gift.

"But what did you do for it?" I persisted.

"I just smoked along with them, that's all."

"They were older boys, you say, and they found you that companionable at fourteen or fifteen?"

"They liked me," he said indifferently.

I thought of that maddening television commercial. "You must have been doing something right," I paraphrased lightly.

He moved his thin shoulders slightly. "I'd rather not discuss anything personal."

With this cozy little circle of homogeneous benefactors, he had smoked opium for nearly a year.

Hadn't it been difficult to quit?

He gave that thin-lipped smile, "I had reasons for quitting." His eyes traveled to the girl sitting fondly near him. "Some purpose finally came into my life."

The girl nodded understandingly. She had made him promise to go clean.

I marveled at the affection this wisp of a boy had evoked in this apparently well-adjusted girl.

"I felt Dirke had a lot to save," she said self-consciously, "and I had to save it."

They were already thinking of marriage, but she was only seventeen herself, and her family wouldn't consider their consent at this time.

"What makes you so sure that Dirke won't go back to drugs?" I asked.

"He won't," she said confidently. "He realizes now how stupid it all was—to destroy himself just because he doesn't like the way the world's run."

The blonde from Berkeley mulled this over. "Marijuana smokers and drug addicts—even drug users—are two different things," she said. "Anybody who uses hard drugs has got to have big personality problems."

Dirke staunchly defended himself. "I never smoked so much opium that I picked up the habit physically, though I may have been psychologically affected. Actually, the stuff was cut so much it would have been hard to become physically addicted."

The blonde was still shaking her head disapprovingly. She

came from an old family, prominent in the California economic and social world and she had a strong sense of what was fitting.

"Don't tell me," she said, "that marijuana leads to other things. Nobody in my group would smoke it if it did." She gave Dirke a baleful glance. "People like you," she said, "give marijuana a bad name."

The sociologist broke in smoothly. "I think he has done fine to come out of it like he has."

The business executive had been eying the blonde curiously. "Do you really believe your commercial for pot?"

"Of course."

"When was the last time you smoked?"

"Not for six months," she said. "The kids do it more secretly on the campuses in the East."

"Not really," he said. "Harvard, Columbia, Cornell, Yale are all quite active." He gave her a friendly smile. "It's not that hard to get."

"I wouldn't begin to know where around here, without getting mixed up with a lot of addicts." She gave poor Dirke a scathing look.

The executive smiled serenely. "Well, I could give you some."

I looked up in surprise.

"Oh, I have a month's supply or so at home that you are more than welcome to—only you'll have to roll your own. It's in leaf form."

The sociologist looked up puzzled. "How do you happen to have a supply?"

He explained airily. "A lot of the boys in the office were smoking it after hours until somebody complained about the smell that hung over the place mornings. So they got a little nervous and turned the cache over to me." He shrugged. "I don't need it myself. This world, bad as it is, suits me. I don't have any difficulty relating to other people—or myself."

He peered over at the blonde. "Well?" he challenged.

She took out pencil and paper. "Give me your address," she

said, "and I'll be over to pick it up. I don't want any good marijuana going to waste." She looked up with a frown. "It is good stuff, isn't it? If it's green, it makes you sick."

On this uncertain note, the party ended. As we stomped out to the street, she was still expressing her disapproval of Dirke. "The next thing you know," she said tartly, "he'll be on heroin. He's not at all interested in expanding his mind."

I regarded her open-mouthed.

"Do you really believe this is why they smoke marijuana?"

"What else?" she rejoined sharply. "And, of course, LSD is even better, as you see even more of the world and yourself with it."

There was no questioning her sincerity. "I've tried both," she said, "and I ought to know."

This was the last I was to see of the Berkeley blonde, though I heard from her by phone shortly thereafter. "I've just taken LSD," she said, "and I can see it all clearly, my relationship with my family, why my marriage didn't work, why I didn't finish school. It's wonderful, wonderful."

She announced she would soon issue a report on her marijuana and LSD experience so I might learn what these remarkable hallucinogenics did for the venturous young.

Two weeks later, the report had not arrived, and I inquired about her. I soon learned she was in a New York hospital, the emergency ward of Bellevue. She had, for some reason, not fully understood, put her head in the oven, slashed her wrists, and taken pills. Fortunately, somebody, smelling the gas, had broken into her apartment in time to drag her out alive. Of course, it couldn't have been the LSD or pot, for at Berkeley, and other institutions of higher learning around the country, they knew these were harmless drugs.

2

THE SEEKERS

The "social scientist," addressing the pundits at the Center for the Study of Democratic Institutions at Santa Barbara, California, was blandly discussing the commitment of new billions to salvage the slum Ghettos of the cities. "We will have to make ever-increasing efforts to reach the deprived, allotting ever more money, time, and energy to compensate for the social injustices of centuries."

He spoke with the assurance of the scholar whose specialty was the abstract, and he was obviously surprised when an interruption came from an unexpected quarter, the chairman of the meeting.

"How do we know," the chairman said, "that the young generation of today, whom you are pledging to this commitment, will regard this as their bag?" There was the least suspicion of a twinkle in his eye.

The social scientist faltered but briefly. "Like previous generations," he said with renewed aplomb, "they are going through
a phase, and they will come out of it as others have, taking
the lead our generation has given them."

One or two others around the big conference table seemed
to share the chairman's doubts. "Why," a visitor asked, "should
they pay any attention to the generation they consider the 'failure generation'?"

It was apparently an entirely new concept for the social
scientist, who could not conceive of a world that did not believe
as his world did, that social science, whatever that was, and
money, more and more money, would not in time solve the
gnawing ills of the poor and the disinherited—in the face of
overwhelming evidence that these panaceas were accomplishing
nothing.

The speaker again wavered only momentarily. "I have talked
to students all over the country, and they recognize these obliga-
tions, as we do."

The visitor's experience had been entirely different.

The distinction was quickly recognized by Bishop James A.
Pike, a working resident at the Center. "We are apparently
talking of three different days," he said, in an analogy of the
roughly three different types of young. These were the hippies
and the alienated on one extreme, the "straight arrows" or tradi-
tionalist "Horatio Algers" on the other, and the great bulk, the
impressionable middle group in the center, drawing on either
faction and contributing as well, in a vast flux of interchanging
ideas and values that might one day form a new, perhaps
radically different society.

The social scientist sat down, unconvinced, as so many contemporaries were, that he had a grandstand seat at a human
revolution that might in his time see the uprooting, modifica-
tion, or demolition of nearly every value and tradition that
spelled out twentieth-century society—church, country, marriage,
education, work.

It was all under attack, the object of not only rebellion but of utter rejection. Its progression was obvious. For the first time in the history of the nation, spurred on by the unpopular Vietnamese war, it was considered patriotic by the protesting young to be unpatriotic. The war protest, beginning with the hippies and the alienated, spread over to the middle group, forming a militant movement engulfing even adults who once had no thought but of serving their country. In this way, the decorated war hero of another generation, actor Sterling Hayden, could comment approvingly when his son dramatically destroyed his draft card in a gesture against war.

In much the same way, couples were cheerfully living together, without the sacred blessing of matrimony, not only unabashed by their parents' disapproval but questioning the very validity of the relationship from which they sprung. "I got so tired of hearing how my parents had kept their marriage together for me," a starry-eyed girl of twenty reported typically, "when I wouldn't have wanted twenty minutes of their marriage for myself."

In withdrawing from conventional society—the Establishment—and in turning to drugs frowned on by that Establishment, the hippie left expressed their total rejection of "cookie cutter" jobs, mass education unmindful of individual values, and a creeping Big Brother statism, which not only benevolently served the individual from cradle to grave, but was also his master, arbitrarily ordering his life, property, and children.

"We elect public servants to serve us," a teen-age adversary of the draft expostulated, "and soon they are telling us how to serve."

With their colorful array, the hippies, the so-called hip, hep, or knowledgeable, had focused the spotlight on their own insular movement, which professed to replace hate with love, materialism with idealism, and the instant enlightenment of mind-expanding drugs—the ballyhooed hallucinogenics—for a dull stodginess that would risk nothing to pierce the frontiers of traditional mentation. They were the pioneers of a movement whose aims were not always clear, whose efforts so often lacked positive direction, and in their restless strivings, they reflected the sweeping change in the nature of the drug user. They had a proud new name for themselves. They were searchers, seekers, and what they were searching for was human experience, even cosmic experience, if they could come by it without undue exertion, by smoking a weed, swallowing a pill, sniffing a powder, or jabbing a needle into the veins.

There were different breeds of addicts or users, just as there were different nonusers. The New Breed, equally at home in the Bohemia of the large cities and the sheltered campuses of the country, disdained the "hard stuff"—heroin, morphine, and other opiate derivatives, but indulged in the mind-expanders—LSD, DMT, mescaline, marijuana and its devil-sister, hashish, arbitrarily lodged in the truth drug class.

They had enough sense to avoid getting physically hooked, though already psychologically addicted to the fantasy world of drugs, without acknowledging it even to themselves. Among this New Breed, there was a disdain for any who didn't have the enterprise or intellectual curiosity to "turn on."

They might not have a job, be failing in classes, or penniless without prospects—yet fancied themselves a superior "type of cat." They could be a success, as the world measured success, but they would then have given in to the enemy—the despised material world which measured success only by material acquisition. They had a standard of their own beyond all this materiality, but were painfully vague and uncertain in limning the outlines of these standards, or their own purpose. They were frequently defiant, bristling at the merest suggestion they shied from the world because they were afraid they couldn't compete on even terms. "Anybody can get a job," they said, not working. "Anybody can graduate from college," they said, dropping out. They were the great iconoclasts of our time, but their criticism was chiefly sneers. They had little constructive to suggest.

So long as they didn't meet the ordinary challenges of workaday life head-on, they could sit back and reflect on their own superior capacities. In Beverly Hills, California, the scion of a wealthy family assured me tartly, "I could have finished college —it just wasn't for me."

He was the head of a record promotion company, which existed only on the letterheads and calling cards he proudly passed out. Meanwhile, he was working as a glorified errand boy for an interior decorator, and smoking up grandiose dreams with pot.

They let their hair grow, because the world they professed to despise equated respectability with neatness and tidiness. They seemed to revel in dirt for the same reason. This cleanliness, that other generations considered a necessity, they considered a superficiality. They laughed at the concept that the body was the temple of the soul, and hence they had no sexual integrity— sexual promiscuity was almost a way of life, leading to not only casual relations between the sexes but to acts of homosexuality rooted in a transcending amorality that found its justification in a meaningless intellectual curiosity.

They were not homosexuals or bisexuals really, but what humorist J. P. McEvoy once called trisexuals; they would try anything—as long as it didn't call for positive study, concentration or work.

Their sneering attitude toward their elders was reflected in the encapsulated air of detached superiority with which they placidly viewed the march of events. For them the massive weight of centuries of learning was a complete zero.

They speciously judged our culture by the annihilating, destructive aspects of the H-bomb—and with wars, such as the war in Vietnam, which others condemned as well as they. Above all, being hedonistic, they lacked faith and most of what they lacked faith in was themselves.

God was only a phrase, and they found it easy to sneer, "If there's a God why does he allow the flower of our youth, innocent women and children to be senselessly destroyed?"

Others were more boldly irreligious. "If there is a God, he is subordinate to the devil."

But while they prided themselves on their intellectual curiosity, they scraped the surface of everything. And what passed for introspection, often seemed a morbid preoccupation with their own shallow sensuousness.

If there was a common denominator in this hippie-oriented group, it lay in a restless striving for an easy way to reconcile the philosophic problems of living which traditionally stimulated man from the time of Aristotle and Plato down through Shakespeare, Galileo, Thomas Aquinas, and Einstein.

In material success, regardless of how it came about, they saw a red flag, a denial of the ever-lasting, never-ending quest for the elusive truth.

"What difference does it make if you worked hard," one devotee of LSD said impatiently, "if you worked at the wrong thing, for the wrong reasons?"

The standard for themselves was not always as stringent. This critic had just been the recipient of nine months of unemployment insurance through the benevolent Welfare State policies of the State of California. He saw nothing peculiarly parasitical about working just long enough to collect these benefits. "It gives me time," he said, "to expand my consciousness with drugs, and the money to buy them with. Hail Caesar."

Still with it all, there was a validity of protest against tottering institutions that no longer seemed adequate in a world moving too fast for its own good. In the honesty of this protest, as it lashed out against social evils leading to war, crime, poverty, divorce, the hippie movement did inevitably influence its own generation and those before and after it.

The feeling of protest was often sharply defined. It was against churches, for instance, but not religion, accounting for the interest of so many Westerners, Protestant, Catholic, Jew, in the Eastern philosophies of Buddhism, Hinduism, Zen, transcendental meditation and, ironically, a primitive Christianity rooted not in sectarianism but in the simple teachings of Christ.

Never in modern society had there been greater mistrust between the generations, with the hippie left generally mistrustful of people and their motivations just because they were older, hence representing a hypocrisy which permeated every activity of that generation.

The gap between the generations was often dramatically revealing. In Hollywood, California, for instance, when a Presbyterian pastor opened his doors to stranded bands of hippies, the first to protest was a horrified Christian congregation, dismayed at the church's inflicting even an echo of drug addiction, sexual misconduct, and slothfulness on their sanctified halls. "You would almost think," a church official observed wryly, "that Christ had not committed His church to sinners."

In this controversial move to serve confused, vagrant youth was clearly outlined the yawning gulf between generations. City Hall warned a Christ-oriented pastor against creating a nuisance, neighboring merchants deplored the creation of a soup kitchen and flop house, attracting young people in garish costumes who often troublesomely begged and squabbled in the streets. One church elder even called for the ouster of the minister who dared to bring his ministry to the scorned "sinner."

The hippies liked to think they were on Christ's side. "Churchgoers," a young novitiate said, "often forget that Christ not only preached Christianity but lived it. They should read and reread the parable of the Prodigal Son. If these be sinners, as so many older people hold, then the church becomes culpable only if it withholds its help. If we must choose between respectability and usefulness, the choice is obvious for a church of Christ."

Although the hippies, and their gaudy getup—long hair, beards, beads, bells, and sandals—monopolized the spotlight, it soon became apparent they were only a spectacular, highly caricaturized, stereotyped manifestation of a human revolution that cut a swath broadly across the oncoming generation, having a vitalizing impact on the impressionable middle group in the high schools and colleges, even stirring the curiosity—and antipathy—of the "straight" right, determinedly cast in the social and psychological image of their forebears.

Nowhere was this influence from the hippie left more apparent than in the spread of drugs, particularly marijuana and the hallucinogenics—LSD, mescaline, psilocybin, DMT, STP. Drugs had become a symbol not only of revolt but of status, with their spread fostered by a dry-rot intellectual materialism, using the prestige of the Establishment to paradoxically stir up a drug-oriented revolt often losing sight of purpose in its absorption with drugs. In colleges around the country, where students had been nabbed by police in marijuana raids, faculty members, abetted by friendly legislators, called for legalization of marijuana or reduction of statutory felony charges to a misdemeanor. The drug was portrayed as no more harmful than tobacco or alcohol by such prestigious personalities as Dr. James Goddard, recent head of the Federal Food and Drug Administration, and Dr. Joel Fort, former director of the Center for Special Problems in San Francisco.

Doctors, Fort charged, have allowed the "moral entrepreneurs" to draft anti-drug legislation without the benefit of objective testimony—this, despite the fact that "crashes" from LSD, "harmless" marijuana and sundry other hallucinogenics were being constantly reported.

Whatever the section, whatever the street milieu, the hallucinogenics, capturing the imagination of the young with their hollow promise of vast new insights, prevailed not only in opposition of the law, but often because of it. Los Angeles, with its fine homes and multiple universities, was typical of the big-city drug spread. "In middle-class Los Angeles," Dr. Duke Fisher, senior psychiatric resident at the University of California at Los Angeles, told a medical symposium, "drugs have become almost a puberty rite—the kids having the idea the only way to become somebody is to use drugs."

As an ironic carryover from the Establishment's own predilection for the medicine chest, the use of marijuana and LSD spread to fad turn-ons: smoking aspirin, injecting Methedrine, or "speed," an amphetamine (component of diet pills), and such bathroom staples as Murine eyewash, Ac'cent flavoring agent, Ban deodorant. Was it any wonder that our youth were already brainwashed when every other medical prescription in this country was for a drug that affected the mind—"downie" barbiturates, "uppie" amphetamines, and untranquilizing tranquilizers? In 1967 alone, some 125,000,000 prescriptions for tranquilizers and sedatives were filled in this country, along with 25,000,000 prescriptions for amphetamines, plus as much again on the sprawling black market.

The use of LSD, glorified by Dr. Timothy Leary and Dr. Richard Alpert, the exponents of an everyman turning on, tuning in, and turning off, had been discouraged by recently reported mental "crashes" and the risk of chromosomal breaks in the genes, disclosed in both laboratory experiments and real life. But this development only served to broaden the interest in amphetamines, at least as hazardous, and ever stronger varieties of marijuana, from the hashish resin of the hemp plant to the more subtle variations of homegrown "grass."

Even as the drug movement spread like wildfire, there was an adult tendency to minimize the incomprehensibles, the extremes, the freaks who could be comfortably dismissed as off-beat. Yet, in the middle group itself, in the high schools and colleges, student after student, not thinking themselves hippie but hip, casually reported that "everybody was on pot." And pressed for a percentage, students of Connecticut, New York, California, Washington State, gave the same percentage in the same offhand way—80 to 90 percent.

Because of its revolutionary symbolism, its often relaxing effects, its mistaken reputation as "harmless," marijuana had won through as the adolescent social drug, at least as popular with its generation as alcohol was with its parents. It spread not only through permissiveness, but through the blindness of school officials who in not acknowledging the problem somehow felt they were escaping responsibility for it. In one West Los Angeles high school, for instance, a principal kept two UCLA drug experts from warning a student assembly of drug hazards on the ground there was no problem. Eventually, the principal was overruled, and the assembly held. Of the thousand students attending, some 80 percent openly admitted using marijuana at least once, 50 percent regularly.

As usual, the parents blamed for everything, were blamed for the spreading wave of drug abuse—by alienated youngsters as well as the experts. "I was looking for unconditional love and couldn't get it at home," a pretty seventeen-year-old runaway observed, "for every benefit, there was a condition."

She rebelled at dating young men from the parental social sphere, of getting good grades because it heightened their estimate of their own intelligence, from, in effect, being extensions of their own tasteless middle-class egos. "I smoked pot," she said, "to get back at them, and smoking pot, I met kids like myself who were too busy doing what I was doing to do anything but love me for it."

Even after the bird had flown many parents looked everywhere but home for the trigger touching off the household revolt. "Ours is not a war against manners or customs, or even institutions per se," a militant hippie told me, "but a stand against the old values, against an almost universal hypocrisy beginning at home and traveling through every aspect of the culture."

As it had for others, it seemed to me an oversimplification to put everything on the parents. In the revolt against the Establishment, they were the nearest Establishment figureheads against which the young rebels could conveniently turn. They stood for an unchanging society, committed to perpetuating itself, and the more successful they were, by their generation's standards, the more intrenched, the more revolt did they inspire.

While today's youth were in some respects like any younger generation, according to Dr. Kenneth Keniston of the department of psychiatry at the Yale School of Medicine, they were also different because they were reacting to unprecedented affluence. They were the most impressionable part of a society, caught up in an electronic revolution, that was changing more rapidly than any other in history in a world capable of destroying itself. "We should not be too surprised therefore," observed Dr. Keniston, "that a portion of the most talented, the most able, the most sensitive and at times the most disturbed members of this generation are seeking new ways of finding meaning, heightening their experience and intensifying their encounter with the world."

Even so, the older generation, hopelessly frustrated by offsprings they couldn't begin to understand, persisted in their mistake of equating their problem children with their own standards and attitudes, thus compounding misconceptions that brought about the generation gap in the first place.

"In our day," an avowed foe of smugness assured me smugly, "the campus rebels of the left were loudest in denouncing the social injustices of the System—the Establishment of those days—and now these very leftists, having made it, are the respectable prototypes of the wealthy ultraprivileged class they were once trying to scatter to the winds. This group will pass through the same phase."

My own delving had led me to an entirely different conclusion: this was not a rebellion or rejection of a preceding generation, as was customary, but a repudiation of nearly everything Western culture had carefully nourished in the name of civilization.

It was obvious to even the most casual observer that drugs, even as they induced a pleasant euphoria, were symptomatic of a flight from normal society. As Dr. Dana Farnsworth of Harvard observed after closely examining the drug phenomena in the human laboratory of his own Cambridge campus, "If drug-taking

were not related to current social conditions and individual's reactions to them, it would be much easier to deal with. But the
issues are complex, and drug-taking means something."

More than others perhaps, as the responsible medical officer
on a campus where the Pied Pipers of LSD had first sounded
the clarion call to turn off, Farnsworth had wrestled with the
reasons behind the rejection expressed in drug use:

"On a personal level, young people tend to suffer intense feelings of isolation and vulnerability . . . the mass-produced is
valued more, the man-made less than ever; government and
colleges are becoming larger and more impersonal, and the individual's sense of being insignificant and helpless is increasing."

As an authority symbol himself, Farnsworth was in an ideal
position to assess the breakdown of authority, from the viewpoint
of the disillusioned young. He was to mention a word I heard
stressed more than any other by the young—hypocrisy. "Social
injustice, the threat of nuclear war, the ineffectiveness of downright hypocrisy of those in authority" had led to an adolescent
confusion culminating in rejection of that which was first and fore-
most at hand—family, school, government in terms of police
and state. "As a result of their confusion they often tend to
reject all authority. Their criticism of society becomes so general-
ized they reject conventional values, refuse to participate in a
system they see as pernicious and focus instead, with drugs as
their instrument, on their own subjective values and experience."

This, then, was the why of turn-on, tune-in, dropout, and marijuana so accessible, so "harmless," appeared to evoke a sense
of greater fellowship with contemporaries and a new stronger
feeling of communication. But more often than not, as Farnsworth pointed out, it was pure illusion. "Drugs temporarily help
young people to escape their feelings of being alienated, under
pressure and helpless . . . and the act of drug-taking places
each individual in a group of kindred spirits. He may feel better
related to others even as objective observation shows him to be
even more isolated than before."

In my own exploration, I had been struck by the fact that hardly anybody took pot alone, as they might tobacco or a drink. There was a ritual of implicit camaraderie, the cigarette passed from lip to lip, until it was practically a butt—a roach—on the pretext of getting the fullest use from each "joint."

Condoned as it were by faint disapproval by prestigious members of the Establishment, it was easy to understand marijuana's spread. Warned that marijuana possession was a felony, imposing drastic penalties, even the millions in youth's conservative middle bloc considered this the "ultimate in adult hypocrisy." Pot, they heard, was less harmful than alcohol, and alcohol was legal. Hadn't Federal Food and Drug Administrator, Dr. James Goddard, stated with all the authority of his recent position: "Whether or not marijuana is a more dangerous drug than alcohol is debatable. I don't happen to think it is."

Those minimizing marijuana's hazards made no distinction between the casual drinker unaffected by his one or two drinks, and the casual pothead, who could, unpredictably, have a bad trip with a casual cigarette that had never had this effect before. And marijuana, regardless of all the propaganda to the contrary, rode piggy-back for something worse. In trying marijuana, many discovered too late they were addictive personalities, and requiring ever stronger stimulation, turned to heroin and the opiates. Admittedly, most marijuana smokers didn't go on to heroin, but most of those on heroin could clearly trace their habit back to pot—and gave it full credit.

As for other side effects, medical authorities dispassionately pointed out that marijuana lodged toxically in the liver, while alcohol, unless excessively taken, broke down into natural compounds and quickly left the system.

Like alcohol, drugs solved nothing, and in this lack lay some hope. Dr. Farnsworth, reassuringly, saw the use of mind-expanding drugs, including marijuana, as self-defeating. "Drug use and its associated forms of behavior have certain built-in limitations. They provide little permanent satisfaction. Short-range satisfac-

tion is derived from peer group approval and publicity. Moreover, the overzealous (and sometimes blatantly wrong) activity
of some law enforcement officials serves as justification or 'proof'
of the rightness of their positions."

When narcotics officials, as did former Narcotics Commissioner
Anslinger, painted marijuana users as depraved dope fiends prey-
ing on society, they lost the confidence of the young who either
tried the weed without becoming fiends or had some very attractive companions on it who appeared anything but fiends. "The
exaggerated concern accorded them by their frustrated and
bewildered critics," Farnsworth pointed out, "may encourage them
to persist with their self-defeating activities longer than they otherwise would prefer. Since most of them seem to have no fixed
income other than what they get from their families, and are not
developing a capacity for responsible employment, they may
ultimately tire of their vagabond existence. There is considerable
evidence that many young people toy with various forms of a
social or antisocial behavior only to return to more responsible
modes of living, often with strong dedication to the righting of
social wrongs."

But before they righted themselves, there was a very real
danger that irresolute youngsters might suffer damage from drugs
in the process of overreacting to values they didn't approve, or
couldn't relate to.

"In their desire to express themselves," Farnsworth said, "the
majority find satisfaction in their studies, their school association,
and the support they get from their families and friends. Others
not so fortunately situated cannot resolve their conflicts (usually
they are not even aware of what the conflicts are) and express
themselves in delinquent acts, or poorly controlled impulse expression, or by showing no sense of social responsibility (or any
combination of these).

"A new and disturbing aspect of hallucinogenic drugs is that
they may permanently impair the judgment of people who experiment with them. These potentially capable young men and women

could thus become permanent casualties of their struggle to give meaning to their existence."

Until some ten years ago, when the human revolution began burgeoning, the drug problem centered in the so-called under-privileged areas, where hard drugs—heroin, morphine, cocaine, codeine—were Dream Street staples. But the new users generally come from the middle and upper classes, prefer pot to heroin, have had some college, and were often caught up intellectually before drug indulgence slowed them to a creative crawl.

In Vietnam, with widespread use reported among the troops, a similar slowdown has been noted. Home-bred apologists for pot notwithstanding, Brigadier General Harley Moore, Jr., artic-ulated concern at the brain-dulling effects of marijuana in combat areas. Several accidental shootings were believed to be the direct consequence of pot parties, as all caution deserted the smokers of the "harmless" weed.

Like opium, marijuana had a long and glamorous history. The Chinese discovered its mind-altering properties five thousand years ago, and the habit fanned out through Asia. The West became exposed during the Crusades, the Crusaders carrying it back with them. A Moslem leader—Hasan—used it to recruit warriors to kill his enemies, and the word assassin was in time bequeathed to Hasan's followers and to the drug itself, hashish, most potent extract of cannibis sativa, the hemp plant.

The drug was not less potent with time. The Greek biochemist, Constandinos Miras, experimenting with chronic users, had re-ported in 1967 that marijuana was another form of hashish, weaker, to be certain, but with a similar propensity for damaging brain, liver, eyes, and the respiratory tract. "There are those," Miras observed, "who have tried to tell me the two are different, but I have seen no evidence of this."

In the Middle East, where it was widely used by the Arabs, marijuana became a top Israeli problem when that country took over conquered areas. "Knowing of its enervating effects on the peoples they had but recently overwhelmed in a six-day war,"

one observer noted, "the Israelis went to some lengths to keep
marijuana from similarly devitalizing their own people." With
some ingenuity, the Israelis trained bird dogs to detect the peculiarly pungent aroma of marijuana, then circulated the dogs through
the crowded market squares. When the dog went on point, barking
and sniffing, police frisked the pointees, and invariably came up
with marijuana.

There was some question, naturally, whether the marijuana
or other, unknown factors had induced the apathy noted by
the Israelis. However, there seemed little doubt, observing chronic
users at home, that after a while, as Miras pointed out, they
constantly talked about doing things they never got around to
doing.

It was hard to see how any marijuana-watcher could dismiss
the drug as harmless unless he were on it so much himself that
his own senses were dulled. Marijuana obviously built up a
dependence, withdrawing habitual users from painful challenges,
and often sexually stimulating the casual user. But the most
common result was a state in which ideas seemed disconnected,
uncontrolled, perception disturbed, minutes seemed hours, and
seconds minutes. Spatial images were distorted, and the near
seemed far, and the far near.

Unlike the alcoholic, who generally offered lame excuses for
his aberration, the average pothead, rather than being apologetic,
had developed such misshapen values that he felt everybody would
be the better for pot, just as so many others had felt that
everybody would profit from LSD.

From his watch-point at Harvard, Farnsworth could clearly
spot the destructiveness of drugs which so duped the user that
his feeling of being opened up was often the rudest deception
of all. "To an observer," remarked Farnsworth, "he appears to
have abandoned the usual efforts to be clean, neat and presenta-
ble; he has failed in college, has no job [and doesn't want one],
yet insists that he has achieved happiness. Like many other users
of the hallucinogenic drugs, he insists that physicians who take

care of those who become disturbed or psychotic know nothing about the drugs, refuse to see their good qualities, and are in no position to judge them because they have not taken them themselves. Clinical reports of persons involved in acute and chronic psychoses, suicide or even murder are discounted by the more ardent advocates of drug usage as being so few in number as to be insignificant."

Just as there was once a softness on heroin, sold over the counter as harmless for years, and on LSD, until its disastrous effects were manifested, so has there been almost a crusade in some quarters to sanctify marijuana though only recently was it possible to scientifically assess the drug. Dr. Sidney Cohen of Los Angeles, pioneer explorer in hallucinogenics, discussing the previous instability of the drug for research purposes, pointed out in *Medical Science,* in February 1968: "Marijuana contains a variety of tetrahydrocannabinols which are unstable. The instability of the active ingredient has retarded research, but a reliable synthetic cannabinol is now available for investigative purposes."

Already, preliminary research, in controlled circumstances with controlled dosages of marijuana, has dramatically shown that marijuana, unpredictably, affects some more than others, indicating, as alcoholism should have made clear, that certain people were peculiarly vulnerable to certain drugs. Nevertheless, on the campuses, in the high schools, and in the fading hippie paradises, marijuana has been protectively isolated from other drugs. In the underground press, answering hippie queries on drugs, sex, and associated problems, Dr. Eugene Schoenfeld, formerly of the University of California Student Health Center, was aggressively pro-marijuana, even while warning of LSD and Methedrine.

"It has finally become known," Schoenfeld stated with a dazzling dearth of authority, "that marijuana is not addicting, and the laws regarding its use are unrealistic. From the legal standpoint" [wrote this doctor], "it doesn't seem appropriate to create a new criminal class by fiat."

Whatever the query, the youthful Schoenfeld managed a kind word for good old Mary Jane.

"I am twenty years old and have to take insulin daily for diabetes. I would like to try marijuana. Will this be harmful to me?"

"As you know," Schoenfeld replied, "your insulin requirements depend a great deal on your caloric intake and the type of food you eat (i.e., high in sugar, fat, protein, etc.). Marijuana is a powerful stimulant to the appetite but the mechanism for this peculiar property is unclear since studies have shown conflicting results.

"One reports that marijuana raises blood sugar, another that it lowers blood sugar [perhaps the investigators were stoned]."

Schoenfeld took time and space to go beyond the question itself—whether marijuana would harm a diabetic—and observe that pot might one day be of value in treatment of diabetes and sundry other disorders, including mental disturbance.

In this, he blandly overlooked the fact that the head of Harvard's medical services, drawing on a vast undergraduate laboratory, joined other colleagues in deciding marijuana had no therapeutic value.

"Someday," said Schoenfeld nonetheless, "marijuana or one of its components might be a proven valuable agent in the treatment of diabetes mellitus [the medical term for 'sugar' diabetes], of anorexia nervosa [a condition in which the victim may literally die from lack of appetite] or as an aid in psychotherapy."

But until that utopian awakening—when somehow the marijuana ingredient would undergo a miraculous metamorphosis—the doctor in Schoenfeld counseled the letter writer to proceed carefully.

"Meanwhile, it would be best for you to avoid marijuana since it might cause an insulin reaction by decreasing your blood sugar, or diabetic comas by raising it directly, or via visits to candy counters in all-night food stores."

Schoenfeld was not as tolerant of the amphetamines, admittedly deadly, and LSD or other hallucinogens, which he felt should be taken only under close medical supervision.

His warning on "speed" or the amphetamines came in reply to the question:

"Tell us about 'speed.' What happens to the body and brain when Methedrine [crystals and tabs] is taken in small and large doses?"

Answer by Schoenfeld:

"Methedrine [methamphetamine] is used in medicine for appetite control, mood elevation and to raise blood pressure when indicated. The drug is usually ingested in five milligram tablets, one to three times a day. Medical research for injecting Methedrine are specific and few.

"Tolerance to the amphetamines develops rapidly and increasingly large amounts must be used to achieve the same results. When large amounts are used, blood pressure may be raised sufficiently high to blow out a blood vessel in the brain, thus causing a stroke.

"True addiction to Methedrine also seems to occur. Recently a patient in a drug abuse clinic stated that it was harder for him to kick the Methedrine habit than it was to get off heroin. At the time he was shooting up 200 milligrams of crystals every two hours. He was found dead a few weeks ago, apparently from an overdose."

The casualty list was varied:

"An eighteen-year-old boy on Methedrine climbed out of a third-story window in Berkeley last New Year's Eve. He is now confined to a neurological institute, completely paralyzed from the effects of a broken back.

"Both general and student hospitals are seeing increasingly greater numbers of sixteen- to twenty-five-year-old people who have caught hepatitis from a needle used to inject Methedrine. Neither boiling water nor soaking in alcohol will necessarily kill the hepatitis virus found in too many spikes [needles]."

Curiously, an almost protective attitude toward drugs has spread through the adult intelligentsia, encouraging use of marijuana and the amphetamines while holding law enforcement up to ridicule. In England, where the "English system" of controlling addiction has proved no system at all, the conservative *London Times* rallied to the defense of two of the Rolling Stones musical group booked for possession of marijuana and "speed." (Another young man was seized at the same time with heroin.) The *Times,* more permissive—and less knowledgeable—than Dr. Schoenfeld, charged that the Rolling Stones' Mick Jagger was being persecuted by a critical adult world, as a hated symbol of youthful "decadence." The *Times* editorialist, medical evidence notwithstanding, arbitrarily ruled that amphetamines found on Jagger were harmless.

There was a similar permissiveness and coddling leading to a climate of violence on American campuses. Rather than deny undergraduates the right of free expression, or embarrass them in any way, unrealistic college officials refused to cooperate with police investigations of drug activity. "Our efforts to curb the illegal flow on campuses is hampered in many instances by the educators themselves," Joseph J. Healy, chief of the State of Illinois Narcotics Division, told a congressional committee. "The idea among some educators that students should be able to experiment and be given the freedom of choice of personal behavior has made it extremely difficult to apprehend law violators among students."

Even when students were arrested for using "soft drugs," there were successful movements to get official arrest records expunged, a new development since drug use became fashionable among suburbanites, socialites, and intellectuals. "Nobody worried very much when police sent thousands of Ghetto dwellers to languish in prison for years for puffing on one joint," wryly observed Alfred R. Kindesmith, Indiana University sociologist and author of *The Addict and the Law.* "But now that the doctor, the lawyer, the teacher, and the business executive and their children are facing the same fate, marijuana has become a *cause célèbre.*"

The academic fraternity seemed almost subservient to the whims of capricious youth.

At Berkeley, University of California researchers, claiming to have penetrated the world of adolescent drug users in a low-economic area, said they could not get the youngsters to give up drugs because, incredibly, they couldn't refute adolescent arguments for those drugs.

The report, following an eighteen-month study with taxpayer money, was made public by sociology professor Herbert Blumer. Heroin was on the wane in this group, marijuana and LSD on the upsurge. Moral suasions against drugs were put down as hypocritical because of society sanctions of alcohol. However, as any policeman might have pointed out, the drunk was relatively easy to handle, while the individual on marijuana, LSD, and amphetamines, seldom recognized the dangerous changes occurring during drug intoxication.

The Blumer study was made in neighboring Oakland. Most of the subjects were poor and from minority groups, in the main, Negro. Nevertheless, even the educationally disadvantaged could apparently outreason the professors. "From their personal experiences and observations," the report said, "they could refute the claim that drugs usually led to health or personality deterioration . . . They were able to show that the limitations on their career opportunities were due to other conditions than use of drugs." And they were almost to be admired for their ingenuity, besides. "They met the fear of arrest by developing greater skill and care against being found out."

While clinical reports elsewhere revealed that a preponderant number of heroin addicts had started with marijuana, the Blumer report indicated quite the contrary. "They viewed with contempt the use of opiates and rejected the argument that using marijuana and LSD naturally and usually led to the use of opiates." And this, when a check at one California drug rehabilitation center disclosed that, of one hundred and thirty-three heroin addicts,

questioned at random, each and every one had begun with marijuana.

Drugs were obviously part of the human revolution, and this
revolution, in its many aspects, appeared to have also wrought
a sexual explosion, abetted by the Establishment's preoccupation
with sex symbols in advertising, plays, motion pictures, novels,
television. There was little positive to be learned from such erotic
exposure, the situations hardly ever resembling anything in normal
living in their "distorted emphasis on physical pleasure and
release of tension."

"Little is said," Harvard's Farnsworth stressed before the Inter-
collegiate Association of Women Students, "about the mutually
responsible relations between a man and a woman, in which
giving and sharing occupy the prominent place, with sexual satisfaction being the index of an otherwise deeply satisfying love for
one another."

With the permissiveness of their own generation corrupted by
the parent generation, they were the uneasy inheritors of a new
morality—or amorality—which had all the old pitfalls of Adam
and Eve. "They go along in twentieth-century attitudes," a college
dean observed wryly, "until the girl gets pregnant, and then nine-
teenth-century morality suddenly reverts."

The responsibility for sex, freely given and received, seemed
to have strangely shifted. "In the past," Farnsworth asserted,
"the young man engaging in sexual relations with his partner
was assumed to be taking the responsibility of seeing that pregnancy did not occur." But with the "pill" and changing values,
the responsibility had passed to the female in the male mind. "He
usually assumes that if his girl permits intercourse she is using
a contraceptive. Not counting on an old-fashioned streak in some
girls, he does not reckon with the fact that many girls feel that
planning to prevent conception is itself immoral and that they
prefer to believe that they have been forced into having sexual
relations."

In the hippie never-never land, apart from the youthful center, the gay happy appearance of the "plastics," the natural beauty of their starry-eyed partners, and their obviously honest and open sexual attitudes, often inspired secret envy in their mocking elders, widening the gap between the generations. Some of this was reflected recently in a calculated confrontation at the University of Southern California between three carefree hippies and a class of stolid schoolteachers.

Turning up in the classroom to answer class questions, the three could have walked right out of Hippieville. Their hair was long and shaggy, they carried bells and beads around their necks, and were clad in colorful raiment reminiscent of the American Indians. They were comfortably barefooted, and very much at ease.

The educators regarded them with set faces, trying to mask their instant dislike and mistrust. The hippies gazed back evenly, as though unaware of the impression they had made.

One educator, youthful and confidently aggressive, focused on a twenty-three-year-old hippie, a promising if unpublished poet in his own circle.

The USC graduate student, barely concealing his scorn, asked, as anybody in the Establishment well might:

"Why don't you go back to school, get your degree? In three years, if you work at it, you could very well be on the road to success."

The hippie poet considered the question carefully, apparently evaluating not only the query but the young man confronting him. He showed no sign of tension. Indeed, there was a whisper of a smile on his lips.

"Right now," he said, "I live in great ease with friends on the beach of the glorious Pacific. I walk the beach whenever I like, eat when I like, and write my poetry when in the mood. I have no wants that are unfulfilled. Many beautiful girls walk through the beach house and I sleep with them at various times, and it is all very beautiful and reciprocating. There is no responsibility, no guilt and nobody feels they owe anybody anything."

His face puckered in a frown. "Now if I understand you properly, you want me to give all this up for some kind of job three years from now that won't give me anywhere near what I am getting now." He smiled and shook his head. "No, man, that's not my bag."

3

THE GENERATION GAP

"What is so terrible about God?" I asked.

The girl had shuddered at His name.

Like most in the room, she was in her early twenties, and almost compulsively absorbed with finding out what life was about.

She eyed me speculatively for a moment. There was no apology in her manner, nor was she rude. She was trying, sincerely, to frame her own thinking about the Deity.

"I've had horrible experiences with God ever since I can remember," she said finally. "I've been flogged and frightened by Him so much that my stomach kicks over just hearing about Him."

"God," I said, "represents an orderly design."

Her jaw hardened. "God," she said, "is what people make Him. My parents made Him a fright, and if I gave Him credence I would go around half scared to death."

She was attractively blonde, looking as thoroughly American as apple pie. She was one of a dozen or so in this Santa Monica group, students and young careerists squatting on the floor around a parlor moderator, discussing anything that came to mind. Two or three women in their forties, conspicuous by the age difference, were perched just outside the circle, as if recognizing they were not quite *in*.

Margie, the Godless, was chatting pleasantly with the young people who seemed mostly in agreement with her.

"How," a gaily clad brunette agreed, "can you accept a God less benevolent than yourself?"

Another laughed. "God is a human conceit; man says he is cast in God's image, so look at the poor thing God must be."

Somebody suggested that man was in God's image, not corporeally, but only as man strove for Godlike perfection in behavior and aspirations.

Margie's eyes flashed. "My father generally invoked his God when he was up to something unsavory. He went to church regularly, but left God at the door."

Her eyes took on a reflective look. "How tiresome to be constantly told God was going to punish you, to be threatened with a Hell of sulphur and brimstone, all in the name of the Lord thy God."

In rejecting her parents, she was rejecting their God.

"How," she asked, "does one separate the image from the image-maker?"

The older women, at the edge of the circle, shifted about uncomfortably, as if shouldering the blame for their generation's shortcomings.

One, a matronly figure with graying hair, diffidently raised her hand, "I don't blame young people today," she said, "we owe them something for putting them into a war in Vietnam that nobody can explain, for the fact that for the first time in history we have produced weapons that can destroy mankind, while talking about a God who has no relevance to what we do."

I wondered what reaction this sympathetic tack would have. The circle of faces was stolidly impassive; even the pretty iconoclast who had teed off on God appeared strangely disinterested.

The speaker sensed the lack of rapport. "Look at the mess we've left you," she said. "Marriages ending in broken homes, social injustice on all sides, the best of our population sent off to kill and be killed, with the blessings of the clergy, speaking for God. What a travesty!"

The legacy of my own generation, I reflected, had not been much different. Born in one World War, it suffered through a great depression, and another World War. It had not been a bed of roses, but it was challenging.

The older woman's voice broke in on my thoughts. "In this confusion, and seeming cross-purposes," she was saying, "it is easy to understand why so many young people have turned to mind-expanding experiences to know where they're at."

I could sense the restiveness of the group, their almost total indifference to what constituted an apologia from one of my generation. These were Dr. Pike's middle group—actors, designers, students, clerks.

Inevitably, the older woman faltered to a conclusion.

One of my companions, older and grayer than myself, observed in a wry undertone, "They're certainly not interested in our group."

I smiled. "Who listens to failures?"

"And they're successes?" she came back.

The conversation of the young had gotten onto drug experiences, and I could only wonder what truths were apparent to the immature with chemicals that their elders weren't aware of.

"It's more in a feeling of awareness than in rational explanations," a young man interposed.

Briefly, the group touched on their psychedelic adventures.

Only three or four had taken LSD, but all had tried pot, with mixed reactions.

"Pot relaxes you," one said, "but with acid, you just don't know where you're at."

The moderator, who had the status of a guru or teacher, pondered aloud whether drugs were essential for normal functioning.

"It all depends," a young man said, "what you consider normal functioning." He frowned. "For instance, if we'd all been on pot yesterday, we wouldn't be sitting around talking now—we'd be sleeping it off or just moping around the house."

The moderator nodded. "You mean, all we'd be good for was more pot."

Amid general laughter, a young blonde, with a thin face and serious mien, said, "I've discovered that if I've been on pot the day before, I just can't take my cello lessons the next day."

There were appreciative smiles in the circle. "And so you have given up the cello?" somebody teased.

"No," she rejoined primly, "I just make sure I have nothing important the next day."

"Like this meeting," another laughed.

A young man with long hair and sideburns, looking more the hippie than any other, seemed annoyed at the conversation.

"I don't see why we sit around discussing pot," he said. "If we're going to spend all this time on it, we might better be smoking it."

Godless Margie gave the speaker a doubtful glance.

"Why deny ourselves discussing anything we want to?"

There was general assent. "Why impose taboos on ourselves," another concurred, "when we get together to share our thoughts?" His eyes traveled slowly around the circle. "I think you all should know about my experience with pot. I smoked it for months, and it was cool. Then one day out of nowhere, I suddenly felt like I was going to blow up, my body, brain, every part of me. I tried not to panic, and kept trying to focus but I couldn't read, relax, or talk, so I ran out into the street and stomped around until it wore off."

He had not smoked pot since.

His experience caused no great wave.

"You just got hold of some bad stuff," a neighbor observed calmly.

"Or maybe some good stuff," another stressed. "Some of this grass is really potent, with very little of the hemp in it."

The young man shook his head. "It was the same stuff I smoked a couple of days before."

There was much shaking of heads, but the youth with the "bummer" experience finally found a supporter.

"I, too, had a nasty experience," a studious-looking youth said stiffly, "and from the same batch as before." Instead of everything appearing slow and easy, slowing up, as it generally had, he began to feel unaccountably nervous. "I had to get up and move around to keep arms and legs and the rest going. It got worse as I kept smoking."

There was still little reaction, even though these first-person reports seemed to contradict claims that pot was no worse than alcohol.

My middle-aged companion reacted much as I did. "At least," she sighed, "with booze we knew what was going to happen to us." `

The absorption with pot again drew a protest from the hippie-type with the sideburns. "We're wasting time talking pot when it's something that must be experienced."

Margie, who had questioned him before, now made the point: "We wouldn't otherwise know now of unpleasant reactions in at least two instances. Perhaps we can learn from experiences of others as well as our own—even in so subjective an affair as smoking pot."

The protester stuck to his guns. "I don't know who got us on this kick, but we should get into discussion areas that challenge our psyche."

My companion wrinkled her nose. "He's worried about his psyche," she whispered, "when these two were concerned about their sanity."

Eventually, the conversation got back to God and the churches. "The hippies," somebody said, "are nearer to God than the churches because they are closer to the primitive religion of Jesus and the Apostles. They believe in helping others, they're not making a status symbol out of churchgoing."

As the meeting drew to a close, with nothing resolved, I reflected on other meetings I had been to all over the country, where the hippies prattled of love and drugs, while reporters like myself avidly absorbed their pearls of wisdom.

"We are like the early Christians," a hippie love-poetess had sighed in San Francisco, "we beg from time to time, like Christ's followers did, but we also share and help one another."

The hippies, too, had made God in their image. Some equated not working with their own flexible creed. "Work's against our religion," quipped a hippie in Toronto's Yorkville paradise. He quoted from Hindu scripture: "God plays, He does not work."

Had disenchantment with religion been true only of the hippies, it would have been a matter of only passing interest. But hippie reactions approximated those of large segments of the youthful population. In Toronto, while making the hippie scene, I had come on a striking article by Allen Spraggett, religion editor of the Toronto *Star,* dealing with this sectarian revolt.

"Like all hippies," Spraggett wrote of a dissenting pair, "Steve and Olga regard organized religion as only a notch above organized crime. Yet, in their own far-out way, they are unmistakably religious."

The hymns of the new faith were the protest songs of Bob Dylan and Joan Baez.

"Its sacraments," Spraggett went on, "are LSD and marijuana which promise the true believer a trip to heaven (although sometimes he gets rerouted to hell). Its worship is the love-in. Its churches are parks and the great outdoors in general (when the weather's good)."

While describing hippie rejection of traditional religion—a rejection all too often shared by more conventional young—Spraggett was nonetheless impressed by their spiritual outlook. "They may be more radically Christian in some ways than our society cares to admit. Certainly they are not anti-Christ." His Steve and Olga, sharing their apartment—and poverty—with another young couple, were even more militantly anti-traditional religion than Margie, who spurned God.

"Jesus was a beautiful man," said Steve, "but the church is un-Christian.

"A bishop is about the farthest from God I can imagine anyone being. You didn't see Jesus walking around in velvet robes while people starved."

Curiously, the hippies were critical of symbolism and façade, while enjoying both. A California mother had sent her son to Berkeley, only to have him return in six months with long hair, a beard, and a sneer for the fine shops lining downtown Beverly Hills. "Façade, that's all, façade," he scoffed.

"And what," she snapped, "is that beard but façade?"

The hippie movement, like the adolescent revolution in general, was clearly more significant because it sprang out of the prevailing middle-class.

Both Steve and Olga came from ordinary backgrounds. "He was sixteen," Spraggett said, "when he decided to heed Timothy Leary's advice to 'Drop out and turn on.' He left home—over the strenuous objections of his parents—and set out for Yorkville in the spirit of a Muslim pilgrim on his way to Mecca."

Steve went back home a few times, until his father ordered him not to return until he had cut his hair.

He never went back.

The long hair was a symbol to Steve. "I cut it once and felt like a traitor. If you want to find out what it's like to be a Negro in the Deep South, just let your hair grow. People will give you dirty looks. Drivers don't stop for you at crosswalks. Police pick on you. Because you look different, you're inferior."

What about drugs?

There was some intramural conflict here. Where folksinger

Joan Baez attacked LSD and Marijuana as a crutch the young could do better without, Steve saw it differently.

"Does Joan Baez take aspirin for a headache?" Steve asked. "Well, LSD's a drug for heartache."

In the ego release of LSD, Steve experienced his God. "To see God, to discover the God within you, that's the only place."

Steve had the answers, his answers, about chemicals, and when the findings of others differed, there was no question whose findings he accepted. "He pooh-poohs the medical warnings that LSD and other hallucination-producing substances are potentially dangerous to mind and body," said Spraggett. "He put such drugs in the same class as fasting, sensory deprivation, and other aids to meditation used by mystics in the past."

The only difference : LSD was quicker.

The hippie need for some spiritual belief was quite apparent in the hippie press, especially influential in the San Francisco and Los Angeles areas. *The Oracle,* most mystical of these publications, produced a characteristically personal version of the Ten Commandments:

"Love all things equally, forsaking not yourself.

"Revere all Nature equally, not forgetting your own body as flesh.

"Whatever harm others have inflicted upon you, remember these and strive in your own person to be the end of that harm: to effect such an end of the harm by not repeating it in your own actions.

"To love God as you know Him, or as He chooses you in whom to reveal Himself.

"To share your visions as you are blessed with them, but never to coerce those growing into their own around you.

"Cultivate a gracefulness of person. In this, as in all things, the Supreme models are in the natural world.

"Instruct yourself, and most particularly, the children in the virtue of adding to the beauty of life through the creation of beautiful things. Yield always to the creative forces within yourself, and take care to care for these gifts.

"Teach, if possible, always by example, but failing that, be vocal in decrying any outrage perpetrated against life and love.

"Be not afraid, Nor take shame if fearful. To voice a fear is to diminish it, for man is a child of nature and Nature-in-Him understands the foible of fear.

"Seek patience, for patience is a place: The City of God!"

In the adolescent revolution there were many gradations, and even on campus there were sharp distinctions among the rebels.

"Alienated students," noted Dr. Seymour L. Halleck, director of student psychiatry at the University of Wisconsin, "should not be confused with genuine campus activists. Occasionally, an alienated student will sustain an interest in a cause for several weeks or even months. This is most likely to happen when the cause is one of direct attack upon a firmly entrenched social institution. When he does become involved with activist groups, he can be characterized as the most angry and irrational member of that group. He is unwilling to cooperate with other students, or to follow an organized plan, and if unchecked by more mature activists will lead the group into battles that have no chance of being won. The alienated student differs from the revolutionary student insofar as he is not motivated by utopian ideals and is more concerned with means than ends."

Did this explain the senseless campus riots, the violent protests of the draft, napalm, Vietnam, social injustice?

The alienated students, many brought up on Dr. Spock baby books, were large created by parental coddling. "The alienated student," said Halleck, "is usually of middle-class background. His parents have considered themselves psychologically sophisticated people and have raised him in a rather permissive manner.

"While the family seeks to create an image of loving permissiveness, a more careful look at their interaction reveals critical flaws. The aura of love which supposedly has surrounded the child is more often talked about than provided. In a quest to resolve their own problems, one or both parents have frequently identified with their child and have imposed role responsibilities upon him which more appropriately belong to their own spouse.

"The latent problems of the alienated student become manifest when he leaves home and begins his life at the university. The most salient experience of the newly arrived college student is that of his freedom. Not all students are prepared to deal with this abundance of freedom, and the student who has been subtly controlled by his parents is especially perplexed. Not sure of his own identity, he felt guilty at the realizaton that 'his affluence is unearned and that many other people in our society can only dream of obtaining the privileges he so routinely enjoys.'"

Was this why so many inexplicably gave up comfort for the squalor of hippie communities?

After guilt came withdrawal.

"It is as though he perceives that a world in which anything is possible is a world in which no goal is really important. When confronted with unlimited choice, he refuses to choose. Having failed to develop an internalized value system which allows him to determine his direction in life, he is paralyzed when the external world removes its guidelines and restraints."

If not on drugs before, he soon would be on campus. Marijuana or LSD, Halleck felt, was definitely tied in with adolescent alienation, related to feelings of being unloved by parents. "Smoking marijuana has become almost an emblem of alienation. The alienated student realizes that the use of pot mortifies his parents and enrages the authorities."

LSD was so often the ultimate in the expression of an overwhelming sense of frustration and futility. "Many alienated students perceive the reality of their existence as so sterile and unchangeable that they expend much of their energy searching for a rapid means of changing themselves. They seek a basically autoplastic adjustment in which they can create a new inner reality simply by taking a pill or smoking a marijuana cigarette."

The ferment on campuses around the country was indicative

of the widespread nature of the student revolt. At many colleges that protests were sparked by serious students of a militant middle group, and it took an orderly and reasonable course. At others, like Columbia, encouraged by a craven administration which coddled lawbreakers, protest demonstrations by a small student minority got out of hand and destructively shut down classes for the suffering majority.

By knuckling under to ridiculous undergraduate demands, such as the claim by Negro students for segregated quarters at Northwestern, university officials seemed to unwittingly substantiate student charges of general unfitness. At Stanford, where pot was prevalent, student officers won the right from a feckless university administration for one Vicky Drake to run for president of the student council. The ruling was unique, inasmuch as Miss Drake was not only a topless dancer at an instructive night club, but not even a student at the university.

In some instances, student demonstrations appeared admirably motivated by a desire for educational reforms. At Florida State University, a mass protest was triggered by administration censorship of an undergraduate literary magazine, but it soon became apparent this was only a side issue. The real issue was academic freedom, whether undergraduates, many of whom had fought for their country, would have a voice in undergraduate affairs.

Students, it was felt, should have the same right as other citizens, and they were willing to share similar responsibilities—adhering to lawful censorship—following the same libel and obscenity laws as anyone else.

Again, there was the familiar attack on adult hypocrisy. Laurel Akers, editor of the college magazine, which precipitated the controversy by publishing a short story with some obscenities, contended that the university administration had no integrity. "It is up to our generation to change it," she said, "to strike for freedom."

Thousands of students joined in the censorship protest, pointing out that while they didn't aspire to a student-controlled university, they wanted one run by responsible officers in sympathy with students, not a politically oriented Board of Regents which arbitrarily censored a student television program because it considered it pro-North Vietnam.

Even while protesting, student leaders susceptible to adult opinion, resolutely remained activists in the normal framework of society. "We are not a hippie movement," one wrote. "Our leaders come from all areas of the university—honor students, fraternity and sorority members, respected faculty members, and religious leaders from the community. Our ranks are filled with ordinary students; students who have just now awakened to a serious situation which threatens the whole foundation of higher education."

These students, as they insisted, were keeping their grades up, were "still taking daily baths, and were clean-shaven." They were vastly different from the plastic-stereotyped hippie extreme which was seen wandering around aimlessly, unscrubbed and unloved in the doubtful paradise of San Francisco's Haight-Ashbury. These were hardly the Flower Children I had read so much about. Talking love, they still hated, with a deep-seated resentment they hid even from themselves. "Their feelings," noted Dr. David E. Smith, youthful head of the Haight-Ashbury free clinic, "are expressed primarily in an alienation from society, with a corresponding conscious rejection of accepted social standards." This rejection showed itself in the almost total absorption with drugs. "The use of alcohol was minimal, but the use of marijuana as a social drug approached one hundred percent," Smith disclosed. "LSD and other psychedelic drugs were used for mystical purposes, predominantly to facilitate the philosophy of 'turn-on, tune-in, dropout.' Methedrine [methamphetamine], however, was the major drug 'abuse' problem—a drug that nobody had a good word for."

"Meth-heads" didn't rationalize their habit like acidheads or potheads. They were frankly interested only in "kicks," intravenously "mainlining" their drug for the speediest effect.

But marijuana was the great staple. And it was harmless, they told themselves, even as the habit hardened into a definite life style. They couldn't listen to music without "turning on" pot, couldn't have sex without it, nor appreciate a sunrise or sunset. And yet they assured themselves, succumbing to this hedonistic ideal, that pot was neither physically nor psychologically habit forming. At times, considering the squalor of Haight-Ashbury, it almost seemed as though they were seeking out the lowest human denominator, where there would be nothing to remind them of the enterprising culture they had left behind. This was no utopia, but a noncompetitive world, where they whiled away their youth in destructive idleness.

Burgeoning resentments were equated with the parents who served the God of manna, preaching one thing, they said, and doing another. "Their parents," said Alan Rose, a Haight-Ashbury clinic director, "tell them not to use drugs, then reach for a tranquilizer or barbiturate, or a shot of whiskey. And what are diet pills but amphetamines, another name for speed?"

Young Rose was himself an authority on the generation gap. He had dropped out of college to the dismay of his parents. "They said I lacked responsibility," he reported dryly, "and now that I'm showing some, they want me to come home." Rose felt he was finding himself in helping others. Certainly he had gained fresh insights. "The older the kids get, the more the parents treat them as children, particularly when they should be helping them break out instead of smothering them."

From daily observation of the clinic assembly line, it was obvious that the production of dropouts began early. "All through childhood, the parents kept telling these kids, 'I want you to have everything I didn't have.' Essentially, these kids wanted love, not money or gifts, not substitutes or bribes. By the time the parent recognized his mistake, he had lost his son or daughter."

Few parents, Rose felt, took trouble to understand their children. "They were involved in work or recreation, and the kids soon realized they came into being not because they were wanted but as an expression of sex." As Dr. Halleck had pointed out, in the insecurity of not feeling loved, they soon weren't sure of who and what they are, and resentfully ranged outside their parents world in the hope of finding themselves.

One father, Rose related, had gone to his teen-age dropout and tearfully asked, "What can I do for you?"

The boy coldly turned away, "What have you done in eighteen years?"

Long before college, even high school, the seeds of alienation were recklessly sown. "Until the children were ten or eleven," offered Dr. Louis Rangel, a distinguished Mexican authority on adolescence touring Haight-Ashbury, "the parents were unquestioned heroes. But as the children grew older and more observing, they started to examine parental behavior critically. They began to notice how seldom their parents told the truth—about income tax, business dealings, relationships with each other. Consequently, the child gradually questioned the parent whose authority was previously unquestioned."

At fourteen or fifteen, Rangel found the child floundering dangerously. While physical maturity often came at this age, psychological development was normally deferred to eighteen or twenty, creating a hazardous personality gap. "In this period of four or five years," he stressed, "the adolescent was prey to every passing pressure."

Were only hippies involved in soul-searching reappraisals of old values, the impact could hardly have been as revolutionary as it obviously was. The changes in the large middle group of youth were often as deep, modified only by recognition of their responsibilities to the Establishment and to themselves. They, too, were in revolt but their insurrection was of a private nature, and usually they fought it out alone. In the beginning, there was generally little to indicate the underlying stress and insecurity. In high school, for instance, Judy appeared the typical All-American girl: cheerleader, honor society, student council member, football hero boyfriend, the most popular in her class. An only child, she had all the clothes she wanted, a car, money, and a plethora of love. But she was secretly unhappy even then.

"I hated all the rah-rah to get an education, get married, live in the suburbs and send our kids to the same schools."

It was like a breath of fresh air to get out of high school and off to college. By now Judy was beginning to understand that her parents, particularly her father, were trying to make her an extension of themselves, and she began, almost involuntarily, to resist. She wanted desperately to achieve her own values, and they were not always her parents'. "My father had struggled to survive during the Depression and he wanted me to have everything he didn't have. But he could never do anything without imposing his old values, which put me in the same bind he was in."

At twenty-three, now out of college, Judy was attractively dark and petite with brown saucer eyes, smooth skin, and a pert nose. She was a designer, had her own apartment, and could hardly have been called a hippie. She had gone to Washington to participate in an anti-war demonstration, but had been as offended by the violence of the demonstrators as the violence of war.

The deterioration of her relationship with her parents had plagued her all through college. They felt so badly over her desire for independence that, not wanting to hurt them, she compromised. After graduation, she went back to her hometown to be near them. But she took her own apartment, and made her own rules during the week.

"Weekends at home," she recalled, "I played nice little Judy, gratifying my parents secret wish I grow up in their image."

But what gave them security held none for her. "My father had worked all his life for what he thought would make him and his family secure. But the material things that spelled out security to him were meaningless to me and my friends, since we had

never wanted them, and had done nothing for them. So all the
luxuries he wanted to shower me with only made me all the more
aware of an insecurity dependent on his largesse. I understood
now what the hippies meant by doing your own thing. That was
the only security anybody could find, within himself. Nobody can
give another person a feeling of true security. You have to do it
for yourself."

Revolting, she gravitated to a new circle of Bohemian friends,
dressed differently, and quite naturally turned to pot and LSD.
She was not extreme in attire—black stockings, wild prints and long
hair, all seemed to modishly suit her personality.

Perhaps because he was so different, she fell in love with Jim.
"He was a pot-smoking musician from the wrong side of the
tracks," she recalled, "and all my parents' dreams for me would
have gone out the window if they had known how serious we
were. And we lived together for two years without their even
knowing about it. We set up house; bought dishes, furniture, a
car, the works. And my parents never knew. Can you imagine
living in the same town like that? It was like walking around on
broken egg shells."

They had taken their own marriage vows, and while this satisfied the Bohemian musician, there was enough bourgeois in
Judy to want the union formalized. But the shock an open an-
nouncement would impose on her parents always restrained
her at the decisive moment. Eventually, with all its strains,
the relationship foundered. "I suppose I had failed him by not
loving him enough to throw off my parents, and he failed
me when I needed him most, when I was expecting a child and
wanted to know I was loved." There was an abortion, and the
idyll was over. Suddenly, what had seemed beautiful became
cheap and tawdry.

With Jim, she had occasionally tried pot. Now, feeling lonely
and empty, she thought of taking acid for the insight she might
gain. But she was afraid of a bad trip. However, a young professor, who had taken it, talked about how helpful it was and

exciting. "And so the first moment I felt strong enough to stand on my own, I tried LSD with him as my guide."

She had a pleasant trip. "I felt fertile and open. And that was great. I'd been frigid and alone for so many months. Now everything was so comprehensible. I remember just sitting there and laughing at nothing."

The trip lasted six hours, but it seemed longer and shorter at the same time. Each hallucination had been a gratifying one. They had turned on the record player, and the music was like nothing she had heard—or seen—before. "There was a crack in the wall, and I saw the notes coming out of the crack. These were Indian notes—I was just getting interested in Indian music and they floated out, one after another, through the crack. Then we put on some Bach and the notes were too thick to get out. It's funny, but I've always had this thing about being too thin. But it was the thin notes that got through the crack, not the fat ones. Maybe it was a sign that I liked myself."

It was her only experience with LSD, as she was soon frightened off by newly published reports of chromosome changes in LSD users.

But she still thought the experience helpful. "It made me realize I had to be myself, whether in relation to Jim, my parents, or my job."

Being herself was doing what she wanted, as she wanted, in accordance with her own standards and ideals. It was not being commercial, or materialistically motivated, like her father and others, even though her actions were invariably misunderstood.

She smiled. "The other day we had a big crisis in the fashion center where I work, and I offered to work late to get clothes out for the collection."

The boss had eyed her suspiciously.

"I can't pay you overtime," he said shortly.

"I don't expect to be paid," she said.

He was even more suspicious. "Then why stay over?"

"I like working here and I want to help."

He made a face. "Stop putting me on," he said stiffly, and walked away.

But Judy had tried.

"He's older," she said, "and he doesn't understand."

Everywhere, in the lives of Judys, and in the newspapers there were signs of drastically changing values. It was on the front pages, the back pages, the columns, wherever a live newspaper mirrored a community in ferment. In an electronic revolution there was no longer isolation anywhere. Television, radio, and press moved all too rapidly. The young throughout the world could now gain strength from the certain knowledge they were part of a momentous movement. Had the Colonials the same swift access to each other's thinking, the Revolutionary War undoubtedly would have occurred long before it did. In common knowledge of unity, lay boldness of purpose and action. Obviously, permissiveness at Berkeley had done much to encourage drugs and demonstrations on other campuses—Columbia, Florida State, Northwestern.

In all this disquiet, drugs were but one issue. Virtually all of youth was caught up in a milieu of spiritual searching, programs for peace, educational reform, stemming out of a surging desire to cast their lives in a peculiarly personal mold.

The story was all in the newspapers, and pieced together, it clearly spelled revolt. There on Page One was a commentary on the sharp questioning of church tradition: *Crisis of Obedience in Catholic Church Deplored by Bishops.* In a collective pastoral letter, the Roman Catholic bishops of the United States appealed for "a renewal of that love for the Church that has characterized the faithful of all ages."

The Bishops had a point: "Not everything old is bad, and not everything new is necessarily good."

Inside the fold of the newspaper, the revolt continued: "UC Student Association Gives Declaration of Independence. The student government at UC Berkeley [the University of California] declared itself independent of the administration of Chancellor Roger W. Heyns."

In a chatty column, reporter Art Seidenbaum discussed "The Yap Gap 'Twixt Teen and Adult." "As a wise friend worried recently," the columnist noted, "there are adults who now worship words from the young, precisely because young people uttered them. Such adults want to be whipped by youngsters. Want to revel in shouts of 'hypocrisy,' taunts about drunkenness, puncturing of material security."

There was little youthful respect for authority, institutionalized or otherwise, for the White House or the least of the bureaucratic establishments. And in this revolt, drugs were the name of the game. It was often difficult to tell who was altering who. The Santa Monica *Evening Outlook,* interviewing an inmate of a juvenile center, reported "dope all over the place."

Another youth, sixteen, reported that he could acquire drugs by performing homosexual acts with the detention staff.

But the big news was a militant hippie uprising. They were turning-on, tuning-in, and taking over, or at least trying to. The locale was Venice, the honky-tonk beach community adjacent to Santa Monica.

"Venice hippies, engaged in a bitter beachfront conflict with police," the story went, "have formed their own small 'government' and a patrol force they claim is better than Venice police."

The hippie action was actually a reaction. There had been complaints of hippie misbehavior, ranging from possession of marijuana to panhandling and drinking in public. The police swept down on the beach, rounding up some seventy-five persons, mostly hippies, accused of shaking down senior citizens for the privilege of walking down the public beach.

Hippie vigilantes soon "claimed that there were no instances of tolltaking anymore and that the long-haired patrolmen were outpolicing the police."

Hippie leaders, meanwhile, in a pamphlet, the *Sounding Board,* counseled broader understanding for the guardians of the law. "The police have reasons for what they do. Inadequate and irrational laws, leaders and training, pressures from areas of society, fights with the wife and kids. Frustrations from all these things are compounded into a thing called cop. He has all the problems evident in our society, plus a few extra since he needs to be a type of person to take and get the job. However, we need the 'man,' but not with the stigma that's beginning to surround him and his miserable job. A paranoia has grown in many people toward him. Instead of trying to understand his problems people are just hassling him back, which just forms a mutual paranoia that spirals on."

To be a hippie, and real hip, was to be aware, and war, most odious of Establishment hangups, was "The Tragedy of the Unaware." "Recently," wrote one young editor in the *Sounding Board,* "I received word of the death of a young friend. One is always sad to learn of death, especially when it claims someone close. To compound my grief, if this is possible, his death was senseless.

"You see, my friend was killed in Vietnam. With what must be the most sorrowful comment on the impersonal bureaucratic society, his government said he died defending Hill 561. He was a very young and beautiful person. He was three years short of being able to vote."

The indictment of adult society bitterly continued: "In these days of uncertainty when nothing is clear, when the President lies with impunity, when half-truths are not, cannot be questioned, my friend made the fatal mistake of being innocently unaware.

"Like many of his contemporaries, he left high school before graduation. He thought that he had learned all that he needed to learn to partake of the American Dream. He could not see wasting his time in school when there was so much money to be made, so many new cars to be bought, so many good times to be had. Alas, he came up short of credentials and connections.

"My friend joined the Marines which, as everyone knows, builds men. In no time he was a man, and in Vietnam. He wrote to me often during his brief tenure. On one occasion when he was no longer able to conceal his disillusionment, he said that the

Vietnamese people were a wretched lot more deserving of pity than of napalm. He said they were a dirty, scrawny, skinny people who deeply hated the Americans who were simultaneously defending and killing them. He thought the war a 'mess,' and had no idea why he was in Vietnam, except to fight 'communism.'

"I wrote to him and expressed my sincere regret that he had to be a part of it. I asked him not to kill and also asked him if he didn't honestly believe that he was closer spiritually to these wretched peasants than with the American people in whose name he was fighting.

"Now, I'll never be able to know whether he did consider the thought or, for that matter, what his last thoughts were as he died in defense of Hill 561. Nor will any of us know the last thoughts of many like him, sent thousands of miles from home to an obscure little country with scrawny little people, to kill and be killed, while avaricious cowards at home wave a flag and send more young men, all the while making a profit out of war."

The flood of underground newspapers, unprecedented since the French Revolution, was symptomatic of the gestating human revolution. Each paper reflected some distinct phase of the revolt. The recklessness of certain aspects was frankly stated in the Los Angeles *Underground:*

"We want out from your 9 to 5 jobs. We want out from your cookie cutter schools. We want out from your tight white collars. We don't mind if you don't let us drink because pot is a groovy thing and LSD can take you on trips to places you never dreamed of. Where is everything at, man? It is in a cap, man! It's in that sugar cube. God's there, man. Get off your bum trip and join us! Look, take one, here have a head band, join the tribe, will call you morning star or morning glory."

The LSD sweep of the land was proudly hailed:

"Maybe a million American minds blew themselves on LSD this past year. Mostly, you won't even notice it because it ain't that kind of crazy. We monkeyed in our chemical labs until

we came up with this thing, this simple thing that could ZAP!
Change reality! Make it into anything you want to. See that wall?
It ain't really a wall, it's a rubber band! See? I'm stretching it.
Want to see it snap into place? Look! Ain't that funny?

"Or maybe the wall didn't go back into place—a bummer, man.
A bummer. Or maybe if you're lucky someone will hold your
hand and talk you down—but keep talking man, keep talking.

"They came up with this thing LSD and somehow it brought
you closer to your fellow man. You got a good look through the
door but there was a price you paid."

Admittedly, a stiff price.

"For some it was to babble in a straitjacket but for countless
others it was to mean a much more subtle form of psychosis that
will never end in a cell but gently damn you to wander in seeming reason bereft of real will, going through life like a painted
marionette in a puppet show."

And so they spoke of war, LSD, money, church but mostly
they got on hypocrisy—hypocrisy in the home, society, the schools,
business, government.

There was the usual outcry against parents preaching one
ethic and practicing another; people cheating the government and
the government shortchanging the people; the sanctimony of liberals advocating school integration while patronizing private
schools; the absence of loyalties; the dullness of jobs; the anonymity of the classroom; the sharp business practices that perhaps
more than anything typified a sham society.

They spoke derogatorily of the butcher, the baker, the can-
dlestick maker; the automobile merchant, the TV repairman, the
landlord, the preacher.

"In a society," one epitomized, "where it is folly to care for
one's fellow, it becomes the mark of wisdom to beat one's
neighbor."

Was there validity in their scorn of a Golden Rule conspicuous
in its absence?

"If we didn't take drugs to open ourselves up," another shrugged, "we'd take them to shut ourselves off."

Not since Christ drove out the money-changers had the outcry against manna been so strong and clear. It was not so much a cry in the wilderness, as a whole wilderness crying out.

"Diogenes," one youth commented bitterly, "would run up quite a light bill today trying to find an honest man."

Since everybody needed food, shelter, clothing, and transportation, they, too, were consumers. And, as consumers, spoke sharply of a chicanery they considered the by-product of an outrageous social order.

"You don't have to look far," one said, "to know what's wrong with *your* world."

And, I suppose, it was my world, the only world I had ever known—the world of Caveat Emptor—buyer beware.

And so I looked around me to see what it was that they saw. I did not look very far. That same day I decided to buy a used car.

I had a friend with a "connection," who took me to one of the finest motorcar establishments in Beverly Hills. The manager of the used car division received me with a warm smile. He showed me three cars. I thought them overpriced compared to the cars noisily advertised on TV.

He smiled pityingly. "With us you know what you're getting, and the price is realistic. You get what you pay for."

Through my "connection," I was permitted a car for a trial run. The manager patted the hood affectionately. "There's only thirty-three thousand miles on it," he said, "and you can bet that's one speedometer that's never been turned back."

"But," I said, "isn't it against the law to turn back the mileage meter?"

He shrugged. "Some dealers are unscrupulous, what more can I tell you?"

The car was three hundred dollars above the ordinary range for that year and model, a 1962.

"But you know what you are getting," he pointed out patiently, again patting the hood, "a real buy."

For eight hundred dollars, I thought I might get a more recent model.

"It's not the year that counts," he said, "but what's under the hood. Now this is a lot of car, and only thirty-three thousand miles, remember that."

In a weekend to remember, I tried out the car.

The first evening, Old Reliable stalled on the highway, and had to be towed to the nearest garage. A mechanic thoroughly checked it over. He ran it around the block, and pointed to a disagreeable noise emerging from the front. "It's the drive shaft," he said, "there's something radically wrong with it."

"Will that take much doing?" I asked.

"Only three or four hundred dollars," he said, "more than the car is worth."

"But it has very little mileage on it," I protested.

He carefully scrutinized the motor.

"For one thing," he said, "the carburetor has been rebuilt."

"But the mileage," I objected, "that's certainly legitimate."

He snorted. "They didn't have to turn it back. It got up to 100,000 miles and started all over again."

That should have ended my used car experience, but it didn't.

"Your mistake," a friend advised, "was that you didn't buy from a private owner. You save the middle man differential, and in knowing the owner, you know the car."

Together, we scoured through the classified ads of a Los Angeles newspaper. "Ah," my friend said brightly, "there's one; five hundred dollars, same year as your dealer wanted eight hundred for."

I called the number listed, and a woman answered.

"We just overhauled this car," she said, "gave it everything, including a new generator."

The husband introduced me to the car. "Take it out on the freeway," he said, airily, "it travels with the best."

"Why are you getting rid of it?" I asked.

"We already have two cars, and we have a chance to pick up a more recent model."

It sounded reasonable.

The car seemed to drive well. Meanwhile, remembering what my friend had said about a car reflecting the quality of the owner, I tried sounding him out.

He came from the Midwest, and had not yet acclimated himself to California ways. "They're very grasping out here," he said.

Since I had just found this the case, I was agreeably impressed.

I made up my mind on the instant. "You're obviously an honest man," I said.

He gave me a friendly smile and a warm handshake. I was the owner of a "new" used car.

That first day the car picked up a strange buzzing noise. I took it to the garage, a new bearing was put in a front wheel. The next day I had the gas tank filled, and the service station attendant reported I was out of transmission fluid. It had all leaked out. I got some sealer. The following day, I had trouble starting, and stalled across busy Pacific Coast Highway, blocking both lanes of the two-way traffic. I needed new spark plugs, an air filter, an oil filter, a new smog valve.

The mechanic worked on the car for hours. When I arrived to pick it up, he asked, "Have you been using a lot of gas?"

I had, but couldn't understand why.

"There's a leak in the gas tank," he said, "so big we had to put something under your car to keep our platform clean."

"Can you fix it?" I asked

He shook his head. "It'll have to be pulled out and soldered; take it to a dealer, they can handle it."

I sighed unhappily, reflecting on what a hippie had said about Diogenes and his quest for an honest man. Diogenes must still be out there—looking.

Whatever their drug habit, youth couldn't be all wrong.

4

THE PASSING HIPPIES

The hippies came, and went.

They were part of a changing scene, which all too often they didn't understand themselves.

They were the excrescences of a human revolution, popping out of nearly every area of contemporary youth.

Originally, picturesque garb, long hair and beards were only symbols of withdrawal. But soon, through the accent on appearance, the cult stressing anti-materialism gave way to a hippie stereotype—and the symbol became the cult.

Even so, there were scattered manifestations of individuality, but the mainstream of the hippie movement appeared hopelessly static, except as it provided the intellectually immature with justification for dropping out. Oddly, despite their blatant disavowal of society, the hippie stereotype—the plastic—had no qualms about applying for public relief; medicaid, free clinics—

not seeing the hypocrisy of accepting help from a society they rejected as hypocritical.

Ostensibly, taking drugs to release their egos, they were still ego motivated. Banding together, in their communes and hovels, they found a curious emotional security in a common lack of achievement.

It was not easy to meet them on an equal footing, since I was compelled to acknowledge a distaste for the slovenliness of body and mind pervading hippielands in Chicago, New York, San Francisco, Los Angeles, Washington, and other congregating centers. To void any lack of objectivity on my part, I engaged a researcher contemporary with the hippies, to go over pretty much the same ground I had.

In Yorkville, Toronto's hippie center, twenty-three-year-old Olie Westheimer met, as I had, the usual mélange of plastic hippies, druggies and voyeurs, adolescent and adult. "I found few seemingly genuine hippies," Olie reported, "dirty, strained expressions [the result of pep pills] or glazed, fey expressions [from LSD or pot] and all of them, tired looking. The hippie life may be one of leisure, yet restful sleep doesn't seem a part of it. But the high school 'pretend hippies' were all cheery and peppy."

One of the first to catch Olie's eye was a tall, bearded youth in sandals, tight khaki pants and dirty wrinkled shirt, table-hopping in an outdoor café on Yorkville's main street. He moved slowly, his shoulders stooped so that he didn't have to shout down to those sitting down. Olie fancied him as a very young Walt Whitman. As it developed, he was a poet, selling copies of his poems.

He handed her a mimeographed poem in free verse about true love.

"After reading it," Olie reported, "I told him I didn't want to buy it, but that I would like to talk to him because he looked like a hippie and I was under the impression that hippies disdained money and didn't work."

He was in no way offended. "Well, I guess you could call me

a hippie. As for working, how could I live if I didn't work? I don't do too much, just sell my poems so that I have money to pay my rent and phone and eat."

"I always wondered how the hippies survived," Olie said. "I guess they work just enough to get along. Do you live with a group of people? What I'd really like to see is a community of hippies."

"I live alone," he said, "and while I'd love to talk to you, I'm working right now, and this is losing me money. See me during the day."

The poet moved on to the next table. "Not very loving or people-oriented for a hippie," Olie noted ruefully. However, two youths at a nearby table, overhearing the conversation, offered to help. "I know hundreds of places around here where you can see people living together," one said.

His name was Steve, and the other, Rudi.

"The two didn't look as if they went together," Olie related. "Neither was talking to the other, and they didn't look as if they'd have much to say to each other if they did talk."

Rudi was a sort of mesomorph going to seed. His face was pudgy but interesting because of bushy eyebrows and big black-rimmed glasses and a broad, lazy smile. He was dressed in a clean white shirt and slacks, loafers and white socks. He was conventionally mediocre down to his thick school ring and huge round watch. Steve at this point was staring nervously into space and seemed totally out of it, despite the fact that he was the one who had offered to show Olie some hippie communities just a few minutes before.

"Rudi, you don't look much like a hippie," Olie said, almost accusingly.

"Oh, I'm not really," he said with a smile, "just a weekend hippie. I come down to Yorkville for the weekends and just walk around, meet Steve sometimes, and pretend I'm a hippie. I get so bored during the week, working in a bank as a teller. I go home at night though, not like Steve here."

"What do you do?" Olie asked, studying Steve closely. He was her idea of a hippie. He was slight of frame and fair, blond hair hanging down around his ears and neck, narrow angular nose, blue eyes, thin lips. He could have been an impersonation of Christ—the Sunday school picture book image, except for his expression which was tense. His clothes were dirty, and horribly wrinkled: a blue work shirt, brown corduroy pants and a thick black leather belt.

He seemed unaware of her scrutiny. "Oh, I walk around, sit, think."

"You don't sleep?"

"Yeah, sometimes; the trouble is the cops are always pushing you and telling you to move on when you rest. So now I don't sleep at night, except at someone's pad."

"And you're not tired?" Olie seemed immersed in personal hygiene.

"No, I take pep pills to keep me awake at night and then I sleep outside during the day when the cops don't bother me."

"What do you do when you need to eat?"

"Whatever I want to when I have to—first I try to get it from someone else, food I mean. But I'm on to something good now. You see my hair?"

Olie gave him a long look.

"Yes," she decided, "it's trimmer than most except it's dirty."

"Well, I had it cut. You should have seen me two weeks ago, it was below my shoulders." He sighed. "It cost me four bucks, but it looks good, doesn't it? I could have cut it myself, but I couldn't get it to look this good. It was a lot of money but it was worth it. Like I say, I had to."

Try as she could, she couldn't see any style to it whatsoever. "Why did you have to have your hair cut? I thought hippies didn't feel they *had* to do anything."

"I told you I was on to something good." He paused dramatically. "I'm selling dope. The contact said I couldn't unless I got my hair cut—too suspicious otherwise."

"You sell dope?" Olie was incredulous; he looked so harmless.

"Yeah. I just started. I wouldn't sell any to you though, only to friends I can trust. That way you don't get caught."

Olie frowned. "Aren't you afraid that maybe I'm an agent or something?"

"No," said Steve, "you're too young to be a 'cover.' Besides I can tell."

At this point, the poet repassed the table and slipped Olie one of his mimeographed poems. On the back he had written: "One thing I remember your saying interested me. When I told you I lived alone, you said, 'Good for you, I don't understand how hippies can stand to live so many together.' I'd like to discuss this with you. Call me during the day." At the bottom was a phone number.

Olie tucked the note away and turned back to Rudi and Steve. "It's true, I'm not a 'cover' as you say, but I still don't understand why you have to sell dope or beg to get money. I like to do the same things you do . . . sit around, talk to people and think. And what's more, I get paid for it."

Their eyes bugged at this.

"What do you do?" Rudi asked.

"I work for a magazine, and do a little free-lance work besides."

"You're lucky," said Rudi, "I'd like that instead of banking."

Steve was back staring into space and tapping his foot. His moodiness intrigued Olie.

"How old are you?" she asked.

"Eighteen."

"Are you from Toronto?"

"No, Calgary. But I haven't been back in two years. I left school when I was sixteen. Went to Vancouver. That's the place, man. Thirty, forty, to a house—right on the water. Get up in the morning and run out to the ocean for a bath. That's the scene. I'm just in Toronto to see what it's like."

All this random moving around intrigued Olie. "Do your parents know where you are?" she asked.

"Yeah," said Steve, staring down Yorkville's main street. "I send 'em a post card every once in a while. They must have stopped worrying by now. They're used to it. Even when I went to school, officially, I'd never go. There was this place down by the railroad where we used to hang around. That's where I tried pot."

Steve's plastic façade was wearing down; part of his problem, Olie thought, was sheer exhaustion and nervousness as a result most likely of pep pills—amphetamines—he was using to stay awake. But she plowed ahead, unconsciously relating her questioning to her own rationale.

"Do you have any plan?" she asked. "Do you want to do anything in particular?"

"Oh, sure," said Steve, "I got it all over these other guys. I got a trade. I'm a painter, a house painter. Learned from my dad. I'll travel around for another couple of years and then go back to Calgary."

"I was asking him questions," Olie concluded, "that made him realize that he didn't have a just live-for-the-moment hippie philosophy, nor a conventional middle-class stick-to-the-rules study—marry-work-live-in-the-suburbs philosophy, either. And this made him nervous, as he wondered uneasily, 'Who am I anyway, what am I doing here, what am I going to do in the future?'"

There must have been something about Olie, her age, her looks, her being perhaps what they secretly wanted to be, that sympathetically drew out these aimless young people. For Steve now made an admission that had never been made to me in conversations with hundred of hippies. "Oh, I don't know," he said with a grimace of disgust. "I'm just mixed up, I guess."

She looked over at him suddenly with new, speculative expression.

"Have you ever taken LSD?" she asked.

"Yeah, often," he replied. "But be careful if you take it. I've seen guys right here on the street try to kill themselves to get rid of the things they were seeing under LSD." He looked up challengingly. "But you can still learn something with it."

"And what did you learn?"

"Lots of things, like responsibility for myself; it's up to me, everything is, and how to relax, and enjoy, and sympathize. It's hard to explain."

If it was so enlightening, why was it so hard to explain?

"You may be doing very well, but it all seems false to me," Olie said. "I understand you—and what you learned, but it all seems fake to me because it's synthetic. A chemical made you see that—you didn't work and struggle to come to terms with what life's all about. That's what I have against LSD, aside from the harm it can do to the body. I struggled to learn all those things, and you just take a cube of sugar, lie back and the meaning of life comes to you. It's too easy to be true."

Steve mulled it over. "Sure, there are other ways, but this is one way, so what's wrong with that?"

She regarded him doubtfully.

"You don't look like you're enjoying yourself or me right now," she said.

Steve suddenly stood up and motioned for her to follow. "I'll show you," he said.

Rudi was left alone, staring glumly into space.

"We walked a few blocks until we came to an old ramshackle wooden house on a rundown block full of other big rundown houses," Olie recalled. "Steve called into the first-floor bay window, someone rang the buzzer and we entered a huge, smelly room filled with one bed and a clutter of orange crates, boxes full of books, papers, underpants, a torn shirt here, a pair of jeans there. Yellow paint on the walls was peeling, the mirror above the fireplace, which was being used for garbage disposal, was smoky and so thankfully didn't reflect anything caught in its line of vision." The newcomers hardly created a stir.

"Steve introduced me to the hippie lying around on the one bed, two overstuffed and coming-unstuffed armchairs, and the floor."

This was a small community of hippies which grew or shrank depending upon who was on the road, what friends came to town, how many hippies they needed to get together the $63 a month rent.

Grace, an advertising layout girl for a newspaper by day and hippie's girlfriend by night, was lying on the bed waiting for her boyfriend George to come back with help. This was a crisis night in the life of these hippies—the landlord had evicted them, and they had an hour to pack up and get out. No one was lifting a finger. Nor was anyone talking to anyone else; everyone was in their own private world of what seemed to be sheer emptiness. Perhaps they were thinking underneath blank stares, but their faces showed no sign of mental activity. Olie was the only one disturbed by all the packing and moving that needed to be done within the hour.

"After a while Ed, the sociable one of the group, got up to get coffee for all of us. He smiled. That distinguished him from Steve. Ralph, seemingly the leader, sat hunched up in a pile of dirty laundry, and Mike, the huskiest, had made the scene in Toronto and was taking off for Vancouver, the hippie paradise of the world according to him. Varying heights and lengths of hair from ear length to shoulder length were common to all as were dirty tight pants, and wrinkled shirts. Inside, no shoes was the password and everyone's feet appeared black; no longer dirty, just plain black as the dirt had penetrated the skin.

"Do your own thing, be free, was the hippie slogan; in terms of outward appearance all these hippies were doing the *same* thing. Conformity to the nth degree. Ed came back with coffee and generated some conversation by asking who I was and what I was doing in Toronto. I told him I was visiting and meeting hippies, and reporting on them. And what was he doing?"

Ed answered matter-of-factly. "I do whatever I have to do and no more. First, I beg to get money for food, or go to some of the kitchens around that hand out stuff, and then, if I can't get enough that way, maybe I sell paper flowers to the tourists. Ralph here (pointing to the guy hunched up in the laundry) organized a paper flower factory. We make 'em here and sell 'em out on the street at night. Sometimes when I'm high on pot or LSD, I steal stuff, nothing big, whatever's around and easy to get; food from stands, or pick up stuff in stores."

Olie's sense of propriety was offended. "That's not hippie, that's just wrong," she protested.

Ed smiled. "Well, like the world's all one on LSD, we're all part of the same thing, the same family, so it's not really stealing then."

His sophistry was lost on her.

"Do you have any plans for the future," she asked, "or will you just go on living this way?"

"The hippie thing is to live each day. How do I know what I'll do? I'm getting married some time soon, that I know, and I'll do whatever I and we feel we like."

Olie, an Establishment girl, was frankly nonplussed. "You're getting married? How are you going to support a wife?"

For a moment, she was afraid she had overreacted. "Ed just looked at me as though I was really the most hopeless case he'd ever come across and nothing he could say would help. But he tried anyway: 'I'm not supporting my wife, we're going to live *together,* we'll both work as much as we have to and want to and do whatever we want.'"

Olie's middle-class background suffered a wrench. "Okay. But what if your wife gets sick, and you get in debt or have a baby? Things happen and you need money. It would be nice not to have to worry, but the world isn't set up that way."

Ed was not easily roiled. "There are lots of ways—I'd borrow, use state help, work if I had to."

Suddenly, he turned away. Just as the conversation with Steve had ended when it got too pressingly direct, so did this one. With nothing else to do, Olie started looking around the room. On the table next to the bed which she was sharing right then with Grace, she noticed a package of birth-control pills. She asked what happened when someone wanted to make love and others were in the room.

"What would you do?" asked Ralph.

"Well, I'd ask everyone to leave, leave myself, or wait until some other time."

Ralph laughed. "It's not very polite to ask people to leave their home, especially when there aren't many other places to go and it's cold. And there is nowhere else for you to go, either, for privacy, and if you wait you'll never do it because there's always someone around. In Vancouver, dozens share a house."

"So you just make love with everyone else around?"

"That's the idea," said Ralph.

With all her Establishment hangups, Olie was obviously beginning to seem ancient to them, and they were turning her off. There was no point in staying on.

"Steve was getting restless again, and said he was going out. I looked at my watch and found to my great surprise that it was 2 A.M. so I left with him. On my way out, Mike gave me a book of Spenser's poems. He couldn't get them into his suitcase and didn't figure he'd need them in Vancouver. No one got up or said goodby. I just left. Once we got back to the main street, Steve took off, too. 'See ya round,' he said. When I looked around to say goodby, he was lost in the crowd."

Where I had scouted the Yorkville surface, Olie had with her open appearance—and mind—quickly brought the utter futility of all the underlying human ferment into focus. She now looked forward to a weekend with an "elite community," not far from the Canadian border. "There will be three college professors there," she said, "and it should be stimulating to see how they react on each other." On this bright expectation, I traveled north with her.

As she did, I met the faculty members, all youthful, all articulate, all liberally oriented, and all looking forward to a weekend of pot. In about an hour, I had learned about all I could from these paragons of "higher education," and after a lecture from one, a sociology professor, on the chauvinism of the American press (and everybody differing from his own special brand of permissiveness), I drove on to the Montreal Expo, while Olie stayed dutifully behind to put her report together.

For Olie, it had not been a completely fruitless weekend, as her report indicated.

"Communities: Hippie life often involved groups, boys and girls all living together. So when Frank, a psychology professor at a liberal university, invited me to his farm in upstate New York for an intellectual weekend discussion of community living, I was quite enthusiastic. The idea baffled me. Living with a group out of necessity? Okay. Orgies? Okay. Living with *some-one?* Okay. All of this was comprehensible. But living with a whole bunch of people whom you don't know beforehand? Why?"

Olie's awakening came slowly. "I like to think I realized five minutes after I arrived that this was not to be my weekend of enlightenment. But, really, I think it took a bit longer. Frank, I knew, had problems or rather pretensions. I didn't know the pretensions were problems until this weekend. My first thought when I arrived was: the people who Frank told me he invited couldn't come, so he got others. Where was the wife of the sociology professor? I learned the next day that the sexy girl who was always posing herself in calendar positions whom I thought was Frank's date and who seemed to have her eyes on every male in the room was the sociologist's wife. Her husband, Tom, impressed me at first. He seemed polite, was clean-looking in a country club sort of way and didn't seem to interrupt the way Frank did. It wasn't until liberal-minded sociologist Tom had the floor to himself the next morning that he turned me off. His conversation concerning the value of a professor's time ('There's no reason why I shouldn't read when a student comes to see me, they need me and I don't have as much time to waste.') and his angry dismissal of anyone in a position of authority reflected more hostility in one human being than I thought tolerable."

Hannah, a professional student, seemed oddly incongruous in this group. "At twenty-six," Olie reported, "she reminded me of a terribly mixed-up college sophomore, the kind who drops out. She had done this five years ago and she hadn't progressed since.

"As for Frank, he was not pretentious," it developed, "but all confused about his mother and women and life in general and was generally obnoxious but nice despite it all."

They sat around half the night, smoking pot, and discussing what was wrong with college and country, but saw nothing wrong in themselves.

The weekend left Olie depressed. "I'd been looking forward to enlightenment. Instead, I listened for hours on end to people defending their lives and ideas and saying in essence, 'I'm great, I've got the answers.' I wondered for a whole week afterward how in God's name I'd survived a college education and in the end decided it was luck. I vowed that I'd never send *my* daughter to a university. Or if I did, I'd explain to her first that college professors do not have all the answers by any means—or—perhaps any answers."

One thing came out of the dreary weekend. Through Hannah, who lived in New York's East Village, Olie was introduced to that unchartered hippieland on the edge of the slums. Hannah had been Olie's roommate in the upstate community, and had helped make it a memorable weekend. She was an overage hippie, reflecting what younger hippies could look forward to in time, without some development. "There were lots of Hannahs around the country, building up on college campuses," Olie decided. She was certainly no Flower Girl.

She was dumpy looking, with unshaven legs, long, shaggy, dirty hair, dirty feet and fingernails, a very round face and a very fat body. Hannah had been lying in the bed next to Olie's when she woke up that weekend. Having forgotten her toothpaste, Olie asked if she could borrow some.

"Sorry," Hannah said proudly, "I never use toothpaste."

Olie bravely accepted Hannah's invitation to dine the following week in the East Village. But her appetite left her as soon as she walked into Hannah's crowded flat. "I've been in slum apartments before, but never one so truly dirty," she recalled. "Clothes, food, and books littered the floor in all three rooms, and every other surface except a makeshift couch and chair. Everything was crumpled and tattered. It seemed to me that in Hannah's world there must be a law: 'Thou shalt create havoc, let filth lie where it may, and remain oblivious to the disorder around you.'"

Hannah followed this commandment faithfully. A trail of books, mostly opened face-down, led from under the bathroom tub to the kitchen table to the bed (a mattress on the floor partially covered by a gray sheet and big coat).

Olie gingerly sat down. "So this is a hippie pad," she said.

Hannah guffawed. "Hippie, are you kidding? Because of the communication speed-up, new generations are formed every five years instead of the traditional twenty, and their values differ accordingly. I'm too old to be a hippie. Most of my friends nineteen and twenty feel they're too old too. The hippies around here are fifteen and sixteen."

Olie was caught up in labels. "What do you consider yourself?" she persisted.

"Nothing, really. I guess I'm a member of the Lower East Side community, otherwise known as the East Village. Only place I feel comfortable anymore. You get used to trusting people down here and being open about things and people just aren't friendly or even communicative elsewhere. You forget what life is like outside this area. Now it's a big shock for me to go uptown."

Olie was not as favorably impressed. "I walked over two or three blocks from Third Avenue and didn't feel I was in such friendly territory—guys sidled up to me with propositions, and Puerto Ricans were saying God knows what as I walked along."

Hannah dismissed her remarks with a laugh. "They resent young white girls walking around alone. To them it represents free sex, only none of it for them. In their culture, a decent girl just doesn't walk around by herself. So they're pretty nasty but harmless."

Olie was not so easily reassured. "You're not afraid of being robbed or broken in?"

Hannah shrugged. "You can see all the bars on the windows and it's getting worse. Speed [Methedrine] makes people dangerous, and real dope addicts are moving in now."

Olie looked around the room. "What do you pay here?"

"Fifty-five dollars a month, not bad for three rooms."

"And you're not working?"

Hannah smiled pleasantly. "I haven't been working for a year now. Before that I was sick for a few months in the hospital and before that I had a copy editing job for a medical journal. So I collected disability insurance for a while and now I have welfare. You get your rent and living allowance. I spend about $25 a week. It's amazing how well you can live on welfare. Everyone does it. They give you plenty of money especially if you know how to handle it; which most of the real slum people don't. They just waste it. And if you have a kid, you've got it made. It's close to $100 a week then; you get to buy clothes and everything. Everyone here lends stuff (drugs) to friends and so you can pick up an extra $100 that way, selling the stuff."

She sighed dreamily. "Once you've got your welfare card, everything is free. It's a great way to live. I've been doing it for a year now."

Olie, free-lancing for extra money, was properly abashed. "You haven't worked for a year? What do you do all day?"

Hannah gave a graphic picture of the hip young lady on welfare. "It's amazing how my days have changed. At first I didn't know what to do and sort of did nothing, really. I'd spend the whole day washing or buying food or something. And then I got regulated. I've been going to group therapy sessions twice a week and one dance therapy class. And movies. I'm interested in film and want to make a movie. I go to a class about moviemaking, too. I read a lot. Everybody should have a year like this. I'm thinking about finishing my degree or maybe just studying film and maybe teaching."

Deep down inside, Olie winced. "Don't you have to plan anything?"

Hannah shrugged nonchalantly. "It depends on what I decide I really want to do. It's too late to start school now, so I'll just wait and see."

Olie kept plodding along. "Why didn't you get your degree before?"

Hannah was in and out of college. "I went to Swarthmore, it was a compromise. My parents wanted me to go to Radcliffe, and I didn't want to, so Swarthmore seemed the place. But I hated it, and left. That was the first time I did something a little out of the ordinary. My parents couldn't believe it. I'd always been perfect in high school, top student, nice little middle-class Jewish girl. So then I went to Columbia and that was worse. I got involved in a community of anarchists; college kids and older people, married, unmarried, living together. They lived, dreamed, thought anarchy. Columbia wasn't much better than Swarthmore, so I came down here and shared a loft kitchen and helped put out a little magazine. I got sick of that and pretty soon it just broke up anyway."

Still the straight-arrow, Olie asked, "What did your parents think of it all?"

Hannah's mouth tightened. "They weren't too happy. But they couldn't do anything about it. We weren't on good terms at home, but once they didn't have control, they were okay. Now they're having a blast, buoying up their ego, I guess, by writing this newsletter on youth. It's done quite well, it helps middle-class businessmen and clergy, and whoever would be interested in what youth was up to, feel they're *in*. It's their way of showing me, I guess," she laughed. "They ask me what I think of something sometimes and I tell them it's junk and they print it anyway."

Olie returned to the East Village and all its shoddiness. "What do you feel you've gained by living here?"

Hannah seemed pleased by the question. "I know not to believe all the tripe I read about slums and poor people and hippies. They're really happy here." She thought a moment. "You really know what it's all about when you've got the same money to spend as a slum person. Pot isn't the great thing to talk about here, it's just a pleasant thing to do. LSD used to be all over but now they're getting scared to take it because of all the reports of chromosome changes."

As usual, Olie was conventionally oriented. "Do you ever want to get married?" she asked.

Hannah's frown made her even plainer than before. "Someday. I used to feel sorry for myself because all of my friends were married, but now they're all divorced." She moved her dumpy shoulders slightly. "If girls aren't married here, they have babies anyway. But it keeps you at home too much. Later on, maybe . . . I couldn't give up my freedom now."

Not all hippies waited for the future to overtake them. San Francisco was crawling with hippies turned activists. They were staging peaceful—and unpeaceful—demonstrations for peace, and a segment, the Sexual Freedom League, was advocating what everybody was doing anyway.

An Oakland anti-draft demonstration, across the bay from San Francisco, was a model of hippie activism. Ringing an induction center, the Flower Children sang Christmas carols (it being the Yuletide), and waved flowers as they were carted off in the paddy wagons. "Communicate," their leaders advised, "not with anger or hatred, but with love and respect for each person."

Protest singer Joan Baez went joyfully to jail, with her own version of the African song, "Kumbaya"—"no more drafting, My Lord Kumbaya, no more napalm, My Lord Kumbaya." As she marched into the police van softly singing, "Silent Night, Holy Night," police and demonstrators alike stood quietly in hushed tribute, for this was the season of the Prince of Peace.

Not far away was the hippie paradise of Haight-Ashbury, where the hippie stereotypes, plastics, as distinguished from the activists, dominated the grotesque scene.

Love had ostensibly filtered into Haight-Ashbury. Young men and women stood in fond embrace on the walks and in hallways; male or female combinations strolled the streets, giggling together as though enjoying some delicious secret. In hippie shops, pungent with the bittersweet aroma of marijuana, posters sharply reflected the ugly mood of revolt. One bitterly flayed the Great Society, showing its supreme architect, Lyndon Johnson, standing determinedly on a rock pile of human skulls. In another, marijuana was sardonically represented. KEEP CALIFORNIA GREEN, one poster stated, GROW GRASS.

Sex was not overlooked. *Chastity,* a poster announced, *Is Its Own Punishment.*

Ironically, health stores were everywhere, while malnutrition was commonplace.

A hundred thousand hippies had stormed Haight-Ashbury, with some twenty thousand clogging the narrow area at any one time. They brought not only a drug problem, which immediately worsened, but a syndrome of familiar disorders—hepatitis (sometimes hippie-itis), venereal disease, upper respiratory infections, and sundry nervous indispositions.

There were strong divisions within the hippie movement. The activists, for instance, disdained the stereotypes they felt were hurting the hippie cause with their sloth, squalor, and flagrant drug abuse. Others, less militant, still deplored the conventional image of the scraggly bearded, unclean hippie. Some of these were far less tolerant of Haight-Ashbury than any outsider. Howie, up from Houston six months before, was of the do-nothing hippie aristocracy. He was a clean-cut looking young man whose long auburn hair framed a well-scrubbed countenance. His clothes were freshly laundered, if frayed, and he professed to have taken LSD and pot for mind expansion only, put on to the former by Aldous Huxley's Door of Perception, and to the latter by a professor who thought marijuana no worse than alcohol or tobacco.

Howie felt he had control of his drug habit. "There's nothing wrong with drugs," he said with a determined authority, "so long as you know your own limits." He felt the "plastics" had neither limits nor standards. "Haight-Ashbury is a dirty, miserable pesthole for escapists and weird-os which has given the whole hippie movement a bad name."

Across the dinner table, Howie looked healthy, but apparently wasn't. He had worked at various odd jobs but was jobless for months now because of a recent bout with hepatitis.

I had read somewhere that dirty hypodermic needles were often infectious, causing hepatitis.

He shook his head scornfully. "Occasionally, they shoot 'speed' or the 'barbs' [barbiturates], but not me. I wouldn't take those chances."

"Then how did you get it?" I asked.

He shrugged. "How do you get anything?"

I mentioned that marijuana apparently lodged in the liver for five or six days, and the accumulating toxics could make that highly sensitive organ susceptible to infection.

Howie chuckled mirthlessly. "What nonsense," he said. "Would all these university people be saying it was harmless if it wasn't?"

His drug habit was formidable. He had had more LSD trips than he could remember; two or three hundred perhaps, and he smoked five or six cigarettes—joints—a day.

It seemed an expensive habit, at the going price of fifty cents to a dollar a joint.

He gave me a pitying glance. "I have friends who share." Whoever in his group that happened to be working at the time provided the "bread" for the LSD or pot shared almost as a ritual.

"Suppose there was no pot?" I asked.

He looked at me incredulously. "How else would you feel good?"

Other people had obviously found peace and contentment in faith and a sense of achievement.

Howie's face set in a stubborn mold. "I see things more clearly than ever," he said flatly.

"What are you doing with all this clarity?" I asked.

His eyes flashed. "I intend to do something at the proper time."

"Nothing ventured, nothing lost," I observed glibly.

He flushed. "I'm not afraid of competing."

Still, he had dropped out of college in his final semester, just short of graduation. It all seemed rather pointless.

He smiled almost pityingly. "It was because I was nearly through that I quit."

That didn't seem to add up, either.

He patiently explained. "It suddenly struck me that if I finished up I would become part of the Establishment, a college graduate looking for a job, any old job, with sick benefits, promises of promotion, pension benefits, and all that Establishment pap."

It didn't sound catastrophic to me.

He smiled thinly. "I would have been caught, trapped, by my degree."

I studied him closely. "And what do you have now?"

He shrugged. "I'm free."

"Free from what?"

"For anything I want."

"Just so it doesn't require doing anything?"

"I won't be sick forever."

He looked healthy enough to me. "Perhaps you wouldn't be sick at all if it weren't for the drugs?"

He eyed me sullenly. "Marijuana is not a drug."

"What is it then—a substitute for thought?"

He apparently didn't consider the question worthy of an answer.

I wondered next when he had picked up the habit.

He grimaced. "It's not a habit."

"Then why not stop."

"What for, it's not harmful?"

"And neither, I suppose, is LSD."

He laughed. "They did a survey at Berkeley, with twenty-three parents who were on LSD, and sixteen of them had super-babies; quick, active, alert."

I mentioned other surveys where the finding were diametrically opposed to Berkeley's.

He wagged his head contemptuously. "Berkeley shows there's nothing to it."

In this frame of reference, it was laughable, of course, to postulate that "harmless" marijuana might damage anybody, even when it appeared to do so.

"Hell," he said, "the groovier professors even take pot."

"And doctors and nurses," I pointed out, "quite frequently take heroin. Does that make it therapeutic?"

He shook his head. "You just don't understand. You're"—he groped for the right word—"prejudiced."

I disclaimed the label.

"On the contrary," I said, "if you were functioning on marijuana; productive, healthy, and optimistic, I would acknowledge that marijuana was good for you."

My eyes fell on his hands, nervously fiddling with a glass. On the second finger, left hand, the marriage finger, I noticed two plain silver bands.

He caught my glance and smiled.

"Have they any significance?" I asked.

"One," he said casually, "was a gift from a girl, another from a man. They're symbolic."

"Of what?" I asked.

His smile broadened. "Of something you wouldn't understand."

He was twenty-two, no longer a child, yet he seemed caught up in secret childish games.

He smiled bleakly. "Your generation doesn't understand. The joy of life is in its being, not in trying to get somewhere or something. And there is joy in love, just plain ordinary loving. That's my commitment in this life, showing people I care for them."

It sounded like so much claptrap to materialist me. "And how do you do that?"

He regarded me solemnly. "Would you be surprised if I told you that I loved you?"

"I'd be overwhelmed," I said.

He smiled. "Happiness is fleeting, joy everlasting, and that is why I must love you, and everybody else."

It was quite sporting of him to include me, as he had little respect for me as a writer. He had run through my book, *The Sixth Man,* described as a *Study in Homosexuality,* and had not thought it much of a study. "Rather superficial and trite," he decided loftily.

The book had been lightly regarded by many homosexuals, though commended by some psychiatrists and clergy.

I wondered why he took so sharp a stand. "Do you have any misgivings about your own sexuality?" I asked.

He smiled disdainfully. "Actually," he said, "there is no such thing as a homosexual, only people."

"Sexually," I said, "people are considered heterosexual or homosexual—or neuter."

He laughed thinly. "That's just another label."

And using a label, for want of anything better, which did he consider himself?

He shrugged, and then squarely caught my eye and held it. "I've had heterosexual and homosexual relationships—they're not conflicting."

He had none of the traditional earmarks of the overt homosexual; his voice and mannerisms were masculine, his reactions calm and deliberate. His features were rugged and still too youthful for any of the lines or planes that in time would mirror his personality.

All through his conversation, he had stressed love and sharing, the importance of caring for even people he didn't like.

It had suggested another thought to me. "Are you promiscuous?" I asked.

He smiled tolerantly. "I've never had a relationship with anybody I didn't like."

He had not answered the question.

I couldn't resist. "And like Will Rogers, you have never met a man you couldn't say something for?"

He had never heard of Will Rogers.

Perhaps because hippie boy and girl duos had seemed so lovingly commonplace, I had not considered homosexuality a factor in the hippie movement. I was in for a surprise.

"The whole hippie movement is homosexual," he said enjoying my discomfiture. "The whole idea is to love one another. Why should we cut off half the population from this love?"

It was an interesting thought, but I still couldn't get over my surprise, remarking on the soft, lustrous femininity of so many hippie beauties in their gay attire. "It must be difficult for them to adjust to the idea of their boyfriends being homosexual," I said, finding it hard myself.

He almost choked on his beer. "What do you think *they're* doing?"

I looked at him in open-mouthed disbelief. "How can you say something like that?"

"How can I help saying it, when we're living all together. I'd have to be blind."

He stared at me moodily for a moment. "And it's easier for them," he said resentfully, "for nobody thinks anything of two girls kissing or hugging, or even snuggling in bed together."

From sex, thankfully, we went on to money. Howie had complained about being too broke to buy a Christmas tree for his friends, and I, perhaps rising to the bait, had given him a few dollars and an extra sweater to wear against the cold night. He had thanked me perfunctorily.

My mind had flashed back to the indigent Hannah and her East Village friends.

"Why not go on welfare for a while if you need help?" I asked.

His face tightened angrily. "They turned me down."

He had not met resident relief requirements.

"You would think they would help anybody," he said bitterly.

I looked across the table at this sworn enemy of the Establishment. "I wouldn't have thought you would want this help," I said.

He regarded me sharply. "Why not?"

"You even quit college to steer clear of Establishment entanglements."

He made a face. "That's different. When you're sick, you need help, and should be able to get it."

"How about the Haight-Ashbury clinic?"

"Oh, yeah, I got treated there, but you don't get 'bread.' "

"Well, aren't your friends happy to share?"

He looked at me sourly. "Most of the group are sick, only my roommate is working."

They had colds or hepatitis, and a chronic malnutrition aggravated by an overdiet of soft drinks and candy bars, apparently in response to the marijuana smokers' insatiable hunger for sugar.

Our dinner had not been particularly pleasant, and I was tired and ready to turn in. Howie offered to drive me back to the hotel. In the car, he was silent a while, seemingly mentally preoccupied, and then said suddenly, with a wheedling voice, "You know, I don't need much to get on my feet and get back to living a wholesome life." He regarded me speculatively out of the corner of his eye. "Would you know anybody wealthy enough to get me started?"

My guard went up. "The wealthy," I said fatuously, "don't give anything away for nothing."

"I might be able to do something for them." His eyes held

mine. "A benefactor would give me the chance I need until I get well."

We had drawn up to the hotel, and he gave me a last beseeching look. I clambered out of the car. "If I hear of any benefactors, I'll let you know," I said, not quite meeting his eye.

I heard the scrape of his car taking off. He was headed back into the darkness that covered him so inadequately. In the hotel elevator, I suddenly realized my mistake. I should not have given him the money or the sweater. He had judged my generation by his own.

Despite Howie's bland report on homosexuality, I had reservations about the prevailing rate among the hippies. It just didn't seem possible. In Los Angeles, away from the ephemeral fairyland of San Francisco, Patricia, an ex-hippie, now hip, received my misgivings with a smile.

In one respect, at least, Howie was right.

"I don't know if it's total," she said, "but it's pretty damn comprehensive." The scene was a familiar one. "The boy bombs out on LSD and pot, and with his fresh insights," she laughed, "turns on with other boys."

And the girlfriends?

She shrugged. "All the losers—the leftouts—get together."

It seemed a rather sick society.

Patricia's eyebrows went up. "Is anybody insisting it's well?" Almost in the same breath, she had coupled LSD with pot.

"As a matter of fact," she elaborated, "pot is worse because it creeps up on you when you least expect it, whereas even the looniest acidheads realize they can have a bad trip at any time."

She had taken LSD a dozen times before she had a bad trip; whereas pot had never given her an uneasy moment. "But, smoking pot, I always found myself with the wrong people at the wrong time, and never got anything done."

It had not been easy for her to give it up.

"But nearly everybody on it," I observed, "insists it isn't habit-forming."

She laughed. "They keep saying they can stop whenever they want to, but they never seem to want to. I've seen actors and writers break appointments, and miss the very opportunities they had come out to Hollywood for, just because they were so busy talking about the things they were going to do. That's pot for you."

It did have its uses. "A lot of the boys, of course, have sexual problems, and they can make it with a girl for the first time, relaxed with old Mary Jane."

It sounded rather contradictory.

"You were saying that so many hippies were homosexual?"

"Oh, sure, but not everybody on pot is a hippie, and some have guilt feelings the hippies don't even know about." Her voice had a bantering inflection. "Hippies don't worry about homosexuality, that's love, man."

She smiled slyly. "Why do you think some of these boys find it so easy to let their hair grow, even though they may not know why they're doing it themselves—at first?"

She brought out a copy of the Los Angeles *Free Press,* an underground newspaper which was a hippie favorite, and checked through the classified ads.

"This paper is full of it," she said.

I followed her finger to column one:

> Very Pretty Young Bi-Sex
> Fem Looking for Fem Only.
> Please Enclose Photo if
> Possible.

My eyes traveled briefly on:

> Young groovy goodlooking
> gay guy would like to meet
> same in Orange Co. All
> replies ans. Send photo if
> possible.

And, intriguingly:

> Small young man w/elfin
> appeal and liberal artsy-
> craftsy gutsy intelectual
> cx life-style desires to
> meet same: will answer
> all literate replies.

Just as San Francisco appeared more sophisticated than Los Angeles, so was the ad appeal more suave in the hippie-favored Berkeley Barb:

> Hip Berk Student seeks
> roommates. No one-night
> stands or non-students.

> Need Male roommate
> discreet semihip gay grad
> student with broad. Near
> campus, own room fireplace
> piano garden $60.

Still another:

> Male seeks male object For-
> ever Cleopatra and the Tam-
> ing of the Shrew. Looks un-
> important as object is finding
> true love!

At times, the argot was quite in:

> Male needs rm-mate semi-hip
> discreet acdc male/fmle.
> femmes must be butch ok if
> male no sx nr camps gdn fpl
> pno own rm.

This last had a special message for Pat. She looked up with a smile. "They're real hippies, anything to save bread."

Her finger again ran down the column, and a grin slowly spread over her face. "Now, there's one":

> 2 Beautiful Little Cats need
> homes. Call . . .

A telephone number was given.

It all seemed very enigmatic to me, but not to Pat. She carefully wrote the number down. "I'll just try it for the hell of it," she said with a smile.

5

LOVE ON THE RUN

In view of the love principle which presumably guided the Flower Children I was often intrigued by the hostility greeting friendly overtures of interest. I had been more pleasantly received by politicians, police, thieves, killers, and gangsters. They were at least civil. For most of the hippie extreme, I typified the generation over thirty, and they connected me with the rejection and disillusionment that was theirs at an early age.

Imperceptibly, perhaps through a subtle process of osmosis, they sensed my own reservations about drugs which were almost sacramental to them. Fortunately the hippies were only a small part of a much larger scene, a human revolution, which they influenced and were in turn influenced by. One had to wade into the turbulent sea of life, often tawdry and tinselly, to grasp the dynamics underlying a rapidly changing scene. Human values were afloat, and it was in the ceaseless human struggle that they

were gradually crystallizing, not in formless interviews in the
armchairs of savants and philosophers. The so-called experts—
psychiatrists, sociologists, churchmen—generally saw but one slice
of the melon, the slice they cut for themselves, and that slice,
while chewy, was hardly the entire meal.

Psychiatrist Norman Zinberg, Harvard lecturer on social relations, equated the drug habits of children with those of their
parents.

The parents took tranquilizers, sleeping pills, wake-up pills,
aspirin, insulin, the children marijuana, amphetamines, LSD.
"Drug-taking as an issue," Zinberg said, "doesn't come out of
the air. The parents say righteously, 'I wouldn't do it if I didn't
have to,' and rebellious teen-agers retort, 'I'm only doing what
you're doing.'"

Dr. Harry R. Brickman, clinical professor of psychiatry at
the University of California College of Medicine equated hippie
espousal of "nonviolence" to a "good trip."

"The psychedelic episode," he explained, "forces him to acknowledge his own death and he accepts it. This drastic emotional
experience then leads to a symbolic rebirth and development of
a new self which no longer needs to externalize destructiveness."

The Reverend David K. Wilkerson dumped the load squarely
back on the parents, and a lack of spiritual values. "Parents
who have done their best to raise children under the banner of
God need never feel the invasion of addiction," he said in his
Parents on Trial. "I have never met a drug addict whose parents
had succeeded in instilling sound spiritual precepts in his life."

Harvard's Farnsworth, an articulate observer, related drug-
taking to an overriding dissatisfaction with authority. "Young
people are keenly aware of social injustice, the threat of nuclear
war, and the ineffectiveness or downright hypocrisy of those in
authority . . . Because of their psychological effects, drugs temporarily help the young to escape their feelings of being alienated
under pressure, and helpless. Simultaneously, the act of drug-
taking places each individual in a group of kindred spirits. He

may feel better related to others, even as an objective observation shows him to be even more isolated than before."

Joan Baez, folk-singing hippie advocate of nonviolence, believed that more enduring values could be assimilated without drugs, through love, understanding, positive action. "There's no short cut to enlightenment, and drugs, besides being a bore, can be terribly harmful, physically." She proposed a new drugless activist cult dedicated to "unbrainwashing" the youth of America of the hangups of war and hate, fear and flight. "We want to overcome what school has done to them, to allow them to think."

An anguished parent, typical of so many who had toiled all their lives for their families, said almost tearfully: "My son hates me because I entertain my boss and other business associates whom I have criticized—not appreciating that I have put up with a job I hated so he could have the start I never had."

And the son? What did he say?

"He didn't do it for me, I didn't want it—I'm checking out of this phony world."

And so they checked out, scattering over the country, into Canada and Mexico, sometimes in communes, or Bohemian resorts, sometimes slums, often in a spontaneous converging under one roof.

By chance, I was unexpectedly exposed to a hippie microcosm at grips with the cold, cold world. An eccentric friend, a homeowner, had taken in many, otherwise homeless, renting out rooms to the "long-hairs," as she called them, in the various compartments of her own commodious Hollywood house.

"You should see them," she exclaimed indignantly, "like animals. One day I'll throw the whole pack into the street."

However, there seemed little danger of a mass eviction as one considered the cumulative rentals from her curious assortment of cubbyholes.

"I can't figure them out," my landlady friend said with a shake of her gray head, "they're so repulsive, and they get the cutest girls." She shuddered. "You should just see these girls, beautiful, and they're crawling all over these things with the matted hair and the beards. It's enough to make you throw up."

There were presently six in her ménage, and if she turned her head, the number would multiply.

"They have larceny in their hearts," she said, "they're always sneaking their friends in, and, of course, never pay for them. There would be five in a room, if I let them."

"Why put up with it?" I teased.

"Well, they're not all that bad," she said grudgingly, "as long as they keep the place clean and pay their rent."

Had any beat her for the rent?

She laughed grimly, "Not this lady, they pay in advance or they don't stay."

She had recently had words with a hippie of seventeen, from nearby Santa Monica, who had insisted that a fourteen-year-old girl staying with him was his sister.

The landlady was horrified. "I didn't care if it was his mother; I wasn't going to have a kid that age around, and bring the cops down on me. I run a respectable house."

"Suppose she was his sister?" I asked.

"So what? These kids are like rabbits; it's sex and marijuana all the time, they're escapists." She shrugged. "All I know is, sister or no sister, she wasn't staying without paying."

Like the hippies, the landlady noisily professed the rule of love.

"Why don't you try loving them?" I asked.

"Love them!" Her ancient nose wrinkled in distaste. "It's all you can do to go near them."

Did she have any idea what made them tick?

"They're escapists, like I said. They're constitutionally opposed to work."

Then where did the rent and food come from?

"They scrounge from one another," she said tartly. "Some get checks from home, others chisel from the girls who visit them."

Had she sat down and tried to understand them?

"Of course, I have. I'm a mother myself, but I would have shot myself before giving birth to these monsters."

She thought a moment. "Why don't you talk to them—they're great talkers."

Her house was on a small side street off Hollywood Boulevard, near the heart of the film capital. It was a modest dwelling, and I didn't quite see why her overhead should be so great.

She sniffed. "Whereas they're always looking for something for nothing, I have water, light, taxes, and the bank to pay. I can't be a hippie."

She had tried to put some discipline into their lives, and shoo them out to job appointments. "If they're working," she said, "there's more chance I'll get my money."

Actually, how could she influence them when their own parents couldn't?

She laughed. "Oh, they'll move around when they want things, and can't get them anywhere else. They just think it's smart, putting one over on you."

She had put a head charge on each hippie visiting overnight. "Even if they sleep on the floor, they have to pay a dollar apiece."

The protests had been instant. "You're money hungry," one hippie told her disdainfully.

More reasonably, another pointed out that tenants elsewhere had overnight guests without being assessed for them.

She was not easily intimidated. "Then go and live in these other apartments."

Her present lineup was a typical mélange:

Dick, the mouth organist, from Chicago.

Jay, the rich man's son, from Beverly Hills.

Lewis, "from nowhere," a poet.

The Lizard, a Texan with a rock 'n' roll combo.

Eric, the Swede, with a "model" studio.

John, a fresh-faced refugee from the Canadian cold.

"You better start with Dick," the landlady advised, "Jay and Lewis are up tight."

I laughed at the hippie expression.

"You're groovy," I said.

I phoned later to see whether she had made any appointments. She was beside herself over the phone. "They're real creeps," she exclaimed, "no good to anybody, including themselves."

In a few moments, she simmered down sufficiently to acquaint me with the problem.

"They want to know what's in it for them," she said. "Can you imagine?"

"What do they want?" I asked.

She had landed on them like a ton of bricks. "I told them to pay up, and then be independent." One of the boys was inexcusably a week in arrears.

I surmised they were only trying to appear important.

"Maybe you've got them thinking like the Establishment," I said.

Her voice crackled over the phone. "What do you mean by that?"

"Everything has a price."

She relaxed. "How do you know you'll get anything out of those numbskulls? I wouldn't give them anything until they produce."

That afternoon, I stopped by the rambling frame house in Hollywood. The landlady was out, but she had left a note for me to proceed to a basement apartment in the rear.

I rattled on several doors, before one opened a chink, and a flowing red mop of hair showed through the narrow opening.

"What is it?"

The opening widened, and a tall, lean figure followed the hair. The owner was about nineteen, with thin lips and sullen gray eyes. He held an astrology magazine in one hand, and shaded his eyes with the other. He stood tautly on guard.

This was Dick.

A pretty girl with blue eyes and long blonde hair, a lovely figure in stocking feet, had followed him through the door, and was now standing protectively at his side. She had a clear open countenance and a friendly smile.

I was the first to break the silence, mentioning my interest in the generation gap.

He looked up with a sardonic smile. "What's that," he said, "another Establishment label?"

I smiled back. "What's the Establishment, but a hippie label?"

He frowned a moment, but I caught a glint of amusement in the girl's eye.

"How do you get on with your family?" I asked as an overture.

His lips tightened. "Why do you ask that, because of my hair?"

His hair was longer than the girl's, falling in rich folds over his shoulders.

"I'm not interested in your hair," I said mildly.

"All everybody cares about is appearance." His eyes moved briefly to the girl. "I keep clean and mind my own business, and that's what matters."

I had met him in the late afternoon, the landlady pointing out that her tenants stayed up nights and slept days.

"What is your business?" I asked.

He smiled crookedly. "That's my business."

The girl looked at him reprovingly.

"All right," he said, "I'm a mouth organist, we're trying to get together a group."

"Are you working now?"

He shook his head. "I'm not going to cut my hair for any job."

"How do you know you'd have to?" I asked.

He laughed harshly. "Can you imagine me in some office or shop?"

He had left home three years before.

"Do you hear from your mother and father?"

He shrugged. "Why shouldn't I?"

"Do you get along with them?"

"They're all right."

His father, a machinist, had worked for a newspaper in the Midwest before moving to northern California.

"Did they repress you in any way?"

He said, almost reluctantly, "They tried to understand."

"Did they object to your going off on your own?"

His eyes flickered to the girl, gazing at him with a glow in her eyes.

"Why should they?" he said grumpily. "I can take care of myself."

"But you're not working?"

"I'm willing to work, but I won't cut my hair."

"What's so important about an exterior?" I asked.

"I like it," he said firmly.

"It's your symbol of revolt."

"It's me."

"If you cut your hair, you're no longer you?"

"If I compromise, yes."

He believed in self-expression, "doing his thing" without hindrance.

"Pursuing your present course," I asked, "where will you be in ten or fifteen years, when that beautiful hair is turning a little gray and you no longer have the bounce of youth?"

He smiled thinly. "I'll have a career by then."

"But you're not getting any education."

The girl fairly beamed at my remark.

As the girl Terry stood there, friendly, open, alive, and looking quite country clubbish, I asked, "Are you a runaway from the terrible Establishment?"

She laughed. "You can run away, without leaving home."

"Oh, you're a rebel?"

She tossed her head. "If you want to call it that. I'm tired of being a status symbol for my parents."

And what were their horrible demands?

She grinned good-naturedly: "They have it all laid out; a new car when I get through high school, the country club, the right boy, and, of course, the snootiest college."

She seemed very fortunate to me.

She snorted. "I'm their social status, along with the big ranch house on the right block, the Cadillac, the club, even the gardening society."

I gave her a candid glance. "Are you mature enough to establish your own standards?"

"I'm mature enough to form my own values."

It was hard to reconcile a lovely home, jammed with creature comforts, accessible to mannerly eligible males, with the disreputable young man she was trying to be a part of.

I nodded toward Dick, glowering by now.

"Would you take him home?" I asked.

She smiled. "Why not?"

"And," I turned to Dick, "would you be willing to meet her parents?"

He shrugged. "What is there to be afraid of?" he paused. "But I wouldn't cut my hair."

I wondered how this incongruous pair had met.

Her face again lit up with a smile.

She had been sauntering along Sunset Strip with two girlfriends, when Dick had spoken to her.

"I noticed him instantly," she said with a caressing smile, "he was different."

I was willing to concede as much.

"Would you marry him?" I asked.

Dick gruffly interrupted. "Now, don't put her on a spot, we've only been together on four occasions."

"I was just wondering what she thought about you."

He was only slightly mollified. "She's too young to decide any-thing like that, anyway."

Terry was seventeen, a few months under the legal age of consent.

"Aren't you taking chances?"

"Oh, I don't think she'd turn me in—would you, Terry?"

She shook her head, smiling.

Obviously, whatever Terry was, she wasn't a virgin.

What future was there for Dick, and the others?

"I have to know where it all is first."

Was he getting help?

He looked up suspiciously. "What do you mean?"

"With drugs."

"Drugs?"

"Marijuana."

He snorted. "That's no drug, that's grass."

He smoked it all the time, as his friends did. "It helps you think things out."

"Out of where?" I asked. "That little hole you live in?"

He glared. "I like that pad, it's clean and neat, and it's mine."

"And so what is pot doing for you?"

"It makes you see things the way they are."

"For instance?"

"How everybody's chasing a buck, without giving a damn for anybody else."

I turned to Terry. "Have you tried it?"

She nodded.

"With him?"

She again nodded.

"Did he teach you?"

She smiled brightly. "No, I've been smoking it for three years, with my girlfriends."

"Do your parents know?"

She shook her head. "They wouldn't understand."

She spoke with the easy deference of a well-bred younger

person for one older than herself. "It really doesn't harm you at all, it's no worse than the cocktails my family guzzle, and we don't get as silly."

I found myself bridling at teen-age omniscience. "Do you think the lunatics the best judges of the asylum?"

Dick looked up from his astrology magazine, and grunted, "Aren't they?"

"What do your parents think about your hair?" I asked.

"My mother understood completely," he said, turning back to his book.

"And your father?"

He was silent a while. "My father would never understand my hair."

"Did he think you were trying to hide something?"

"What would there be to hide?"

I recalled hearing that long hair was a proclamation of unreadiness for adult responsibility.

Dick blinked incredulously. "I wear my hair long because I like it long."

I smiled. "And because it makes you independent of your father?"

He turned a page. "You can think whatever you like."

Terry was beginning to show signs of restlessness. "I better get home," she said, "before they send out a search party."

Dick stuffed the astrology book in a side pocket, and awkwardly held out a hand. "It was all right talking to you," he conceded.

On an impulse, I said, "I'm lunching with an astrologer this week, would you care to join us?"

He looked at me closely. "You really mean it?"

I nodded, and mentioned a time.

"Fine," he said, "I really would like that."

He disappeared into his hole, Terry following after him, apparently to retrieve her shoes.

The landlady called me the next day. "Well, what did you have to give him?"

"He didn't want anything."

She growled. "I guess they knew I wouldn't stand for it."

I expressed my surprise at the caliber of Dick's girlfriend.

"Oh, sure, they're always getting these girls who hate their parents because they've made things so easy for them." She laughed. "These boys push them around, and they love it. They fight over them, give them money, pay their rent. It's incomprehensible."

"At least," I slid in, "you get your rent out of it."

"I better, or they won't be around long."

I mentioned that I planned to see Dick again, with an astrologer friend.

"Oh, sure," she said, "I heard all about that. He was around bragging how an important writer had asked him to lunch with a famous astrologer."

"What's wrong with that?" I asked.

"Oh, nothing, except they're such hypocrites. They want everything we want—except they're afraid to go out and get it. That's why they're on pot. It's an excuse for not doing anything else."

At the appointed time, I turned up, but Dick was not at home. The landlady, apologizing for him, compensatingly presented me to her other luminaries.

"This is Lizard," she said, almost proudly, picking out a tall, dark, cadaverous youth of eighteen with a pimply face.

The Lizard tentatively extended his hand.

I mentioned waiting for Dick.

The Lizard's lips curled. "He won't show."

"How do you know?"

He shrugged. "He's a hustler."

The landlady clucked reprovingly. "These hippies are always squabbling."

The Lizard made a face. "He's just making the scene."

The landlady rallied, perversely, to Dick's defense. "I think he's out looking for a job."

The Lizard grunted. "Looking to scrounge would be more like it."

She gave the Lizard a sharp glance. "Now, I thought you boys were getting together in a musical group."

The Lizard gave her an exaggerated stare. "We have a musical group, but he's not in it."

"Why not?" I asked.

His eyes coldly engaged mine. "Because he has no talent."

"One can't do much with a mouth organ," I conceded.

"Some can," he said.

Two youthful companions, silent till now, nodded agreement.

One, the fresh-faced Canadian, observed with just a trace of a Scottish burr, "There's really no awareness about him, no idea about a better life, just an opportunity to tie in with a glamorous movement that may give him a phony identity."

I had thought Dick truly interested in a job.

The Lizard sneered. "He won't work while these chicks are giving him 'bread.'"

I didn't quite see Dick as a Romeo.

"These girls are just making the scene, too." He laughed. "They complain about being stifled at home, the poor things."

The landlady regarded him quizzically.

"They want only the same thing you want," she said, "individuality."

It was still not clear why Dick was disliked so by the others.

The three young men looked stolidly ahead.

The landlady pointed to a heavy wooden bracket covering a large part of a bedroom wall. "He kicked that in, one night." She shook her head in bafflement. "He's good at karate, that's why they don't like him; they're afraid."

The Lizard didn't seem to agree.

"Who drugs don't like shouldn't use them," he said enigmatically.

"And who can handle them?" I asked.

He thought a moment. "They make me relax, I see things more clearly."

The Lizard glibly followed many intellectuals who differentiated between drug use and abuse. "The abusers," he explained, "like the flappers in Prohibition Days, drink to get rid of inhibitions."

The difference between the plastic and bona fide hippie got down to drug attitudes: "The difference between knowing the scene, or knowing yourself."

The hippie scene was obviously on its way out, because it had little or nothing constructive to offer.

The Lizard partially agreed. "The scene is out because phonies losing themselves in drugs have tended to identify the movement with pure façade: beards, beads, bells, sandals, bare feet and the long hair bit."

And what else was there?

"The original protest is still there, and will eventually be felt. So many people die a little every day because they didn't give their dreams a chance."

Out of this frustration came the discontent that led on a grand scale to wars, matrimonial infelicity, estranged parenthood. "How can an unhappy person help anybody else?" the Lizard said.

For one expressing himself so well, the Lizard had little formal education. He had barely finished high school, and then, at sixteen, had flown the coop. He was not looking for a free ride. "My combo rehearses every day." He frowned. "We had a few plastics, but they quit after the novelty wore off."

Being on his own appealed to the Lizard. "I don't resent my parents," he said, "they're products of centuries of bad thinking. My father's whole life was built around the business of supporting his family. He was like a prisoner, never able to do what he wanted to, and living vicariously in movies, adventure stories and, occasionally, booze."

He spoke quietly, with a natural grace and eloquence. "I never want to look back and regret not having done something I should have, something that would have broadened me as a person even if it had not worked out to my satisfaction."

The landlady had been studying the Lizard in frank admiration. "That boy," she said, with a shake of the head, "would have made a great lawyer."

The Lizard smiled. "But I want to be a musician."

The Lizard's group had already had several engagements in Strip clubs. "They don't pay much," he said, "because they don't have to."

The group were presently on their way to rehearsal.

"Are they on marijuana?" I asked.

He went blank.

I tried again.

He looked at his companions and smiled. "What musicians aren't?"

"I suppose you think you play better?"

"Of course you play better."

I mentioned a recent experiment, in which a jazz combo, swinging on marijuana, had made a recording before an audience also on pot—contact high. At the time, both performers and listeners were convinced the performance was superlative. When they were sober, the recording was played back. The dismay on their faces told the rest of the story.

The Lizard had listened, frozen.

"How about the Rolling Stones?" he said, referring to an English combo, which, like the Beatles, had become musical millionaires. "They were busted for pot."

The Lizard and his friends didn't drink or smoke tobacco. They compared marijuana to booze, with booze the loser.

The Lizard repeated the litany originally sparked by Berkeley in the West and Harvard in the East. "It's not as dangerous as alcohol, and it won't give you cancer." The fact that there were six million alcoholics in the country, constituting a major social problem, didn't appear to suggest that one devastating drug was more than enough.

The hippie scene was sharply changing. The Lizard and his friends were no longer talking dropout. They looked forward to participating in the Establishment scene, anxious to reap the material rewards of the Establishment, while living in such a way as to modify its values.

"It's the phoniness we'd like to get rid of," the Lizard said, with hearty affirmation from John and Frank.

"But isn't there something phony about all this stress on appearance?"

The Lizard nodded. "Originally, it was only a symbol of protest, but the weird-os got hold of it."

The landlady suddenly came to life. "There's as many hypocrites in your generation," she said tartly.

"Perhaps," the Lizard agreed, "but hypocrisy is still not the standard."

At this moment, a tall, slim figure hove into view—a young man of nineteen or twenty, with a thatch of yellow hair framing his face, and a psychedelic shirt of many colors covering his slight frame.

"There's the biggest hypocrite of all," the landlady announced, "but I admire him for it; that one's really turning a dollar."

Eric, the Swede, quietly accepted the tribute.

"I have to shove off," he said.

The landlady beamed. "There's the modern success story for you. He came over less than a year ago, and he's rolling in the mint."

Eric smiled deprecatingly.

"I do what I have to," he said with but the trace of an accent.

"And what you have to is very good," the landlady said.

"What do you do?" I asked.

The landlady answered.

"Eric," she said impressively, "runs a model studio just off the Strip."

One of the boys laughed. "It's the 'Strip,' all right."

The landlady silenced him with a glance. "He's just trying to be funny."

She looked at Eric with obvious respect. "Now tell the gentleman how much money you make a week!"

Eric seemed inordinately shy. "Oh, I don't know, I've never figured it out."

She turned to me. "He gets paid by the day, that's why."

"What kind of studio is it?" I asked.

He thought a moment. "Oh, girls pose, and men come and take their pictures."

Was there money in this sort of thing?

"Haw, haw, haw," the landlady cackled, "is there money in this? Tell him, Eric."

Eric obediently complied. "The girls do very well," he said.

"What is their fee?" I asked.

He shrugged. "The money is in the tips."

"Tell him how much," the landlady prodded.

He hesitated. "Well, one girl made one hundred and sixty-five dollars last night."

The landlady's jaw fell open. "That much," she said incredulously. "Of course, she had to split it?"

"Oh, no," he said, "that was after the split."

I suspected the worst.

Eric shook his head. "Oh, no, they just take pictures."

The landlady came to Eric's defense.

"They don't pose in the nude, do they?"

"Oh, no," Eric said, "that would be unlawful."

"Are they prostitutes, hippies, or what?" she asked.

"They're just ordinary girls," he said. "Hippies," he added disapprovingly, "are busy giving everything away." He paused. "Of course, if a girl wants to meet the photographer later, the tips are generally bigger."

The landlady turned to me. "They pose in all kinds of positions, of course, but they have to keep something on."

She turned, almost deferentially, to her Swedish roomer.

"Who are some of these photographers?"

He gestured vaguely. "Lawyers, doctors, architects—the pillars of society. We have the best."

The landlady's head bobbed approvingly. "Isn't that nice," she said, "all that money, without anybody killing himself for it."

One of the boys smiled impishly. "Sometimes the girls get pneumonia."

The landlady gave him a reproving glance. "That's not funny," she said. "Eric is doing a good job, and making good money. He deserves credit."

Eric smiled uncertainly. "I have to be off to work."

The landlady watched his retreating figure for a moment. "There's a good hard-working boy," she said warmly.

I couldn't help but add, "Who pays his rent on time."

She looked at me sharply. "And what's wrong with that?"

She consulted her watch. "That Dick has no idea of obligation, after all I've done for him."

The Lizard was inclined to be tolerant of the preceding generation, even while repudiating its values. "They tell you about being a Christian, doing the right bit, then at eighteen, they give you a number and a gun, and tell you to go out and make a kill."

Two previous generations—his father's and grandfather's—had similar problems.

The Lizard nodded. "No guts." He thought a moment. "They're never going to get me, I'll go to jail before Vietnam. That's not my number."

He squinted into the sun.

"Why don't we bomb everybody and get it over with? I could understand it, wrong or not, if we used the Big One on them. But we're fighting a war we're not even trying to win, and they're asking us to die before we've lived."

As we talked, the Lizard's girl approached. He looked at her. She was tall and shapely, with a mini skirt and glistening hair. She reminded me of Dick's girl. "I want to make music, love a few chicks, and do a few numbers of my own—isn't that what it's all about?" The Lizard shrugged expressively.

The girl entwined her arms around the Lizard and gave him an adoring look. She must have seen something I didn't, for the Lizard was certainly not handsome. But I glimpsed in him a confidence, an assurance, unnoticed before the girl's arrival. She had brought the priceless ingredient—love.

He turned to her now with a smile. "I thought I was going to lose my drummer today, but he made it."

The drummer had appeared that morning for his physical in the draft, and had passed with flying colors—in reverse. "He had been wired for 'speed' for three days previously," the Lizard explained, "and his heart was like a triphammer when they put the stethoscope on him."

The Lizard laughed as he recalled how groovy the drummer's performance had been. "They asked the Kid if he felt all right, and he looked at them with surprise in his big blue eyes, and said, 'I never felt better in my life.'"

The doctors had been bowled over.

"You mean, you always feel this way?"

"Usually, not this well," the drummer replied.

They had kept him a couple of hours, examining and re-examining, then ordered him to report a week later for another examination. He would have to continue on "speed"—Dexedrine, or Benzedrine—but the Lizard saw no alternative. "Either that or a cell," he said, with an appreciative grin.

I watched as the Lizard and his girl strolled off down the street, their arms linked. Nature had brought them together, society would rend them apart.

The other boys started to trickle off, but not before the landlady gave John, the Canadian, a hard look.

He regarded her calmly with big blue eyes.

"I'm looking for a job," he said, "and I'll get the rent to you."

Her jaw tightened. "I need it tonight; who pays my bills?"

His face dropped. "Even if I get a job, I won't have any money then."

Her words snapped out. "Do like Dick. You're a good-looking boy, find some girl who can help you."

The boy frowned. "All right, I'll have the rent tonight."

She pointed a finger at him. "Now, mind you, anybody staying over, that's a dollar extra."

As the boys sauntered off, she made a face. "They're just no good, no sense of responsibility." She shuddered. "That Dick, standing you up."

I had mixed feelings about my landlady friend. She was a good sort, addicted to money, but only because of her fears about insecurity and old age. She was interested in the young people who used her flats, or she obviously wouldn't have rented to them, but not sufficiently to disassociate herself from her own "bag," which was putting money away for a rainy day. She was no worse than most; better perhaps, for she did have a genuine concern for the youthful population floating through her flats, when and as she could afford it.

"That's what makes the world go around," she said, "money."

"Well, you can't take it with you," I said.

She regarded me darkly. "No, but it's useful while you're around."

Perhaps the hippies had something in their rejection of a world turning on money and power?

The landlady snorted. "Without it, you'd be out in the street, and then discover how many friends you have." She frowned. "There's too much leisure time, and not enough intelligence to know what to do with it. These kids sit around all day and smoke pot because they have nothing better to do."

Was there any difference between Dick and the others?

"He's lazier than the rest, and he's never had discipline, so I suppose it's just a matter of time before he's in trouble."

She telephoned the next day to explain Dick's not keeping his date. "He had to meet a friend at the airport, can you imagine that?"

I laughed. "Well, we can make it any day."

Her voice rasped harshly over the line. "I told him to make it tomorrow, the same time."

Unfortunately, Dick was again unable to make it.

He had been arrested the night before, and was being held on charges of assault.

The landlady explained. "He was on speed—whatever that is —and it made him really pugnacious. He was up on the Strip with this friend, and I suppose showing off. He got nasty with the hostess in this restaurant when she didn't seat him right away, and he pushed her. They called a cop, and he took a swing at the cop."

I recalled evidence that regular use of speed—amphetamines —led to almost uncontrollable irritability and violence.

"Did they nail him for drugs?" I asked.

"Disorderly conduct and resisting an officer. The kids said they never get them on speed, unless they find the pills on them."

"Will he be coming back?" I asked.

She smiled grimly. "I don't think so. His girl was over, she'd been trying to raise bail, and she said it looked like one to five years. He's been in trouble before."

It seemed a pity that nothing could have headed off disaster.

The landlady shrugged. "They're always blaming the family, but what can the parents do, when there's no outside discipline and all these intellectual boobs are saying there's no harm in drugs. You just know if that kid hadn't been on LSD, pot, and speed, he would never have reached a point where he could hit a cop."

For the first time I saw a glint of anger in her eyes. "They ought to skin alive the pushers feeding this poison to our youth."

I shrugged. "I don't think organized crime has much to do with this type of drug traffic."

"Then who has?" she challenged sharply.

"The kids seem to enjoy sharing," I said dryly, "as part of their interest in each other."

She wouldn't be put off. "But who's behind them?"

I agreed that somewhere, somehow, some profit motive was involved in spreading the soft-drug habit.

She stood watching me as I climbed into my car, and I caught a suggestion of moisture in her eyes. "I told that Dick," she said with a catch in her throat, "that he had it too easy."

I turned my car into Hollywood Boulevard, and noticed a short slight figure at the light, thumbing a ride.

I opened the door and he got in.

He was only going a few blocks.

"Couldn't you walk?" I asked.

He was thin, with a pasty face, and could have been no more than fourteen or fifteen. I noticed that one eye was red and rheumy, and he had a hacking cough.

He spoke quickly, with a noticeable wheeze. "I have to be there before my friend leaves."

I made a random diagnosis of his symptoms. "Do you smoke pot?"

A slow smile spread over his sallow face, and he showed me the darkly stained fingers of his right hand. "That's from roaches," he said. Roaches, it had been explained to me, were the precious nubs of the cigarette where the intoxicating ingredient had collected and was strongest.

"You must have an expensive habit?" I said.

He gave me a quick, appraising glance. "Do you live around here?"

"No, I'm from the East."

"That's what I thought." His voice became confidential. "Actually, my habit doesn't cost me anything. I push the stuff—just among friends—and at the high school down the street."

"Where do you get it?" I asked.

"From my friends, they're waiting for me."

"And where do they get it?"

His lips twisted. "Down Mexico way—why bother with a middle man when it grows all over the place?"

He was not particularly well-dressed or prosperous looking.

"Are the hippies your big customers?" I asked.

He snickered. "You can't be serious; they got nothing but the habit."

Who then, I wondered?

"The school kids like me; they save out of their lunch and date money."

He was still amused by my reference to the hippies. "Hell," he said, "I'd starve if it was for them, they want everything for nothing, the creeps."

However, a certain amount of missionary work was necessary.

"You do have to give away a lot of stuff free," he concluded, "because of the competition. But I should have a good night tonight."

"Why tonight?" I asked.

His grin widened. "It's a weekend, and the kids will be out full force." He rubbed his hands in satisfaction, as he squinted down the street at a lone figure standing before a shop window.

"Let me out here," he said, "I see my friend."

I was not quite through with the jailed Dick.

For all her failings, the landlady congenitally had a good heart. She had contacted the chaplain at the Los Angeles city prison, and asked after Dick.

"Tell him," she advised the chaplain, "that if he cuts his hair, the judge is liable to be more lenient. At least, he won't think that he's a chronic rebel and troublemaker."

The chaplain conveyed the message.

But it was no use. Dick's jaw had hardened. "Nobody is going to get me to cut my hair."

The landlady was beside herself with frustration. "Can you imagine that," she said, "he won't even be decent to help himself —and when they send him away, you just know they're going to cut it anyway."

Dick had asked her to give his personal things to his girl, and she had come over to collect them.

"The only problem," she said, "is that Dick will be coming around to her after he's out."

How about Dick's parents, while all this was going on?

"I should have thought," I said, "that they would have gone bail."

She grimaced. "They don't even know about it."

The chaplain had suggested contacting Dick's father in San Francisco.

Dick had only shaken his head.

The chaplain had insisted. "It's only fair to let your parents know where you are."

Dick had smiled grimly. "What for? My father always said I was going to wind up in prison."

6

ALONG THE STRIP

Some called themselves hippies, though not at all sure what the name meant. They congregated on a five- or six-block strip on Sunset Boulevard, stopping securely just east of the forbidden boundary of Beverly Hills, the fashionable home of the Hollywood stars, and the most highly manicured suburb in the world. The trademarks of the youthful males were the long shaggy manes, and the equally shaggy beards so often unkempt, mangy, and straggling. They usually formed in knots of two or three, and mingled with their female counterparts, teeny-boppers with gleaming hair, and a radiant appeal. At fourteen and fifteen, the boppers were physically precocious, keenly aware of their allure for not only the hippie set but for the straights who almost wrecked their cars gaping at the long-legged girls skipping up the Strip.

Beads adorned their necks, flowers their hair, smiles of expectancy their faces. The males rarely wore jackets, generally blouses or sweaters of the gaudiest aspect, and the girls invariably sported slacks or the briefest of shorts—mini skirts were square. Like the boys, the girls wore their hair long, it was of a lustrous sheen usually, and swished around on their shoulders as they padded down the Strip in their sandals or bare feet.

They were clearly the most attractive generation of American women, and they seemed to sense it somehow, without quite knowing how to take full advantage of it.

These were, I had been warned, the pseudos, the exhibitionists, the kids who wanted to cop out, shifting from one scene to another, where without criticism they could turn-on, tune-out and get lost.

They managed to eke out an uneasy existence. Some hawked the hippie papers, others got money from their families, or begged. Still others, real plastics, lived nearby with their families, foraging out into the Strip after dark. They came from every state in the Union, and from many foreign lands. They were all over the Strip, floating up and down, hitching rides, flocking outside small, intimate "in" spots, occasionally hitting a square for spare change.

They were alienated high school and college students, runaways, honeymooners, dropouts, the flotsam and jetsam of a drifting society. Nearly all had one thing in common. All smoked pot, and saw no harm in it. And all knew—just knew—it was less harmful than alcohol or tobacco.

Once, listening to this comparison from a freckle-faced fifteen-year-old authority with red hair and a toothy grin, I couldn't resist asking as he sat complacently next to me.

"How do you know?"

He looked startled. "What do you mean?"

"Are you an authority," I asked, "on booze and tobacco, as well as pot?"

He became suddenly watchful. "What do you do?"

I mentioned that I was a reporter.

He seemed to relax.

He was not the usual "Strip Cat," but a sightseer like myself, and was just making the scene for the day. His parents were permissive, believing in progressive education for superior students, which, of course, they were sure he was. He was not so sure, though he did well in high school, and expected to go on to college. "Berkeley or Harvard, if my grades keep up—they're cool."

Once at ease, he seemed almost eager to discuss his extracurricular interludes with drugs and drink. He was the Voice of Experience.

"I've gotten loaded at parties," he said, "and I must say I felt much better with marijuana."

"What kind of parties?"

"Oh, we'd go to some kid's house after school and get on the old man's liquor."

"Was it easier than getting pot?"

"Not really, the kids at school sell pot, or give it away."

"They must be great friends," I said.

He nodded brightly. "Yeah, that's how you know."

He also smoked at different homes, taking pains to air the house thoroughly before the unsuspecting grownups got back.

"Did it ever have any ill effects?" I asked.

He shook his head. "That's propaganda."

"By whom?" I asked.

"By the cigarette people. I understand the tobacco companies already have registered the brand names; Acapulco Gold, Panama Red, and Mary Jane. They're hedging—against the day it goes legal."

Was this information as authoritative as that about marijuana being harmless?

"I have reason to know it's harmless," he said evenly.

"How often have you smoked it?"

"Five or six times."

"And that makes you an expert?"

"It didn't do anything but relax me. I just felt I could do anything; it was all so clear."

"Is it still clear?"

He nodded. "I think so."

The younger the pot smoker, the surer he seemed of pot's mixed blessings.

"You know," he said easily, "it's not addictable."

"How do you know?" I asked.

"That's what all the experts say."

"Don't you realize," I said, "that you break the law every time you smoke."

His blue eyes squarely engaged mine.

"In order to change the law," he said, "you must break it first."

"How do you figure that?" I asked.

"It's always been true, as it was in Prohibition, when constant violation of the law finally led to its repeal."

"Where do you get your ideas?" I asked.

"In school, studying the French Revolution you learn that respect for outmoded law and authority broke down before anything got changed."

"Do you predict a breakdown of law and authority?"

"Only where marijuana is concerned." He looked up with the faintest smile. "How can they enforce a law that a whole generation doesn't respect?"

At this point, he got out, and I drove on, musing . . . a law, any law that a whole generation doesn't respect.

For the most part I had been struck by the easiness with which my Strip passenger responded to a stranger's curiosity, and the depth, at times, of their own observations. There were apparently as many variations on the Strip, even in a plastic society, as in the Establishment. One day, two young men, obviously unknown to one another, clambered into my back seat. One had an unruly mop of bushy hair which merged with a dirty scraggly beard. He looked weird. The other was a tall, lean, neatly barbered youth, who looked like a recent college graduate, ready to make the job rounds.

Both casually reported recurring use of marijuana and LSD, as though it were a routine matter. "Once you've gone high on LSD, you see what it's all about," the Beard said.

I couldn't resist. "And what's that?" I asked.

He groped for a moment. "You see truth."

"Truth about what?"

"About everything, all your hangups—sex, parents, school, your whole bag. Where you're at."

"And where are you at?"

"I'm doing what I want."

"You're not really doing anything."

He smiled indulgently. "I'm being—that's enough for me."

I looked at him doubtfully. "Does that beard and long hair make you being?"

"That only announces my state of being."

The other youth gave him a brief glance, and said dryly, "And the chicks like it, don't they?"

The Beard smiled. "Yes, I do much better with long hair."

The Beard's corner came up first, and he got out with a courteous wave of the hand.

The other moved forward into the seat next to mine.

"You don't look like a hippie," I said.

He groaned. "I'm an individual, like you or anybody else, whose biggest concern is the world of himself. Why label myself?"

As we chatted, it developed that he had attended universities on both the East and West coasts. "I took LSD and pot at Berkeley, but flunked in homosexuality."

He spoke with a dry irony that seemed to acknowledge the gulf between our generations as a very natural phenomenon for which one group was particularly to blame. And he had a humor about himself—rare in the hippies I had encountered on the Strip.

"I don't see anything constructive about this whole movement," I said, "nothing is emerging from it."

He disagreed. "If a whole generation—my generation—withdraws from a set of essentially false values, those values must fall."

Even granting the values were false, what was to take their place?

He thought a moment. "Rousseau's *Social Contract* started a chain of events that swept away a thousand years of false culture, but even Rousseau didn't realize he was preparing the French Revolution."

What puzzled so many in my generation puzzled me equally.

"But what are you doing about it?"

"Withdrawing from falseness that has brought nothing but unhappiness and misery."

This was a familiar line. "Are you on drugs?" I asked.

He frowned. "Not right now—you take marijuana to help yourself see the world, LSD helps you see yourself."

"How about all the 'trips' that failed—the kids that wind up in sanitariums and hospitals?"

"They shouldn't have taken it; the decision was theirs. They should have known themselves better." He shrugged. "Actually, I had a bad 'trip,' and wound up in an institution for a couple of weeks myself."

I asked if he could have lunch with me. He checked his watch. "I have a couple of hours." He was on his way to one of the movie studios for a job interview. He was a writer, and had done several scripts without selling one.

"Maybe they're not bad enough," I suggested dryly.

He laughed. "They're about hippies, and the market is glutted."

I had made my own interest clear, and he was helpful. "One of the basic problems," he said over salad, "is disillusionment. All his life a kid is told about doing the right thing, and then he gets to an age where he can see what's going on for himself, and he realizes he's been given a bad bag. And who's done it? His parents. They told him one thing, about honor, honesty, and all that junk, and it's an entirely different scene. Everybody's out to beat everybody else, and the hell with the hindmost.

"He looks around, and he sees all these bad marriages, including the one at home, and he decides he doesn't want any of that scene. So when he's eighteen or so, he takes off, and begins to shack up with chicks. It's all a big escape because there's no values, and it's all bodies. There's no real communication. But he manages to feel superior, because he hasn't made any phony vows to love, honor, and protect. He saw the chicks cheating on their husbands, and decided nobody was going to do it to him."

Despite his "crash" he felt that LSD had helped him understand himself. He had taken three trips. "Actually, I had an instructive experience with acid, but just couldn't seem to act on the insight I had gained." He had clearly seen his relationship with his father for the first time. "I had this compassion for him, because I saw now how he fouled up. He had wanted to be a screen director, and he was on his way, working around the lots, learning as he did scattered jobs, but then he married my mother, and she wanted security. So my father caved in and took any job he could, and my mother took over from there, and that's why he kept pushing his kids, urging them into college, going without things, just so we could finish up the life he never had."

He had seen all this under LSD.

"I didn't respect him for it, but I understood."

He had a clear picture of his own relations with girls now. "Ever since I was fifteen, I was out to nail them; it was like a competition, how many I could bowl over. I never had a meaningful relationship, and I didn't think there could be one." Under LSD, he suddenly recognized he was expressing his secret resentment of his mother, not letting any woman get close enough to one day do to him what she had done to his father.

With all this clarity, why then had he crashed?

The young man smiled ruefully. "It didn't tell me how to bridge the gulf with my parents or establish a sound relationship with a girl. It was like opening a Pandora box and seeing every-

thing slimy crawling around at the bottom. You realize what a
copout you are, and you hate yourself for it."

But why couldn't he have reacted positively?

He gave the same smile. "Because there's no wisdom coming
out of these drugs, merely moments of expanded perception, all
tumbled together with a profusion of other things. I just couldn't
cope with it all."

He pondered a moment. "You don't get anything without earning it, and there's nothing earned about swallowing a pill."

He had been introduced to LSD in college. "My friends were
making the scene, and they convinced me that I would never
know what it was all about until I took acid. They quoted
Aldous Huxley and Timothy Leary, and the rest of the intellectual brigade, and for every objection you had, they had
countering reasons."

His friends, too, had withdrawn from the humdrum of the
campus. Some were making the scene at Big Sur in central
California, living an almost aboriginal existence on the fringes
of this fashionable artist colony. He had visited them recently,
and it had only reinforced his resolve to never again experiment
with LSD.

"I saw my friend Randy, who had guided my first trip, and
he was on acid every day now, as was his wife." He smiled
wryly. "I went for a walk through the forests with Randy, and
he appeared to be floating in air. I asked how things were going,
and he said, 'Fine, I'm a redwood tree.'"

He thought he hadn't heard correctly, and he repeated his
question. Randy spread his arms, and said with a look of beatific
serenity, "I'm a redwood, a beautiful, beautiful redwood."

With some concern, he later repeated this conversation to
Randy's wife. She regarded him placidly, forming a fingered
steeple over her head, and said, "And I am a beautiful marijuana plant."

He had left within the hour.

He had reluctantly given up pot. "When a drug, a habit takes over, the individual invariably loses something of himself." He frowned. "The more people smoke, the less they do, and the fewer things they are interested in. And they're the last to see the change in themselves."

It had been an interesting session, and I was sorry to see him off.

I hesitated before stopping for my next rider. He was older than most, dirty and grimy, with a thatch of unkempt black hair and a tuft of soupy beard and bleary eyes. He had a knapsack over his shoulder, and when he got in carefully placed it down on his lap.

I had picked him up at Sunset Boulevard, at the junction of Pacific Coast Highway. He was headed for the Strip.

In the light of a street lamp, I could see more clearly the rough hands coated with layers of dirt, the face dark with soot from the road. His shirt, jacket and trousers looked as if they hadn't been aired for weeks.

"I'm down from San Francisco," he said.

"Do you live there?"

His teeth chomped into the butt of a cigar. "I'm from Chicago originally."

The inside of the car was soon afloat with a foul aroma.

I couldn't help but cough. "That smells worse than marijuana," I said.

He gave me a quick glance. "Ever try any?"

"Cigars?"

"No, marijuana."

I shook my head. "Smoking bothers me."

He nodded understandingly. "There are some who don't."

"What will you be doing in Los Angeles?" I asked.

"A lot of the boys have come down to get away from the cold."

"I thought material things didn't bother the hippies."

He laughed. "Everything bothers the hippies."

I mentioned San Francisco's reputation for hospitality.

He smiled faintly. "I never got picked up there."

"For what?"

His smile broadened. "For selling pot. The cops just don't bother anymore."

He had pushed marijuana and LSD in Haight-Ashbury, working streets crowded with drug-happy youngsters from all over the country.

"When the frost came," he said, "I lost most of my customers, but it'll warm up."

If Los Angeles was dull, he would go on to Mexico, and make connections for future supplies of grass. Business had not been all it should lately, what with the seasonal exodus, and credit problems, and he was interested in maintaining price and quality.

"Somebody has to pay for it," he said. "It can't always be free."

When it was warm and the Haight-Ashbury population was up, the wealthier had shared with their less fortunate brethren. "You could afford to pass out some free," he said, "as they would generally remember where they got it."

He lost customers only through death and other sudden departures. "Nobody stops smoking pot," he said. "Why should they?"

We rode in silence. He kept looking ahead, his long hair and beard giving him the shadowy profile of some Victorian character.

"Do you have any reason for growing that beard?" I asked.

"It seems to suit me," he said. He smiled coolly. "The girls like it."

"You mean, it's a badge of mutual recognition."

"Not only with the hippies."

I was frankly puzzled.

"The straight girls come out in droves, particularly on the weekends, looking for kicks and for hippies." His smile broadened. "And they find me." He shook his head in pleasant reminiscence. "Amazing what these girls will do, without even knowing you."

I dropped him off on the Strip with a sigh of relief—only to soon meet a girl quite different from the rest. Her blonde hair was short, and she wore black suede boots, blue corduroy pants tucked inside the boots and a lumberjack's plaid shirt. Even with her high color, it was hard to tell whether she was a boy or girl until she spoke. We had been sitting alongside each other at Schwab's—the Strip rendezvous for small-time actors and characters, when over coffee I suddenly found myself drawn into a rather bizarre dialogue.

"So I asked you for a cigarette," she was saying to a grayhaired man on the stool to her right. "How does that involve me with you?"

His eyes drank in her patrician good looks, for with all her strange attire, she looked finely made and aristocratic. He seemed debating a course of approach.

"How can you not be involved with other people, with our boys in Vietnam, with . . . ?"

She smiled. "I'm involved with what or who I want to be involved with."

He brought out a magazine showing an American GI in a Vietnam prison cell.

"How about him?" he said. "Doesn't he represent involvement to you?"

"I don't care about Vietnam," she said crisply. "I don't know anybody there."

He regarded her scathingly. "What kind of American are you?"

She turned to me. "May I munch on your toast?"

It was lying there getting cold. "You might as well get involved," I said.

The gentleman on the right considered her in perplexed frustration.

"I repeat," he said, "what kind of American are you?"

She daintily wiped her lips with a well-scrubbed hand.

"I'm English, as a matter of fact," she said with a smile, "but I acknowledge that's beside the point." She swiveled about on her stool. "I really don't care what you involve yourself in, just leave me out."

His eyes never left her. "How can you be out of a world in flames?"

"That's it exactly. It's not my world, not my flame, not even my bag. Just stay away from my door, world in flames."

"But you can't really feel that way," he said, "nobody feels that way. You have to be concerned for your neighbor."

"Not when you don't know him," she said blithely.

His eyes still remained fastened on her face. "Suppose," he tried again, "I was set upon by some thugs, wouldn't you help me, wouldn't any decent citizen help me?"

I suggested an alternative. "Why not give up your money?"

The girl laughed. "Yes, what's so important about money?"

His injured look rested on her. "You didn't mind hitting me for a cigarette," he said lamely.

"You didn't have to give it to me. You could have stayed uninvolved."

"But that's my point, you can't remain uninvolved in a world of people."

"Then all you do is react," she said. "I act, within my own horizons. I love who I want, when I want, say what I like, when I like, do what I do, as I please."

He started to say something, blinked, then wiped the watery eyes which had not once left her clean, clear face.

He bent over toward her now, with an air of confidence. "Suppose I was to say I wanted to go to bed with you, would that be all there was to it?"

She was not in the least discomposed. "If that's what I wanted, it would be no more of a deal than going to the bathroom."

He was of a school which apparently thought the battle half won when the act itself came under frank discussion. And yet there were no demure looks, no covert smiles, no tricks of coquetry.

"But love is beautiful," he said. "Where would you be if your mother and father had not made love?"

For the first time, her face lost its easy composure. "All they wanted to do," she said harshly, "is make love, and I don't blame them for it. I just don't have to become involved with them."

She noted my own startled look with amusement. "That's the truth of it—we're all here because somebody wanted to do something to somebody else—if it's euphemisms you want."

She was unusually articulate, and could very well make an excellent study.

"You seem quite observant," I said.

She eyed me doubtfully.

I felt as if I was treading on broken egg shells. "You state the hippie case very well."

Her eyes met mine watchfully. "What do you mean by that?"

"You're a very articulate hippie, fascinatingly so."

Her voice went cold. "Your generation," she said, "is forever categorizing things. I don't like to be labeled."

"We're all labeled one way or the other," I remonstrated mildly. "You just called it my generation, and I no more belong to it than you do."

She apparently had not heard a word I said.

"I do not conform to what anybody expects of me," she said. "I make my 'bread' when I have to, and"—she turned her head to the man to the right—"and I make love when I have to, with whom I want. And it's nobody's bloody business but my own."

I introduced myself as a writer.

"And what is it you're writing?"

"The title speaks for itself, *The Seekers.*"

She kicked it around for a moment. "Why don't you call it *The Journey Man?*" she suggested.

I looked at her blankly.

"We're all taking a trip," she said.

I studied her a moment.

"Drugs?"

She shrugged. "Why not, as long as you see things where they're at."

The answer still eluded me. "And where are they at?"

"Don't you know?" Her voice was faintly mocking.

I was tired of sparring.

"I would like to sit down with you, and perhaps get to see how you live, who your friends are, and what you think about."

"I don't care about people learning about me," she said.

I appealed to her vanity. "You can reach thousands this way, as against two or three here in the drugstore."

She shook her head. "You don't understand—what I'm saying here is what I feel at the moment."

I examined her with new curiosity. Her clothes were clean but frayed, and she obviously was not in good circumstances, or she wouldn't have been cadging cigarettes.

"I could pay for your time and effort," I said.

Immediately, I realized my mistake. She sat rigidly on her stool and said, without looking at me, "You'd better find somebody else. I articulated all last night, and I'm all articulated out."

I tried one last appeal. "But you may find yourself articulating what you had never expressed before."

She shrugged indifferently. "I was with a genius last night."

I recognized defeat. "They're all geniuses," I said.

"I don't know any other genius," she said sharply, turning to the man on her right and cadging another cigarette.

Noticing her check on the counter, I casually picked it up and paid it on the way out.

She watched me in the mirror, out of a corner of her eye, doubtless wondering how anybody in my despised generation could commit even a small kindness without some return.

I had to confess a sharp sense of frustration in not being

able to reach her. Suddenly, I realized where I had missed. I had *tried* to reach her, and the deliberate effort, no matter how well contrived, had been painfully evident. Obviously, I would have to empathize further before I could bridge the generation gap.

Willie was my next subject, and more attractive than most. He was neatly groomed, with conventional shirt and trousers, and an armful of books. He gave me a curious look as he got into the car, but settled back without saying anything.

"How far?" I asked.

He was on his way to school, a few miles along. "You can drop me wherever convenient," he said.

His voice had a clear metallic ring, and he gave the impression of being quite sure of himself.

We drove along silently, until I finally ventured, "You don't look like a hippie?"

He turned his serious blue eyes on me. "What is your idea of a hippie?"

I thought a moment. "Somebody who, without regard for convention, registers an intuitive awareness of the world's problems."

He stared thoughtfully ahead. "The word hippie is definitely a misnomer. It may have fit when the move for personal awareness began, but now every nut, weird-o, homosexual, and slob is a hippie."

"What do you think a hippie is?"

He shrugged. "It's only a label, and labels are restricting. That's why these plastic hippies are so amusing. They run to type, and there's little awareness in any of them."

I had not yet met a hippie on the Strip who was not on drugs. In their acceptance of the drug phenomenon, they weren't even defensive about it.

My passenger was only twenty, but had obviously thought out the scene carefully.

"Why," I asked, "do so many take drugs?"

He glanced at me briefly. "What drugs?"

"LSD and marijuana."

"It's part of their identification. Many started taking it because it gave them a feeling of belonging. And, it gives lots of them the excuse they need not to put themselves in the stream of things. They talk about trying to find out where it's at, and they don't begin to know where they're at."

He spoke with a quiet disdain.

"Have you tried LSD and pot?" I asked.

"LSD gave me a clear insight into the obvious." He shrugged. "I soon discovered that most of the kids taking it were on a psychological hangup, finding some sort of euphoria in trading reality for unreality."

And pot?

He frowned. "That's another copout. They talk about mind-expanding, and yet they have to get sex parties up to enjoy it. All it does is release the inhibitions they want to get rid of. They don't gain anything or get anything done."

One of the things they were trying to escape was the war. The newspapers had carried a story that day about a street demonstration prompted by a public appearance of Secretary of State Rusk, and I questioned the loyalty of hippies demonstrating against Rusk and the war, while hundreds of young Americans were dying in that cause each week.

He jogged his head to one side. "Nobody wants to go to Vietnam; it doesn't make any sense, bombing a country thousands of miles away because we don't like their government." He smiled thinly. "Should the Chinese bomb us because they don't approve our government?"

My own feelings about the war were negative. Nevertheless, I observed, "I was brought up with 'My country, may she ever be right, but my country, right or wrong.'"

He didn't seem impressed. "That's one of the hangups that breeds the chauvinism that leads to wars." He shook his head. "You don't distinguish between government and country."

"The country chooses the government," I pointed out.

"But their aspirations may have parted along the way." He smiled wryly. "Would you say that Hitler and the German people were one and the same?"

"He reflected their will to a great extent."

"As the kids see it, the country is you, your family, your friends, your hometown, your job, your school, what you believe in, and what you want. The government is Lyndon Johnson, Rusk, a handful of generals, and a lot of overage destroyers who never fired a shot in anger." His brow furled with concentration. "Discourage protest, and you could conceivably have a war that only one man wants."

"How about loyalty to a half million troops risking their lives?"

"They're the chief victims," he said, "and we want to bring them home."

I gave him a sidelong glance. "Suppose you were drafted?"

He nodded. "I'd go, I'm still that much part of the system, but only after I'd exhausted every legal effort to stay out."

"But how," I asked, "can we pull out, when we've put so much in?"

His voice rasped. "I hear the casualty figures every day, with the commentators tallying them up like apples."

And his solution?

"Very simple, admit our mistake and get out."

And our economy?

"We could pour billions now earmarked for destruction into eradicating the great slums in our cities, spend billions more on cancer and heart research. Why should killing be more important than living?"

I regarded him curiously. "Could you conceive of any war being justified?"

"It depends on whether you have a choice."

Didn't he feel our security was involved?

He laughed. "You're not serious."

Hadn't he heard of the domino theory?

"That's for dominoes, not people. Historians laughed when

Hitler invaded Poland to resist aggression, and that domino was next door."

He glanced out the window. "People my age have grown tired of wars older people start. It's time we got rid of the old labels, of uniforms, nationalism, and politicians who can't make anything out of peace."

His eyes narrowed reflectively. "Even with victory, six months after we leave Vietnam, they'll have the government they want anyway, and it won't be the one we want."

I slowed down for a red light. "I'll get out here," he said, shaking my hand. "Nothing personal. It's just time the expendable generation had a say about how it should live—and die."

I watched him cross the street, strong and erect, with a quick light step and confident air. There were thousands like him in Vietnam, and many would not come back. I supposed it was only fair they should know why they were dying.

It was often difficult to know what was motivating so many of the drifters. On Sunset, one evening, driving in from the ocean at Malibu, I saw a young man in a thin jacket shivering in the December frost. Gratefully, he got in front beside me, and gave an exaggerated shiver.

"How far are you going?" I asked.

He mentioned a street at the beginning of the Strip.

I was turning off at a side street, a few blocks past UCLA—the University of California in Los Angeles. That would still leave him a few miles to go.

"I would take you in," I found myself apologizing, "but I'm already late for dinner."

He looked straight ahead, as though I hadn't spoken.

I got a clearer look at him as we came to an intersection. His face was pasty and drawn, and he looked like he could use a good meal. He was no more than twenty.

"Do you go to school?" I asked.

He shook his head.

"Are you from out this way?"

His eyes blinked, but he remained silent.

I tried again. "Are you from the East?"

He regarded me evenly. "Where are you from?" he asked.

"New York," I said. "I'm a writer."

That didn't work either.

I stole another look. His long hair framed his thin face evenly, except for the jagged edges. His nose was high-bridged, his forehead well-domed; he could have worn a Brooks Brothers suit and walked onto any Ivy League campus.

I tried once more. "They say hippies don't pay any attention to anybody over thirty, but I haven't found it that way."

He didn't say anything.

"They always get into my car when I stop." I laughed at my own feeble joke—and laughed alone.

"After we pass UCLA," he said, "could you drop me at the first traffic light?"

"That would be the best spot for another lift," I agreed.

We had stopped for a light, when I saw a young man standing on the corner, huddled against the cold. Raising an arm, he edged onto the road, and I could see that he was no more than seventeen or eighteen. As I pulled to the curb, the young man motioned to a girl in the shadows behind him, and she came struggling forward with a big suitcase tied with rope. After helping her, he went back for more bags. Somehow, they staggered into the back seat.

They were tired but talkative. They were headed for the Diggers, a hippie organization offering transient hippies a night's lodging, food, and an employment service.

"Somebody told us it was only a short distance," the girl said with a sigh.

She was a pretty thing and, like the boy, no more than eighteen.

I pointed out that the Diggers were well into Los Angeles, in the Hollywood section. "I'm only going as far as UCLA," I said regretfully.

"What is that?" the girl asked.

"A local university."

"Oh," she said, "the University of California at Los Angeles."

"Where do you come from?" I asked.

"Originally, or just now?" she laughed.

"Originally."

"Fort Lauderdale, we're both from there."

"Why," I asked, "would anybody leave Florida at this time of the year?"

Her pretty face broke into a grin. "We wanted to catch the scene, you know, Haight-Ashbury, and all that."

My uncommunicative hippie friend raised his head. "You just came from San Francisco? How was it?"

"Nothing there," she said, "practically everybody left for warmer parts."

I took a longer look at my new passengers. They were manifestly from "good families." The girl would have been welcome in any home as a prospective bride, and the young man was blond, clean-cut, with a square jaw and pleasant blue eyes.

"He wanted to go, and so we just picked up and left," the girl explained.

"How about school?" I asked.

"I had a few more weeks at Broward"—she named a Florida junior college—"and now I lose all my credits."

She wasn't overwhelmed at the prospect.

"And your boyfriend?" I asked.

"He never got out of high school," she laughed cheerfully.

"How will you live?"

"Oh, we'll get a job through the Diggers. We'll do anything."

"Why couldn't you have done *anything* in Fort Lauderdale?"

She laughed, "Our families might not have agreed."

I consulted my watch. I was already late and my hostess was not one to accept tardiness with equanimity.

"I think you will get a ride here," I said, "young people

should pick you up. But if you're still here on my way back, I'll take you in."

Unconsciously, I had made my own distinction between the young and their elders.

The couple clambered cheerfully out of the back seat, throwing their baggage ahead of them; the hippie at my side hesitated a moment, then said softly, "Good writing."

As I entered the home of my friends, I surveyed everywhere the fruits of great wealth: The spacious Roman-like atrium, the colorful muraled walls and tapestries, the rich, deep carpets, marble statuary, and the heavy tables and chairs.

We sat around a great fireplace having a drink before dinner, My hostess, a woman of some acuteness, sensed my mind was elsewhere.

"Anything wrong?" she asked.

I mentioned briefly the young couple and their dilemma. "I wish I'd had more time."

She looked at me in shocked disbelief. "But they're beatniks."

"It would have made me late," I conceded.

"Hold us up for them." She was aghast. "I would have killed you."

She was not an unfeeling woman, having been a considerate wife and mother.

"Maybe," I said, "the world needs more love and caring."

"Love and caring," she said, "are you out of your mind? They're beatniks. They don't want work, they don't want school, they're lazy, shiftless, you can't do anything for them."

Her husband laughed. "My darling can't bear people who don't hold up their end."

"Suppose this girl was your child?" I asked.

She shuddered. "She couldn't be my child, and if she was, I'd disown her. No beatniks for me."

Her husband laughed indulgently. "They're hippies now, dear, not beatniks."

"Beatniks, hippies, what's the difference—they're all good for nothing."

"They could have used a good dinner," I said.

She winced. "Those dirty people on my lovely things. Why don't they stay home and stop worrying their families?"

"They have their own lives to live."

"Then let them live them, and stop worrying me."

"Don't you think we should try to understand them?"

She looked at me as if I was stark, raving mad. "What is there to understand? Tell me, I really want to know."

I hesitated.

"Tell me," she insisted, "I want to be fair."

"Perhaps we are so engrossed with success and materialism that we aren't interested in people for themselves."

"They're not like us," she protested. "Did anybody give you anything? Haven't you worked for everything you ever got?" She shrugged. "So let them work, if they want things."

"But that's the point," I said, "they don't want the same things we do. Most people punch a clock at some dull job because they're already thinking of illness and old age. These kids think of life as an adventure."

"All right," she said, "let's explore the table."

The meal was pleasant, the food, which she had prepared despite a plenitude of help, was delicious, and the conversation took a safer, pleasant turn.

As I was about to leave, two small children scampered into the room, to be hugged by their grandmother, and then trundled safely off to bed. Her eyes followed them lovingly up a great center staircase.

"Can you imagine," she shuddered, "one of them growing into a beatnik?"

I smiled inwardly. She would have been the last, honest as she was by her lights, to acknowledge that her whole feeling about the rebellious youth of today was vested in fear—fear for the comfortable life she had built for herself, and which she intended to pass on to those hostages of fortune who had just climbed into their cozy beds.

We waved a friendly goodby, passing differences forgotten as they always were, and I cut back to Sunset, my eye on the corner where I had earlier left my passengers. They had obviously got their ride, for the intersection was deserted.

Strangely, I felt an acute sense of disappointment. It would have been nice to have done something for somebody without a thought of return.

7

HOW HARMLESS—POT?

There it was in black and white. Television host Hugh Downs, whose NBC *Today* show had access to millions of American homes, stating in *The Hollywood Reporter* that marijuana was not what it was painted.

Weeks of research for a TV special had led Downs to conclude that Mary Jane was the object of a good deal of uninformed hysteria. "I have been unable," he explained subsequently, "in spite of repeated invitations and appearances of medical experts who oppose a reform of narcotics laws to find any evidence that marijuana is more harmful than alcohol."

Suppression of marijuana, rather than legalizing and controlling it, Downs felt, was the real social hazard. "Most of the evidence unfolded on my television programs," he continued, "appears to point to one immense danger: since young people are particularly sensitive to truth, and since for over thirty years patently exaggerated myths about marijuana have been circulated by an Establishment toward which many of the young already feel rebellious, great harm has been done through the destruction of credibility."

Downs' attitude, naturally, was reflected on TV. "We're being very careful to present both sides," *The Hollywood Reporter* quoted him. "But someone watching the whole show is bound to take a more liberal view toward marijuana."

As for marijuana being the first step toward heroin addiction, Downs had this to say, in reviewing his position:

"In one clinic (drug), seventy percent of the heroin addicts had started on marijuana, ninety percent started on alcohol and close to one hundred percent on milk. You can always find something a group of people have in common."

Dr. Edward R. Pinckney, diplomate in preventive medicine, one-time professor of medicine at Northwestern, a former editor of the American Medical Association *Journal,* and a public health authority, sighed heavily.

"Incredible," he said, "completely and perfectly incredible. What is even worse, it is almost criminal for those so far from the field of medicine or pharmacology to be so dogmatic about something they know nothing about."

There were some, with a semblance of erudition, who were equally uninformed. "Downs' remarks were no worse," Pinckney observed, "than the three sociologists at the University of California at Santa Barbara who wrote a book about how harmless marijuana is—not one of them with any training in what drugs really do to the human body and mind."

The Downs statement not only contradicted Pinckney's own observations in years of medical practice in the film colony, but the flood of pharmacological and physiological research he had examined with growing concern.

Out of a thick file, he pulled a recent *Medical Letter on Drugs and Therapeutics,* prepared by a distinguished group of practicing physicians, summarizing marijuana's physical effects:

"The drug sometimes causes postural hypotension [disturbance of normal blood pressure reflexes]. Mydriasis [excessive dilating of pupils], conjunctival congestion [bloodshot eyes] and photophilia [affinity for light] are frequent. Muscular incoordination, spasms, urinary frequency, dryness of mouth, nausea, vomiting and diarrhea sometimes occur. Increase in appetite is common, and has been attributed to hypoglycemia [opposite of diabetes]. Hypothermia [lowered temperatures] has been observed and some workers have noted a Raynaud-like syndrome [cold extremities and white fingertips]. Large amounts of marijuana depress respiration, which is the first sign of impending death in animals given lethal doses."

There were certain social and psychological changes also, filling physicians with growing alarm: "Advocates of lifting the legal restrictions on the use of marijuana state that it is no more harmful than alcohol or cigarettes [tobacco]. However, reports of serious adverse emotional reactions and personality changes are increasing. Panic, gross confusion, impulsive and aggressive behavior, depersonalization, depression and paranoid behavior have been reported, especially when marijuana is combined with other drugs, such as alcohol and amphetamines. With large doses [or in susceptible persons] delusions or hallucinations can occur. Indolence and neglect of personal hygiene may follow prolonged heavy use. Intellectual functioning and memory may be impaired."

All this was very general, to be sure, but Pinckney could easily be more specific.

As with LSD, some researchers were now beginning to introduce evidence of lasting damage to some marijuana users, genetic damage that might be passed from one generation to another. It seemed incredible on the surface, but what excluding evidence was there to the contrary?

"Certainly," said Pinckney, "the medical evidence supporting this claim should be examined before marijuana laws are made more lenient, in response to pressure from people who are obviously using it themselves—and liking what it does for them, euphorically."

But how could so little be known about such a widely used drug?

Pinckney smiled wryly.

"Heroin, the most dangerous drug on any list, was originally produced, like Demerol, as a harmless synthetic for morphine and other opiates, and for years could be purchased across the drugstore counter without a prescription. That's how much we know about drugs, until they get a thorough checking out on a controlled, scientific basis."

He thought a moment.

"If any other drug had the demonstrable side effects of marijuana, including the high percentage of subsequent heroin addiction, no doctor in his right mind would utilize it, nor would the Food and Drug Administration permit it. The strain of coincidence is just too great."

He had examined the claim of marijuana-inspired chromosomal damage without forming any premature judgment himself. Dr. Luis Souza of St. Dismas Hospital, Paterson, New Jersey, had presented his findings to the Bergen County Narcotic Addiction and Drug Abuse Council for review. They were similar to the studies which had showed chromosomal damage from LSD. Through the use of a chromatograph—a chemical detector which picks up the molecular weight of DNA, part of the gene that attaches to the chromosome—Souza reported that after the first few experiences with marijuana, there was a complete destruction of the DNA component of the genes. His discovery was possible through his use of an ultraviolet microscope, enabling him to magnify the chromosomes one hundred thousand times.

Souza seemed well equipped for his research. He had done some work with the United Nations in the field of mental hygiene, exploring the physical and mental impairment induced by drugs and alcohol, and this had put him on the trail of chromosomal damage. Genetically, he noted that marijuana was unusual in transmitting its effects through both dominant and recessive genes. If any significant number of the three million odd genes were damaged, as noted, the result would affect many generations, possibly disturbing the central nervous system of unborn generations, and resulting in mental retardation and physical deterioration.

Souza's report would of course require considerable confirmation elsewhere. However, it did seem sufficient to point to caution, when evaluated with other, perhaps more tangible reports.

Pinckney had before him a recent report from a council of the American Medical Association, which made it very clear that marijuana was a mental crutch, producing psychological dependence as well as demonstrably adverse physical consequences. "This psychological dependence," Pinckney pointed out, "was frequently reflected in listlessness, apathy, neglect of personal appearance, indifference to accomplishment." Additionaly, the AMA council's statement warned that repeated use could result in "illusions and delusions that predispose to antisocial behavior." Other direct results after long usage were clearly physical—chronic bronchitis and asthma, low blood sugar, sleep disturbance, impaired coordination.

The AMA report was based on evidence accumulating all over the country that marijuana was definitely a medical problem. "It is important," the AMA counseled, "for the physician to remember that a person who has a psychological dependence on marijuana is sick and deserving understanding and treatment, even though he may have been involved in unlawful activity." Doctors were warned that chronic users may be symptomizing "serious underlying personality problems, severe neurotic conflicts or psychotic reactions."

All this, Pinckney pointed out, was the result, not of spot judgment by a television commentator, but a year of study by men whose specialty was drugs and their impact on body and mind.

Actually, psychological, or psychic dependence, could be more of a problem than physical addiction. "Unrestricted use of marijuana produces a significant amount of vagabondage dependency and psychiatric disability," Dr. Henry Brill of the New York Narcotic Addiction Control Commission pointed out. "This psychic dependence—a compulsive desire to take the drug even though it damages the individual and society around him—is more difficult to treat than physical dependence because it can create relapse at any time in the subsequent life of the individual, while physical dependence can be broken in a few days."

Additionally, Brill pointed out, the use of marijuana in colleges was producing a brain drain. "Many students," he warned, "were dropping out of school after using the drug, and going on the bum."

Physical addiction from marijuana was highly controversial. The drug committee of the World Health Organization held that "cannabis [marijuana] abuse comes definitely under the terms of its definition of addiction and is very likely to be a forerunner of addiction to more dangerous drugs."

Nevertheless, marijuana users scoffed at reports that pot was even habituating. "I've been taking it for fifteen years," a chronic user said indignantly, "and can stop whenever I want."

Marijuana's psychic damage was apparently irretrievably interwoven with physiological damage, for it was difficult to understand one without the other. And the scientific explorations of the Greek investigator, Dr. Constandinos J. Miras of the University of Athens, indicated a clear connection between marijuana-induced brain change and disarranged behavior. Nobody had spent more time researching marijuana than Miras. He had experimented with humans and animals for more than twenty years. In his most recent studies, supported by the National Institute of Health, this visiting professor at UCLA ingeniously employed radioactive marijuana to track the course of the drug through the human body. Miras worked almost exclusively with chronic marijuana smokers, those who smoked at least two cigarettes daily for two years or more. His tests revealed abnormal brainwave readings, patterned to behavioral changes. In some cases, with long-time users, Miras noted chronic lethargy and loss of inhibitions for two years after their last usage, indicating, he felt, significant organic brain change.

The experimental radioactive tetrahydrocannabinol (THC), marijuana's activating chemical, passed through the brain in about twenty minutes, and then concentrated in the liver, eventually, after five days or so, passing into the intestines, by way of the bile, and finally excreted. Certain individuals, Miras observed, were obviously more vulnerable than others, and the most susceptible were the easily irritated and irascible. They could even become violent, and kill.

Miras distinguished between chronic and casual users. Long-time users were prone to anemia, eye inflammation, respiratory infections, and a creeping lethargy, impairing normal functioning and aspirations after a while. Many of his subjects were teachers and members of the arts, but as the years passed, with their habit getting an increasing grip, they slipped into less demanding jobs, and preferred to sit around and "sleep and talk philosophy." They were variously depressed and exalted, not always sure when they were hallucinating. Beginners went through a rapid succession of physical changes: laughing, crying, hallucinating, being sluggish, and hungering for sugar.

To discount subjective reactions by those knowing they were being tested experimentally, Miras extended his studies to animals. The results were startling: "Injection of pure tetrahydrocannabinol [THC] or hashish extract in olive oil solution in rats produced a number of effects starting with hypermobility followed by ataxia [nervous disfunction], to the various degrees and types of catatonic stages. The animals, depending on the dose, remained in the sleeping state for hours, the temperature of the body was gradually reduced and they died in the following forty-eight hours if they were not in a properly heated place or if fluids were not administered."

There was marked individuality in the observed symptoms.

"Even among animals of the same sex, age, and weight, the effects were not the same. In some hypermobility was almost absent and catatonia and sleepiness occurred from the beginning."

In conjunction with barbiturates or alcohol, the marijuana drug had a sharply stepped-up effect. "Hashish extract and THC potentiated the effect of barbiturates as well as of convulsion producing drugs . . . Dogs and rats seemed to be more sensitive to motor reactions and corneal areflexia was reported as a sensitive test in rabbits."

The experiments were scientific enough for any scientist. "The distribution and excretion of pure THC was also studied by injection of radioactive THC, biosynthetically prepared by growing cannabis [marijuana] plants in an atmosphere of radioactive CO_2. Radioactivity was concentrated in the liver and excreted in the intestines with the bile. The lungs and kidneys contained an amount much smaller than that of the liver which was about fifty percent of the total injected radioactivity."

Miras tested rats kept on marijuana for a year. The injections were then halted for three months, and the rats given sleeping pills. They slept impressively longer periods than rats given similar pills but not exposed to marijuana previously. "This was an indication," he said, "that something had happened to their brains."

In my own research, more pragmatic than scientific, I had discovered a telltale lack of ambition among constant pot-smokers, accompanied by a bristling resentment of any suggestion that their lethargy was induced by their habit—ironically, one of the few times they reacted with passion. In some cases, young high school and college athletes, taking up pot, soon gave up their athletic pursuits. The passive effect was so strong in other instances that youthful roisterers stopped roughhousing in bars, becoming as subdued in their sportiveness as in positive pursuits. The change in inveterate smokers was rather startling at times. A young graduate student at Berkeley, the University of California, walked out of an impromptu campus pot party when his date, a pretty undergraduate, incredibly lit up a marijuana cigarette. "You're a dope fiend," he said, angrily turning on his heels.

However, at Berkeley, as at so many other institutions of higher learning, many "straight arrows," bombarded with propaganda, sooner or later had their curiosity aroused, and this graduate student was no different. When last heard from, he was smoking pot religiously, growing a beard and long hair, and had dropped out of school. He no longer dated the girl who had taken him to his first pot party. She was too straight.

One of the most revealing studies in Pinckney's collection was that undertaken by Dr. Martin H. Keeler, associate professor of psychiatry at the University of North Carolina School of Medicine, published in the *American Journal of Psychiatry* in November 1967. "In this remarkable study," Pinckney pointed out, "eleven individuals who reported adverse reactions from marijuana were interviewed, and all but two of them said they planned to keep taking the drug despite their bad reactions."

Nearly all those reporting were middle-class university students, of acknowledged superior intelligence, and yet they were continuing an experience which had precipitated "one report of panic and fear, one report of depersonalization, one report of gross confusion and disorientation, two reports of depression, and four reports of paranoid phenomena during the drug reaction." These were by no means passing responses, for as Keeler reported:

"A twenty-one-year-old man stated that after smoking more than his usual amount he became disoriented to time and place, could not think, and had difficulty in controlling his limbs. For some weeks thereafter he intermittently experienced hallucinations resembling those he had had during the reaction. These sensations were accompanied by a degree of anxiety approaching panic."

A change of values was sharply triggered:

"A twenty-year-old man stated that after taking marijuana he recognized that his previous goals, including what he called conventional ambition, conformity, and fear, were not as important as the need to express himself and achieve independent identity. His interest and achievement in academic areas deteriorated and his dress became nonconventional."

Keeler was elaborately scientific in his assessment of the drug, striving to hold the median line of fairness. Even so, it became apparent that marijuana, in its unpredictability, could adversely affect the unstable, and even the stable, if the dosage were large enough. And who was to decide who was stable or unstable, until it was too late? "Perhaps all investigators would agree," Keeler judiciously observed, "that marijuana cannot produce functional psychopathology but can only precipitate it in individuals so predisposed. Many would interpret this as an exoneration of the drug. Others would hold that the occurrence of psychopathology in an individual at a given time requires many factors and that more people have predisposition to mental illness than develop it. In this sense marijuana usage might precipitate trouble that would not have otherwise occurred or would otherwise have occurred at a later time. The use of the drug can initiate changes in style of life. It is left to others to decide whether this constitutes psychopathology."

Apparently the smokers felt in the euphoria of marijuana a positive pleasure, adding that it provided insight, enhanced creativity, and enriched their lives. All this came out of the fugue of the hallucinatory state, with no rigid questioning apparently of their own state, in which the only reality was an adverse physical and mental reaction. "All but two of the eleven individuals reporting adverse reactions," Keeler affirmed, "considered the benefits to far outweigh the unfortunate aspects and planned to continue use of the drug."

It seemed incredible, and Pinckney's reaction was somewhat similar to mine. "Apparently," he said, "they're still hallucinating."

All in all, it was a rather bad rap for a drug so often billed as harmless, but this was only a starter, for true, scientific research, ignored by the pseudo-scientists and the pseudo-intellectuals, was only beginning to materialize. "You must remember," Pinckney said, "that chemists were only able in the last year or so to synthesize the pure tetrahydrocannabinol needed for scientifically controlled experiments."

Actually, this activating element of marijuana was not even identified until 1964, and so laboratory work, with measurable quantities of marijuana, was physically impossible until some time thereafter. Recent tests with THC have shown as little as 18 milligrams of THC, (one/two-thousandth part of an ounce) given to an average-sized male, brought on the psychotic-like responses of the strongest hashish, a form of marijuana whose potency hardly anybody questions. Testing some forty human subjects, WHO drug expert Dr. Harris Isbell of the University of Kentucky recorded hallucinations, loss of reality, visual and auditory distortions. A fraction of this dose, perhaps a fourth, produced a mild euphoria, along with subtle changes in perception and mood. Occasionally, even the reduced dose brought psychotic reactions, but these were obviously vulnerable individuals.

Even with minimal doses, producing a mild euphoria, a slight increase in dosage could bring a drastic reaction. "If you keep turning the screws," Dr. Isbell said, "all of a sudden, they're on a trip watching their own burial."

And none of the subjects, significantly, felt marijuana the cause.

On his experience, not only with his uniquely controlled experiment but as erstwhile head of the government narcotic center at Lexington, Kentucky, Dr. Isbell stressed strict marijuana controls. "The local grass is probably pretty weak stuff, but lower controls and you open the door to more potent stuff."

And it was obviously coming in anyway, an unpredictable weed, of unpredictable strength, for unpredictable people. One of the favorites, "great grass," was Acapulco Gold, brought up from Mexico, and far more potent than the home-grown variety, which could be grown everywhere, from a wooden flowerbox in a New York tenement, to the wheat fields of Iowa, or a backyard in Connecticut. Pot was variously consumed—cigarette-smoked, eaten with spaghetti or brownies, gulped down with booze—and it had a special flavor of its own, and a special name, wherever it was grown. In the Middle East it was hashish, a resin extract; in North Africa, kif; in India, ganja and charas, as well as bhang; China, majen (oddly paralleling the American Mary Jane); in South Africa, dagga; South America, maconha, and in the United States, variously, pot, grass, gange, muggles, grefa, tea, mezz, boo. It was nothing new. The Chinese used it five thousand years ago, as an analgesic, easing the pains of living, the poor man's poppy. But with all the endless debate about it, it was not till 1967 that THC was precisely synthesized, by chemists in Israel, at the Hebrew University of Jerusalem, and at the Wyeth Laboratories in Philadelphia. And so for the first time, research-wise, scientists could determine what effect a specific amount of marijuana's intoxicating ingredient, tetrahydrocannabinol would have on a specific organism, namely man. Almost parenthentically, a recent issue of *Science News* observed: "The strength of pot varies widely; a marijuana cigarette is not a measurable thing; it doesn't always contain the same concentration of active chemicals. Two plants grown in different areas have different amounts of the active chemicals, explains Dr. Daniel Efron, a psychopharmacologist with the National Institute of Mental Health. And depending on where the material is kept —in attic, basement, or refrigerator—the concentration is again different." The method of preparation, perhaps even more than the type of plant itself, indicated the strength of the drug, and its consequent effect on the smoker. "The resin of the female hemp plant, cannabis sativa, produces THC (the male plant produces rope) and according to the method of cultivation and preparation, the resulting drug is either a powerhouse, commonly called hashish, or the much weaker marijuana."

Nobody, not even the grower, could anticipate how the user

would react, now knowing how much THC there was in each cigarette—nor, the user's individual idiosyncrasies.

The deterioration of the individual from constant marijuana abuse was not merely a laboratory exercise. Over relatively short periods, months and even weeks, conspicuous changes were noticeable in habitual users. One originally ambitious young man in his early twenties became so indolent and passive that it was an effort for him to wash his person or straighten his room, not to mention keeping a job and pursuing his original ambitions. In his sloth, he became resentful of attempts to redirect him to productive pursuits. "What the hell difference does it make?" he would protest angrily, as he mooched on friends, "I'm happy."

It had only taken three months with pot to reduce a bright-eyed, bushy-tailed youngster to a blob of inertia.

There were almost as many instances of this reaction as there were instances of marijuana indulgence, which so debased the consumer that instead of opening mystical new horizons, closed him off to a limiting life style that froze off any aspirations he may ever have had.

Older people were similarly affected. Nobody could understand why a housewife, known for her orderly household, had unaccountably grown so slovenly that it was difficult to even maneuver through her untidy kitchen. She stopped seeing friends and neighbors, ceased planning meals for her husband and children—everything was thrown together. The climax came when she eloped with a young man of twenty, fifteen years her junior, in a house trailer, vagabonding around the country. She left no note, nor explanation, merely a cache of marijuana she had slothfully overlooked in one of her closets.

Actually, the most revealing place for marijuana research was not the laboratory, but the cities and campuses and resorts, where the regular use of marijuana was bringing about observable changes in a life style. There was no age limit as older people, fascinated by the hippies, picked up their drug habits, if nothing else. The results were often dramatic—physically, psychologically and socially. For many Southern California observers, the case of the thirty-three-year-old Gridley Wright, probation officer turned hippie, provided revealing insights into the psychological effects of marijuana. Wright, ironically, appealing a marijuana conviction, claimed that he was unable to defend himself properly during his twelve-day trial because he had not been fully aware of what was going on—due to being on LSD and marijuana.

During the Wright trial, expert testimony by Dr. Victor H. Vogel, parole chief at the California Rehabilitation Center, so impressed presiding jurist Mark Brandler that he summarized it in court:

"Marijuana is an intoxicant which in some cases has a slight and, in others, a great effect on the behavior of individuals.

"The users of marijuana maintain a muscular coordination, so marijuana users continue to function, and when under the influence of marijuana, the likelihood of getting involved in dangerous and delinquent behavior is greater."

Vogel also noted that the World Health Organization, composed of one hundred nations, had unanimously agreed that marijuana should be on the dangerous drug list, and set the year 1986 for its complete eradication. There was not a dissenting voice, including the Middle East where marijuana—hashish—has been traditional.

While marijuana users kept insisting their drug was no worse than alcohol, Vogel found differently:

- "He listed three reasons," the judge noted, "why marijuana is more dangerous than alcohol. It is more likely to produce hallucinations. The users have distortions in perception of time and space relations (while maintaining muscular coordination). There in increased susceptibility and suggestibility on the part of users of marijuana."

There were other differences. Alcohol didn't act up all at once, as marijuana so often did; its measurable quality, as well as quantity, gave it a predictable impact, and it was not so clearly suggestive of withdrawal from society. Moreover, the agitation for marijuana was fraught with fraud. Dr. William F. Quinn, chairman of the Committee on Drugs of the California Medical Association, pointed out there was nothing new in the current use of drugs, except that the cultists screaming the loudest were on the college campuses, not in the tenderloin or the Ghetto. There was no contrasting self-deception with alcohol. It was pure pleasure and escape. "Thousands of years ago," Quinn said, "man sought artificial paradise to postpone the harsh realities of life." Now they were trying to surround drug-taking with a halo, while revealing only their own inadequacies. "The use of these substances in the United States today would appear to be an indication that the person involved just doesn't have what it takes, and seeks to make himself think he has what it takes, by achieving instant knowledge and instant happiness artificially."

As for the respective demerits of alcohol and marijuana, it was almost a non sequitur. "Comparisons are made between alcohol and marijuana and it is suggested that marijuana should be legalized as alcohol." Wasn't it bad enough as it was? "The six million alcoholics in this country are certainly no bargain," Quinn stressed, "and the loss of employment, break up of families, and many other tragedies due to abuse of alcohol defy description."

Oddly, the proponents of marijuana, however presumably scientifically oriented, never alluded to the fact that the very prevalence of alcoholism reflected the susceptibility of a formidable share of our population to a specific drug—alcohol. They obviously would not have been alcoholics without alcohol, and many had considered themselves purely social drinkers until they awoke one day with a hangover—and a compulsive need for liquor.

Obviously, in taking marijuana, the susceptible user had no wish to go on to heroin, anymore than the occasional cocktail drinker had to become an alcoholic. But he could not help himself once he started, just as certain marijuana regulars had to keep on seeking ever-increasing highs, once they started with grass. In years of newspapering, I had known hundreds of addicts, who had begun their heroin habit with marijuana.

Was there necessarily a connection?

It seemed obvious to me. Many would never even have thought of Big H, had they not already compromised with the lesser M, which they had already committed a felony for. "If I hadn't taken pot," one addict said pertinently, "I wouldn't have known how to get heroin or how to use it."

"In my circle," a Harlem youngster reported, "pot had nowhere near the status of heroin, and, after a while, pot didn't do as much for you."

Nevertheless, there were many in the Establishment who held, like TV commentator Downs, that marijuana was no more instrumental than milk in setting the stage for stronger drugs. In Los Angeles, sometimes called the marijuana capital of the world, a one-time city counsel argued, "Marijuana is less harmful than malted milk and the users know this." A former Santa Barbara prosecutor, without specifying the dosage, suggested that marijuana be sold in liquor stores, legally taxed so the state could collect revenue from "this remarkably popular product." College presidents, social scientists, a few attorneys, and an enormous number of people on the fringe of the arts—music, writing, painting—had suddenly become authorities on a drug that baffled biochemists and medical experts until its recent isolation for research purposes.

In March 1968, as it was apparent that marijuana was sweeping the campus, the educator who directed the nation's largest federally sponsored drug education project recommended before a Senate committee that laws against the possession of marijuana be removed. "The assumptions on which the laws were based have one by one been proved incorrect," testified Dr. Helen H. Nowlis, director of a drug education project for some four hundred associated universities. "They [the laws] are not enforceable in the sense that any large portion of users can be arrested."

In the prevalent attitude of permissiveness, Pinckney found some of the fault for the spreading drug plague. "Even as academic permissiveness gave the drug habit impetus, the exponents of permissiveness turned around and branded unworkable the law they helped breed disrespect for."

As many other physicians Pinckney was concerned by marijuana's high-incidence heroin side effect.

While not everybody smoking marijuana went on to heroin, a diversity of reports indicated that the majority of addicts had begun with marijuana. "Of 2213 narcotic addicts examined at the Public Health Service hospital in Lexington, 70.4 percent had used marijuana prior to their addiction," reported Gene R. Haslip of the Bureau of Narcotics. "It is true that not all persons who ever smoked a marijuana cigarette have gone on to the use of heroin, but a large majority of addicts began their drug-taking with marijuana."

Other reports showed a strong connection between marijuana and heroin. At the California Rehabilitation Center, in August of 1967, a review of one hundred heroin addicts up for release revealed ninety had previously smoked marijuana.

A definite correlation between the two drugs was affirmed by the Los Angeles County sheriff's office: "Our experience has proved that well in excess of 90 percent of all narcotics addicts in this country have graduated to the use of heroin through the use of marijuana."

It was not difficult to see how this connection built up. In the Laurel Canyon section of Los Angeles, many of the houses in the Hollywood Hills were maintained by floating colonies of fifteen to twenty young people who, instead of paying rent, paid youthful landlords only for the marijuana—and heroin—they used. "After two or three weeks," an ambulatory eighteen-year-old girl said, "you were ready for any drug, including heroin."

Therapists who treated addicts were convinced there was an addictive personality, a person more susceptible to drugs than others, with less tolerance and a greater need. "In other words, as with many drugs," Pinckney pointed out, "marijuana, like alcohol, will have a special deteriorating effect. It will hook some, and not others."

Pinckney had observed a curious distinction between the alcoholic and the marijuana habituate. "Whereas the alcoholic is sufficiently in tune with society to be defensive about his habit, the pothead has so lost a sense of perspective that he feels there must be something radically wrong with anybody who doesn't smoke pot." But whatever the reason users gave themselves—and others —for continuing drugs, it simmered down to pretty much the same thing, according to Pinckney. "Most people who use drugs do so mainly to avoid having to think. This approach parallels the permissive Freudian or psychoanolytic dogma that preaches feeling is superior to thinking."

But, pragmatically, effects cared nothing about differentiating causes. Six million alcoholics were an obvious reflection of the varying impact of drugs. "At least, with alcohol," Pinckney asserted, "we know how much the individual has taken, and that it breaks down ultimately into carbon dioxide and water, which are immediately excretable, and do not in themselves harm the body. On the other hand marijuana is stored in the liver, kidneys and other organs before it is eliminated, and has a corresponding toxic effect." Where marijuana smoking was endemic, hepatitis, a liver disorder, was also endemic, even where the victims had never used dirty hypodermic needles, the usually cited cause.

The presence of a controversial addictive personality became apparent in examining the musty La Guardia study on marijuana, a 1944 report to the Mayor of New York, which was the basis for much of the argument that marijuana was no more hazardous than alcohol.

There was some question, in view of the unknown variability of the marijuana, as to how scientific the tests actually were. However, the response in certain individuals was variably significant. "The doses given were toxic to the individuals in question but not to others taking the same or larger ones." Nine of seventy-eight subjects, prisoners chosen at random, suffered psychotic reactions from a marijuana concentrate. Nearly all reacted to a lesser degree. "A mixture of euphoria and apprehension was generally present. If the subjects were undisturbed there was a state of quiet and drowsiness, an unawareness of surroundings, with some difficulty in focusing and sustaining mental concentration. If they were in company, restlessness, talkativeness, laughing and joking were commonly seen. If the apprehension developed into a state of real anxiety, a spirit of antagonism was shown."

Six of the subjects suffering toxic reactions, with disorientation and mental confusion, revealed a special vulnerability to the drug. "The doses given were toxic to the individuals in question but not to others taking the same or larger ones."

The drug appeared to have particularly disordering effects on the epileptic and the addictable. "After smoking one marijuana cigarette, he (the epileptic) experienced an acute confusional state which lasted a few hours. In the second episode, which lasted six days, there was a more prolonged confusional state." After treatment, the psychiatrists reported: "Psychosis due to drugs. (Marijuana experimentally administered.) Acute delirium, recovered. Convulsive disorder, idiopathic epilepsy."

Paradoxically, hardened heroin addicts were no less prone to the weaker marijuana. The victims of H appeared prominently on the experimental psychotic list, indicating as much built-in susceptibility to one drug as the other. One female subject, a long-time heroin addict, reacted sharply to a marijuana concentrate. "Three hours later she became confused and anxious with periods of laughing and weeping. There were several short episodes resembling hysterical attacks with dyspnea (difficulty in breathing), pallor and rapid pulse during which she felt she was dying and screamed for the doctor and for a priest."

Another, a twenty-eight-year-old woman, a heroin and morphine addict, had varying reactions from her experimental doses of marijuana, sometimes euphoric, other times depressed, moody, irascible. On one occasion there was even a delayed reaction: "On May 8th she was given three cc. of the concentrate and became somewhat confused and unsteady, irritated and upset at carrying out tests, and greatly worried about the physical symptoms. Five hours after she had taken the drug the effects had largely passed off. Six hours later, however, she became restless and agitated, moving about constantly and worried about past conduct. This state continued for a few hours. Toward the end of her stay the subject became depressed and moody, constantly dwelling on the belief that she had committed unpardonable sins."

In the great outside world of addiction, addicts themselves felt that marijuana, or their predisposition to it, had been their own undoing. Questioned by reporters, by doctors, or in rehabilitation centers, they ruefully looked back on their beginnings with "harmless" marijuana. These reactions were often dramatically revealing, as reflected in dozens of authoritative interviews at the California Rehabilitation Center. "You smoke a stick of marijuana in the morning, get lazy on the job and get fired," said one addict typically. "In my case, it led to 'fixing' with heroin."

Another:

"After starting marijuana use, I lost interest in school and sports, was a disappointment to teachers and parents. I finally dropped out of school, all before starting heroin."

Still another:

"The first time I took a heroin 'fix' was when I ran out of marijuana."

The wide difference in individual reactions was clearly evident:

"I was walking down the road with a fellow and we were both high on marijuana, and all of a sudden, for no reason, he jumped about four feet in the air and ran into a filling station and began beating the man. He was like a wild man and *we* had to call police."

In Canada, not as permissive about drug use as the United States, there was a clearer recognition of pot's dangers. Toronto courts sent convicted marijuana users to the city's Alcoholism and Drug Addiction Research Foundation for treatment. "Anyone who deliberately takes a risk against the marijuana law is disturbed," observed a research officer. "It is a negative attempt to establish an identity. The user doesn't like the identities he has, or is aware of. So he withdraws and rejects any kind of identity."

The adolescent reactions to marijuana in Canada were similar to those in California:

"We used to have pot parties. One girl would go to bed with anyone. I've found I was more sexually aroused than ever."

Or:

"I laid down in a bathtub. There was no water in it, but I thought a wall of water was rising around me. Then somebody turned on the tap, and I imagined it was a waterfall."

And:

"One night in a field near my house, I became Alice in Wonderland and ran wildly away from the playing cards."

The Vietnamese war, with its strains, unrelieved exposure to different mores, and the easy availability of a high-potency marijuana, had obviously spread the habit through the overseas fighting forces, and back to the States on the fighting men's return from their hitch abroad. The few returning servicemen I spoke to had all smoked marijuana, and whether Marine or Army, estimated about seven out of ten of their comrades were on it to varying degrees. Despite official disclaimers, this startling figure cropped up repeatedly. In an eye-witness report from the fighting front, twenty-one-year-old Lee Dembart, a campus journalist, observed significantly:

"One group of soldiers whose job is to escort dead bodies from the field into the mortuaries in Saigon and Danang told a reporter that they were taking marijuana from four out of every five American dead during Tet. 'We took a pack of Camels off a lieutenant,' they said. 'Turned out to be full of joints.'"

In contrast to the professional press, Dembart's report to his Queens College newspaper provided a graphic picture of the inroads by pot on the American scene in Saigon:

"In addition to the Tu Do Street merchants, marijuana can be purchased with ease from any cab driver or in practically any store. The bars are all sources of supply, with special bars, like

Mom's, coming in for special praise from GIs throughout the capital area.

"Though Cokes and beers are relatively expensive, the 'free lunch' entices the customers. For here, instead of seeing little plates of peanuts about, a visitor sees little plates of hashish to which customers are invited to 'help themselves.'"

Distribution, as consumption, was no problem. "A man assigned to Tan Son Nhut Airbase just outside Saigon doesn't even have to leave the base to buy marijuana. Little Vietnamese beer stands set up in the rear of the base, outside the Ellis Compound, fill all orders. Sold in what looked like unopened packs of regular American cigarettes, the marijuana has been conveniently packed into what once were Salems or Winstons. Even the cellophane has not been removed from the packages of repacked cigarettes. Only a small piece of Scotch tape near the bottom of the pack indicates that the cigarettes have been tampered with in any way. Such a pack usually sells for $2."

There were all kinds of theories why the habit was so prevalent with the American troops. A general explained that it seemed to be just one more thing to do to pass the time. But others, just back from the battle zones, disagreed:

"You see this guy laying out there," an infantryman said. "Maybe, he's your buddy or cousin. You gotta take something."

And of course, it could always be *you*.

Far from the battle fronts marijuana has become a glamour drug, invading not only the campuses but the social pages. It had traveled far from humble beginnings. Mexican laborers brought the habit across the border in the early 1930s. It caught on with jazz musicians in New Orleans, who felt—erroneously—that it helped them to play better by slowing down their sense of time. The cigarettes were comparatively inexpensive. Reefers were fifteen cents then, and relatively pure, now they're up to a dollar, and nobody knows what they're getting. Only in recent years did pot find its way to the campus. "A decade ago," observed an official of the National Student Association, "you hardly heard about drugs on campus." Then somewhere in the ground swell of a new affluence, or a new student activism—or alienation—drugs went to college. In 1967, surveys by the National Institute of Mental Health indicated that 20 percent of the students on American campuses made a habit of marijuana. Untold others had tried it. Yale put student usage at 20 percent, but the student newspaper made it 35 percent. At Columbia, the dean of students said he "wouldn't be astonished if the number of marijuana users turned out to be one-third of the student body."

Protectively perhaps, the next step, inevitably, was an intellectual defense of marijuana, fanning out from the campus to the educational peripheries. The National Student Association, representing student interests at some three hundred universities, boldly adopted a resolution calling for an end to "all punitive and criminal approaches" to marijuana, soulfully recommending that drug abuse be considered a health rather than a criminal problem.

On the campus, LSD and pot were usually coupled, and the professional pushers, sensing a fertile field, started to move in en masse, indiscriminately recruiting students and outsiders as their agents. If nothing else, it made the college scene lively. "In my last year of law school," a Chicagoan reported, "I was working on a committee with the dean of the undergraduate college. We became friendly and he told me the police had advised him they were watching two eighteen-year-old girls who were pushing dope, and that he had better take action before they had to, and would I help.

"I met the two girls in question and became friendly with them. They were freshmen living in the new dorms. And they had this beautiful friend who was terribly sensitive and played bridge with them and, unknown to the girls, was making it with both of them at the same time. Also unknown to them, he had done time for armed robbery and was a member of the Mafia. He got pot for the girls free. Soon he got some for their friends—they had to pay of course. He set up a real little business in a dorm which housed four hundred people. Meantime, he saw to it that he got something on the girls. He hooked up a camera in a motel room and got incriminating pictures, movies, and stills of the girls. This beautiful person had one other guy working for him, and one day he got caught and the girls got scared. One told me about it, and I discussed the whole thing with the dean. It didn't seem fair for them to be blackmailed and this guy go free. The dean proposed through me that nothing would happen to them, extracting from the police a promise as well, if they would identify the pusher. After his arrest both transferred at the suggestion of the police and the school, and it was all over for a while."

Scenes like the above were not uncommon around the country, as college administrators, defending their students' right of expression, permitted outside agencies, connected with drugs, to gain more influence over their own charges than they enjoyed.

The college attitude was curiously arrogant. Like the English Colonel, in *Bridge on the River Kwai,* engrossed in building a bridge for captor Japs, they lost sight of what the goal was all about: theoretically, they were in the business of training good citizens, and not a law unto themselves. Faculty at the New York State University Center, at Stony Brook, Long Island, were accused of sanctioning marijuana, and tipping off students to a police raid on a campus pot party. Police undercover agents had moved about with ease, unchallenged by campus security guards, as they purchased marijuana in student lounges. One agent reported dealers standing openly in a dormitory lobby, taking orders from students. A bearded agent, disguised as a hippie, made thirty buys of marijuana, hashish, LSD, amphetamines, opium. He frequently observed marijuana smoked in dormitories, as professors unconcernedly passed in halls outside, and girls, turned on, slept the sleep of the drugged in male dormitories. It was a truly bizarre scene. Students would bury caches of marijuana on the campus and then get so high they couldn't remember the hiding places, frantically digging up the grounds. Police estimated that 20 percent of the five thousand students used drugs regularly, others sporadically.

Ironically, professors were more disturbed about police intervention than drug disclosures. "A double-standard exists at the university," a frustrated guard reported. "Campus laws and regulations are applied to the outsiders only and no one can do anything with students without checking with the administration."

The claim of special privileges was endemic. Pediatricians at the Stanford University School of Medicine announced, indeed pledged, to not at any time divulge illegal use of hallucinogenics to police. The decree putting them above the law was delivered by thirty-eight of the medical faculty:

"From a legal point of view, it is true that LSD is included in the list of 'dangerous' drugs. Its possession or use is a misdemeanor under the laws of the state. These comments in no way imply any judgment on the justice or desirability of the law."

But:

"It is our strong conviction that the great majority of physicians take the view that the welfare of their patients demands assurance to the patients that their doctors' *sole* concern will be with the medical problem."

And:

"The pediatricians at the Stanford University School of Medicine *have not* and *will not* report cases of LSD and other hallucinatory drugs to the police."

Unlike the Colonel in the *Bridge,* finally awakened, the doctors never did see beyond their own special problem.

It was obviously bad form to solicit comment from Dr. Pinckney on his authoritarian medical colleagues, but others saw such arbitrary action as part of the national trend for each group or individual to decide for himself what laws he should heed.

Some of this arrogation of jurisdiction seeped down to the fashionable preparatory schools where tomorrow's leaders were presumably molded. After three seventeen-year-old girls at the exclusive Masters School, in Dobbs Ferry, New York, were arrested on a "dangerous drug" charge, the headmaster on his own dubious authority called this an "overstatement."

Marijuana controls obviously challenged a militantly hedonistic society, insistent that its whims be served. "We have a lot of people today trying to convince our youth there is nothing wrong with marijuana," observed Federal Narcotics Chief Henry L. Giordano. "I hate to think what the problem might be if there had been no marijuana controls."

Westchester County, just outside of New York City, and perhaps the wealthiest suburban area in the nation, typified the growing tug of war between "permissives" and "traditionalists" for the minds of the young. Even as Westchester law enforcement officials were proposing a mass educational program to wean their youngsters from pot, a visiting psychologist appeared at a local church to propose liberalization of laws against marijuana and LSD, declaring these drugs less harmful than alcohol. Westchester, meanwhile, had its own "truth about marijuana" report. "Drugs," observed a Westchester official, "have become the sophisticated way to gain social acceptance. No longer is there any stigma. When we talk to youngsters about drug addiction now, their attitude is, 'It doesn't apply to me, I just smoke marijuana.'"

There were other changes in the drug picture. "We no longer have the stereotyped problem of pushers selling marijuana to the teen-agers," the official went on, "for the teen-agers in fine neighborhoods are getting big supplies somewhere and selling it to their friends."

And why not, when the then head of the Federal Food and Drug Administration, Dr. James L. Goddard, asked how he would feel about his children using marijuana, was quoted: "We've discussed this at home, and I would object in terms of the law today and any possible long-term effects." Advocates of marijuana leniency were quick to make the inference that Goddard was satisfied there were no short-term adverse reactions, particularly in view of his stand that "present penalties imposed for use and possession of marijuana are disproportionate to the hazards presented by the drug." An acknowledgment was subsequently wrung out of Goddard by Representative Clarence Brown, Jr., of Ohio, that "we don't know what the long-term effects of smoking marijuana might be."

Scientifically, as Pinckney observed, Brown was very much on the beam when, in October 1967, he sharply wrote Goddard:

"Any relaxation of penalties as established by present law must be founded on detailed and scientific information and official conclusions. Your call for more long-term research to detect any possible serious side effects from chronic usage of marijuana would seem to suggest that such studies and conclusion do not exist."

The corollary was obvious:

"If our knowledge is incomplete, is it sufficient upon which to base your feelings, whether that feeling is personal or official?"

Meanwhile, the "harmless" drug was taking its toll, indirectly as well as directly, in a campus world now suddenly exposed to the violence and skulduggery that inevitably trailed after drugs. At San Jose State College, near San Francisco, a nineteen-year-old student, awaiting trial on marijuana charges, was bludgeoned to death in January 1968. His father, shocked not only by the death but by the disclosure of his son's alleged drug use, reflected the misgivings of many parents sending their children off to permissive universities today. "Apparently, after his first year," he wrote college officials, "my son's friends at your campus included 'kooks' and hippies, although I know this was not his way at all."

He had felt secure in sending his son "into a scholastic climate, which we are entitled to believe would be a healthy, uplifting, academic experience. As it turned out, it was an unscholastic, psychedelic culture, in opposition to the order and progress society has labored to achieve."

8

MARIJUANA—THE SCENE

"Super-groovy," Gloria said. "You couldn't have the scene without it."

"What scene?"

She laughed. "I suppose the scene of changing morality."

I would have thought she was putting the cart before the horse.

"Going home on a date, when a guy brings out the pot, the girl knows exactly what the scene is. And if she lights up, he knows, too."

I had repeatedly heard that marijuana was not a sex stimulant in itself, merely releasing inhibitions, or accenting a mood already dormant.

She snickered. "That must come from a lot of old fogies. Once you get stoned, sex is inevitable."

I looked at her with some curiosity. She was hardly anybody's idea of a hippie or a hophead. In her mid-twenties, she had the fresh radiance of a motion picture starlet, and yet was of a solid New England background in the Victorian code.

It seemed to me that the individual's values were already changing by the very fact of his resorting to drugs for kicks.

"Obviously, they're taking pot to get over their own taboos, and do what they essentially want to do," I said.

She shook her head. "Not originally. You're confusing it with booze. With marijuana, you know what you're doing, but it suddenly seems all right, and"—she grinned infectiously—"like it or not, it does bring a new dimension to sex."

"You just think so," I said, remembering what the experts had said.

She laughed. "And what's the difference?"

She was conscious, under the spell of grass, of every touch, movement, embrace. They were magnified, enhanced, sensitized in every respect. "With whiskey," she pointed out with the authority of uninhibited youth,"the senses are dulled, and so is performance."

She frowned reflectively. "Another thing about pot which becomes devastatingly clear if you're a moralist. It is generally smoked in small groups, where it creates a curiously cozy feeling of camaraderie. You get the idea that everybody is feeling and thinking alike, and"—she smiled—"they generally are." This was "contact high."

Group conversation was erotically plain-spoken, punctuated with hilarity and a titillating spate of four-letter words, which seemed to generate a mood of general sexual rapport. The feeling of closeness had little or nothing to do with the charms or attractions of the people involved. It was as if they were so many electrical anodes or cathodes, joined or polarized by the intimately mystical experience of smoking together, preferably puffing from the same cigarette, not only to fully utilize each "joint," but for the deliciously subjective delight of being on the same psychedelic trip.

With it all, it was still difficult to clearly perceive which came first, the desire for thrills, requiring external stimulus, or a slow creeping decadence emerging out of habitual drug. Or, it could, I supposed, be a bit of each, the basic disenchantment with life reaching out for a compensating euphoric, and the euphoric, in turn, cloaking reality with such pleasantly languorous unreality that the new unreality became the reality.

Still there were numerous other factors obviously weighing on immorality—or more correctly perhaps, the vanishing moral standards of another generation. Where once the male had legislated the terms of a physical relationship, it had become obvious that the female, in her thrust for emancipation, now determined what her sexual responsibility should be. For the first time, she, not the male, controlled her facility to give birth. Thus, I had assumed that it was the pill, diminishing fear of pregnancy, and antibiotics, limiting the risk of venereal disease, which had influenced the changing moral values of the generation born since World War II.

"They're factors," Gloria agreed, "but they still have no direct impact on moral standards, only crystallizing or encouraging a course the person is ready for anyway."

She seemed to have it pretty well thought out.

She gave me a frankly engaging glance. "Actually, marijuana appears to break down the will to resist the sensual, since it is so completely a sensual experience, regardless of the great truths claimed for it."

Perhaps her experience with marijuana differed from the norm?

She smiled. "If you had been to as many pot parties as I have, you would know better."

As a teen-ager, revolting from a harsh home pattern, she had run off to New York's Greenwich Village, met with like-minded young rebels in the easy permissiveness of the Great Bohemia, and taken to light housekeeping with two young men. A course in marijuana had preceded the Great Adventure, and in the cozy togetherness of "copping a joint" together, the idea of sharing a flat had seemed an idealistic venture in sharing.

Seldom had she shared a sexual experience with a partner

who had not shared pot. The two went together, as naturally as black and white, or Bonnie and Clyde.

Unlike the average hippie, she was welded to society, unhappily as it might be. She had a good job, as a stylist, rented her own home high in the Hollywood hills, knocked around in an expensive sports car, and moved in a circle which overlapped all social strata. One common element ran through this actively fermenting society—pot. It was as commonplace as aspirin, and considerably more indispensable.

At times, marijuana seemed virtually a way of life, the busy, attractive people smoking it apparently finding some stimulation they didn't get out of their busy lives. Essentially, it seemed to have its roots in a corrosive intellectual boredom.

Even as Gloria was giving me her briefing, I recalled a lady professor who had told me with a gleam of girlish satisfaction that marijuana had brought a zest to her marriage that had never been there before.

It had struck me as odd that one intellectually rooted could profess such satisfaction over a purely sexual experience.

Gloria, who seemed a true cognoscenti of the weed, smiled indulgently. "The poor girl had probably been up tight all her life, and that's one of the reasons she was on the campus—that's one of the biggest escapes, that professor bit. They're always pontificating about life, without ever grappling with it."

She laughed at a sudden thought. "She was so proper that she probably never realized that women were meant to enjoy sex, too. Now she even likes to talk about it."

Again I gave Gloria a frankly curious glance.

She had no trouble reading my look. "Yes," she said archly, "I too enjoy it more with grass. I'm from New England, and we New England women have our own little hangups."

And how did it work?

She shrugged. "Unstoned, I'm too much of a Puritan to get into it, but any musician on a reefer, experiencing a slower pace while the tempo keeps building up musically, can give you a pretty good idea of the end result."

The fact that pot was against the law no longer worried Gloria, though it had once been a major concern. Still, because of her advancing position in the business world she had more to lose now than ever before. Nevertheless, the very fact that marijuana possession was a felony, exposing the user to ruinous scandal, imprisonment, and loss of civil rights, was not so much a deterrent as a challenge, giving the undertaking the subtle appeal of a cloak-and-dagger experience.

It seemed to me that judgment values had worn pretty thin before anybody would take this risk for something they argued they could do as well without.

Gloria crimped her lips a bit. "Alone, at home, or at friends', it's reasonably safe."

Obviously, through her predilection for the drug, she was building a special world which had little connection with her workaday world. This was the world, the junior jet set, which considered themselves hip without being hippies, sexual without being straight, intellectual without being intellects and whatever wasn't on pot was out—dullsville, square, missing. They moved in and out of the mainstream of society, and at times seemed that mainstream. And for the first time in modern history, the mainstream of a dominant Western society was a drug-infiltrated culture.

But while Gloria lapped over into my world, I only moved into hers professionally. And while I could never become a part of this world of "instant enlightenment," it was apparent that with her physical and mental attributes she could easily cope with the worst of convention without drugs. For even now, except for rare parties, she was a weekend smoker. "Nobody earns my bread for me," she explained with a characteristic shrug and smile.

In her limitless potential she reminded me of what Harvard's Farnsworth had said about it being the elite who were the most tragic victims of the marijuana habit. For they had the most to lose—and lost it.

I looked at her fresh, clear face in frank admiration.

"Why don't you give it up?" I asked on impulse.

She gave me a startled look. "And give up all my friends, what would I do?"

As a college graduate, with some smattering of education, it did seem she might profitably engage a few evenings with a book, a worthwhile play, a concert, or even some intellectually stimulating companionship around a fireplace.

She made a face. "But I do all that, not as much as I should perhaps." She mentioned several poets and essayists of the new Avante Garde.

"Have you read the *Love Book?*" she asked.

I recalled excerpts from this hippie-oriented love poem, replete with four-, five-, six- and seven-letter words, all indicative of a misty head in clouds of smut and an undistinguished vocabulary.

The author, I recalled had smugly, yet kindly, assured me that people who did not know pot also did not know where it was at whatever "it" and wherever "at" was.

I could still recall the love poetess' complacent smile as she condescendingly told me, "You need kicks."

She had laughed scoffingly when I suggested it was possible to develop one's own inner resources through the stress and strain of living.

Gloria was much more appealing, clearly more honest, and not as confident that she had the magic elixir. "It just makes me feel better." Her dark hazel eyes traveled to mine. "Sometimes, I'm so keyed up, I want to sit down and cry, without knowing why, and then I take a few drags, and I'm all right."

I shrugged. "That's the way dope addicts react."

She wrinkled her nose. "Don't compare *me* with *them.*"

Because of her unusual introspective qualities, I had valued Gloria's assistance in my research, volunteered with the bantering jibe that she would convert me before I did her.

She was obviously very much aware of her own scene, and I could obviously profit from her subjectivity.

And so I asked, "How does pot work its manifold wonders?" She gave me a long look.

"Essentially, it relaxes you, and I think everything falls in place from there—sex, conversation, general attitude." She frowned a moment. "The problem of course is that it often relaxes you too much."

"Have you ever had a bad trip?"

She nodded. "I've had several bummers, but my mood was bad at the time, and the pot only accentuated it. You can't blame pot."

Her first experience with pot of any strength had been pleasant, but it had almost led to disaster.

"It was a groovy Acapulco Gold, the best, though I wasn't aware of it at the time."

She had been at a party when the pot, as usual, was passed around. Somehow, this pot was different, quicker, faster, and gave her moments of giddiness. Her partner for the evening noticed the impact, and after a while suggested they leave for the privacy of home. She acquiesced, and they climbed into her car. She had never felt more relaxed, more at ease in her life, it was truly the grooviest of feelings. Whatever her gnawing fears or problems, they were suddenly unimportant or easily soluble. She felt in complete command, sure of herself and of her driving, and was piloting her car through the streets of Los Angeles with unparalleled confidence. There was but one disconcerting note, the cigarette she was smoking, of traditional tobacco, was tasteless and drooped insensibly from her lips, falling finally as she swiftly turned up a winding, rock-rimmed road for home.

Deftly, with the same confidence with which she was driving, she bent over to pluck the glowing ember from the floor of the car. It was an easy motion, full of assurance, but it brought an immediate howl of protest from her companion, as the car roared out of control and clunked into a boulder. In her new confidence Gloria had removed both hands from the wheel as she bent over.

The car bounced off the rocks, then back onto the road, its underside rent with gaping holes.

Instead of being frightened or shaken, she found herself giggling with a sudden access of amusement. It was all so hilariously funny.

The next morning, there was a mild awakening, when she had to cope with the unpleasant reality of having the car fixed and paying for it.

She had never before been in a similar hazard, though she frequently drove with two or three drinks in her. Some saving instinct prevailed with alcohol, short of the numbing point, warning the motorist to proceed with care.

"With marijuana," she explained, "you just *know* nothing is going to happen."

She was smoking more now, and liking it better, perversely impinging the habit on her everyday life. Occasionally, she smoked driving home from work. Turning on in the car was a great "gas," and delightfully symbolized the ease with which potheads could tweak the nose of the Establishment.

The game seemed hardly worth the candle to me.

Gloria was amazed that I did not immediately see how groovy this was.

"Not a chance of getting caught," she said, while conceding that both the smoking procedure and the wispy appearance of the cigarette were suspiciously different.

"You hold the cigarette with thumb and forefinger and exhale just over it, so as not to lose any of the fumes."

It seemed incredible that she should expose herself publicly, when she could have smoked a few minutes later in the security of her living room.

She gave me a self-assured smile. "There's no risk. The police know what's going on, they just don't bother about pot anymore."

Increasingly, she was with people who seemed to float from one pot party to another. It was difficult to be with others, sensing their separateness and disapproval, when it was togetherness and approval she was obviously seeking. Wherever she went, Las Vegas, Palm Springs, San Francisco, Big Sur, her weekends became glorified pot parties with the "beautiful people"—the sensitive people who felt deeply, intensely, the painful vacuity of life reflected in their own vacuity.

In Acapulco, the inspiration for Acapulco Gold, she had joined a party aboard the oceangoing yacht of a famed Eastern millionaire. He had brought his entertainment, musicians, dancing girls, and a bevy of the beautiful people. There they could smoke pot all day, in the warm sun, under the tropical moon. The beautiful people were plucked off like grapes ripened on the vine. It all went together, the languor of the climate, and the languor induced by the pot. They made a cult of the smoking procedure, tamping the weed into the bowl of water pipes, and filtering the smoke through champagne. It was groovy.

For those who wearied ultimately of pot, needing more stimulus, there were paper cones of ammo nitrate, inhaled as the pot wore off. It brought on a rush, similar to the throb of a heroin mainliner, evoking an almost irresistible sexual urge.

"You have to take advantage of the feeling right away," Gloria admonished, "as it only lasts two or three minutes."

The party had gone on about a week, new thrill seekers constantly revitalizing the group, new kilos of marijuana replenishing the rapidly vanishing supplies. All in all, it was a good trip.

I wondered how Gloria had fared.

Her eyes crinkled at the corners. "It was all right."

It sounded like hedonism, pure and simple, I was sure nobody had gained anything.

Her voice was tolerant. "Don't be too sure."

I regarded her curiously. "What could anybody possibly learn?"

She smiled wryly. "I learned I could have a bad trip."

Unexpectedly, she had a "bummer."

She was on deck, sharing a reefer with her host, when, looking up abruptly, in the reflection of his dark glasses, she caught a clear

image of a lion. She stared fascinated into his lenses, a growing
feeling of anxiety sweeping over her. The lion was a threat, growl-
ing menacingly and even when she closed her eyes, he was still
there, snarling, ready to pounce.

She fled to her cabin, remaining there until her nerve came
back.

That day, she left Acapulco. Nobody could ever again tell
her that a bad trip wasn't possible with pot. But even with the
bad trip it never occurred to her to stop smoking.

Even as we spoke, it struck me that the seeds of their own
destruction were in so many of these people, propelling them
perversely into a drug use depriving them of the individuality
and sense of responsibility which they were ostensibly seeking.

Gloria did not agree.

"I make my own choices," she said, "and I could stop at
any time."

"Then why don't you?" I asked.

"Because I don't choose to." She arched her eyebrows. "I
function with pot, and haven't missed a day's work in a year."

I had a feeling that her job was the one saving, stabilizing
influence in her life, and she knew it. Still, her attendance record
didn't quite square with what potheads had told me about being
lethargic the day after grass.

"I may be uncoordinated," she said, "but I make it in. As a
matter of fact, when stoned, I sleep twice as deeply, and am
physically relaxed."

With all her native intelligence, it didn't seem to occur to her
that her whole life revolved around drugs, and drug users.

"Oh, stop being pompous," she said, "I can take care of myself."

She talked frequently of getting stoned, the expression apparently conveying for druggies what it did for alcoholics—a
blackout of normal rationalizing processes.

"Are you stoned often?" I asked.

"When the mood suits," she said carelessly.

"Are you aware of what's going on?"

She shrugged. "Sometimes."

I looked at her with frank curiosity. She was a truly magnificent specimen, a bit high-strung, leggy like a nervous colt, with a high arched neck and a vehement way of tossing her head.

She smiled impishly. "Once," she said, "I wasn't sure. He was in the bed next to me when I awoke, and he said he had, but he might only have been putting me on."

I failed to see the pleasure in an overnight interlude that one couldn't even recall.

"Oh, I'm normally not promiscuous," she said, "but stoned, you react quicker, with more people."

"Do you know who they are?" I asked.

She made a face. "Of course, I know who I started with."

She was rather proud of her record. "I lived with one guy for two years, and there was never anybody else."

The relationship seemed to spell out a pattern. He had sponged off her, beaten her up periodically, and boasted of his adventures with other women.

Obviously, there was a masochistic streak, stemming out of a background I knew nothing about.

She wrinkled her nose. "It's all semantics," she said, "everything's labels."

I observed rather mildly that without drugs her choice of friends might be entirely different.

She frowned. "It does bring you with people you wouldn't ordinarily meet, but doesn't that broaden one's horizons?"

I didn't quite understand.

"With grass," she said, "you realize how great life could be without all your hangups."

She spoke often of her mother and father, sister and brother, and yet with all her family-mindedness, and her obvious charms, she had avoided matrimony into her mid-twenties.

"Most of the girls I know have married," she conceded, "but I know such a complete collection of losers."

Our eyes met, and she broke into a wave of laughter. "Maybe you're right about the people you meet through drugs."

Through Gloria, I had access to the junior jet set. They were by and large a physically attractive group, with more leisure than they knew what to do with, generally functioning in creative fields, and working as the mood or need developed. At one time they were caught up in the pseudo-intellectual craze for LSD, but so many had "crashed" that LSD was automatically a "bummer." However, any suggestion that marijuana might be harmful was hardly deemed worth talking about.

I was to think often of what Dr. Constandinos Miras, the Greek researcher, had said about the creeping paralysis that marijuana eventually laid on the judgment values of chronic users. In their distorted evaluations, they no longer were aware of their own distortions. More insidious than LSD, because of its very insidiousness pot was more hazardous. Deterioration was gradual, and the process clear-cut, even when, as usual, the user didn't begin to understand it.

I had encountered Roger, a young actor, at a friend's home. He was tall, well-built, with even features, and a boyish way. But he had not lived up to his early promise. He attributed his lack of success to not getting the breaks. Yet, even as we spoke, he was obviously under the influence of drugs.

"I've only been smoking pot," he said. "That can't hurt you."

"It might affect your appointments," I said.

He laughed. "You have to make them first."

His eyes were dilated and his face pale and puffy for one aspiring to heroic Westerns on television.

"I am one person," he said emphatically, "that pot has helped."

Squinting over my shoulder he marshaled his thoughts. "Sexually," he said, "it's been a great thing, getting rid of most of my hangups."

"You mean it stimulated you?"

"It did more than that." He hesitated. "I don't know how to

put it, but I was beginning to have definite misgivings of my own sexuality, and it cleared it all up. I just love my relations with women now."

It wasn't clear how the problem had been resolved.

"It's not easy to explain," he said, "particularly when you're talking about yourself. But once when I walked into a room, I looked over *everybody*."

"Now you see only the women?"

He frowned. "To be perfectly honest, if there was a producer, director, or established actor who could do me some good, I don't know what I would do even now."

Was he still homosexually inclined?

His face registered surprise. "In what way?"

"In relating to men who might do you good?"

"Oh that," he said, "that would only be business."

Under the influence of pot, his inhibitions about himself, his misgivings were completely removed, and his zest for the sex act immeasurably enhanced. "It was almost," he said, "as though I was both a spectator and participant at the same time."

Had he considered this might be purely subjective?

He smiled. "What difference if it clears up my doubts?"

Despite many sexual liaisons, he had no solid relationship with any one woman. "It just seems to be a sexual thing," he acknowledged. "I have no real rapport, except physically, and then only with pot." He grinned with amusement. "But I can have three or four relationships with different girls now, and enjoy them all."

"That's pretty promiscuous, isn't it?"

His grin widened. "I think it's pretty good."

"But you really don't have a truly rewarding relationship."

"I just relax more, and enjoy the whole thing, without thinking about anything except how much I am enjoying it."

My eye caught his. "Wouldn't you say that your whole life was disproportionately occupied with pleasure?"

His eyes stared back at mine glassily. "You mean," he said with a slow mocking smile, "that there is something else?"

As I considered this, an older, middle-aged man with a dish face sidled up. He had been watching us with the intentness of a cobra. He spoke in a high-pitched voice, ignoring me completely. "I'm going on home," he said tightly, "will you be long?"

He was Roger's roommate.

Roger shrugged. "It all depends."

The older man gave him a piercing glance, opened his mouth, and then apparently thought better of it. "Don't be too late," he said tartly, striding off.

Roger turned away, and said almost contemptuously, "He was a director, but his connections never worked out for me."

He moved off, and when I saw him last was in an animated conversation with a group of men. Business, I suppose.

Shortly thereafter, I mentioned Roger to Gloria. She shook her head. "Two years ago," she said, "everybody said he couldn't miss—he had everything; brains, looks, build, talent, and now he's just a big slob, mooching on friends, hardly able to get an audition, and not really caring."

It seemed a perfect case of what Miras was talking about. "There," I said, "is an example of how pot can deteriorate individual values."

Gloria was unimpressed. "It hasn't hurt my work."

"How do you know?"

"No complaints and I keep getting raises."

She was only a weekend user, and besides not everybody reacted similarly.

She prided herself on being scientifically oriented, and so as I read from Miras' report, she listened tolerantly.

"After a while," Miras stated, "you begin to see the personality changes that typify the long-time user—the slowed speech, the lethargy, the lowered inhibitions and the loss of morality."

Gloria's expression did not change.

"They will accept," I quoted, "as perfectly plausible things which five years ago they did not even like to hear discussed."

Her interest appeared to perk up, as I read that marijuana might induce brain damage. "The principal danger," added Miras, "lies with young people, who after using marijuana, lose interest in ambition and drive. What will be the future of a nation whose people have no interest in success?"

Looking up, I caught the rejection in the rigidity of her features. "That doesn't fit," she said flatly.

"Marijuana," Miras had said, "does not promote sexuality in itself. This is a subjective impression based on the fact that marijuana lowers inhibitions."

Miras did not wholly agree with Roger. "Sexual performance is actually impaired. Studies with rats show that marijuana decreased reproductive activity by ninety percent."

Gloria was unimpressed. "Nobody has sex just to have children," she said, "remember the pill."

According to Miras, marijuana would eventually cut down on every potential. "It reduces not only ambition, but health and energy, and the users find themselves talking incessantly about doing things they never get to. They were prone to anemia, inflammation of the eyes, and upper respiratory infections—and violence."

Gloria was yawning in my face.

"Another effect," I concluded, "is that it so distorts the individual's perception that he has a distorted view of nearly every activity, including his own reactions to marijuana."

Gloria completed her yawn.

"Why not come to a party? It's really no worse than the average cocktail party, where the boys pour the booze into the girls for the very same reasons."

As I begged off, she laughed. "You really are straight as an arrow. Anyway, come over one night, and we'll show you how little Miras knows about it."

As I was about to leave, the phone rang. Gloria listened a few moments, her face flushing, then angrily hung up.

"It's Sam," she announced, "he's stoned on grass, and he's coming over."

Sam had been Gloria's most recent boyfriend until one night, presumably relaxing with pot, he had unaccountably struck her across the face. Nobody would have believed it of Sam. He was normally so placid.

That had ended it for Gloria, but not Sam.

Gloria stopped me at the door. She was nervous, apprehensive. "Will you stay a few minutes?" she said.

Even as I sat down to await developments, a car screeched to a grinding halt in the lane below her house. There was a flash of lights, followed by the crash of breaking glass.

Gloria poked her head out a window. There was another shattering noise, and the angry scrape of a car taking off. Tugging at my sleeve, Gloria led me down the lane to her car. There we surveyed the damage—small mounds of broken window glass and a car aerial savagely twisted out of shape.

Gloria started to cry, slowly at first, then convulsively. She was a child again; tired, fearful, desperately needing support.

"He wouldn't have done it without being stoned," she sobbed.

I walked her slowly back to the house.

"Why not call the police?" I said.

She dabbed her eyes. "What good would that do? He's already had one marijuana rap, another would be prison."

I thought of the wanton damage, and the threat to the young woman wretchedly sitting across from me.

"He should be put away," I said.

"I couldn't do that." She shivered lightly. "I feel sorry for him—he's so alone."

She closed her eyes. "Funny," she said, "how things keep repeating. Before Sam, there was Tom, and he beat me."

I murmured sympathetically.

"Why," she asked, "why do I find people like this?"

She had a compulsive need to talk, and so I listened.

"Even as a kid," she said, "all I wanted was somebody to tell me I was important to them." She looked at me wryly. "Even now, I keep trying to win Mother's approval."

As a teen-ager, in Connecticut, she had run away from home three times. A stray reaching out for other strays she picked on the dirtiest, scroungiest, most hostile young man she could find before moving on to two other young men. He denigrated her in every way possible, and she tearfully put up with it. He turned her on pot, and in their smoking together, she found a curious rapport with him. She wasn't sure whether she loved or hated him but he was under her skin, and she would go up tight at the thought of his walking out on her. She brooded over his being with other girls, and she "turned on" to gloss over her insecurity. Actually, she could never remember a time, even in childhood, when she had felt secure.

Over the years, she had gained some insight into her own behavior. Downgraded by her parents, she had lived in the image they had fashioned for her. In the formative years her sense of her own value had been cruelly tarnished. She was constantly reminded she was lazy, shiftless, ungrateful, often so subtly that the rejection was all that registered.

One day, she proudly brought home the top report card in her class. Her mother kissed her lightly.

"It is only what we expect, my dear."

She had invited a young classmate home, from the other side of the tracks.

"Where do you find *your* friends, Gloria?" her mother had asked, with a disarming smile.

There had been more, much more.

What did she think her mother had been trying to do?

Her brow knit reflectively. "Keep me safely in her own image, I suppose."

Even connecting alienation to insensitive parenthood, why then did the revolt invariably express itself in drugs?

Gloria spoke from experience. "Nobody is more outraged about their children taking drugs than the outraged parent—they consider it immoral, shameful, sick."

She laughed. "And they feel guilt."

How could she be sure?

Gloria moved her shoulders ever so slightly. "I watched Mom's face when I told her I was on pot. I really enjoyed it."

Human motivation was invariably complex, hardly ever understood wholly by the individual himself, not to mention the unschooled observer. Still, I failed to understand why, if Gloria wanted her mother's approval, she didn't do what her mother would approve?

Gloria's jaw hardened. "I have to be myself."

After that session together I didn't hear from her for a week. She phoned to ask me over to meet a few people. "They might give you a little insight into the problem."

Even as I accepted the invitation I wondered anew about Gloria. She appeared to epitomize the superior individual wasted by drugs. She was living at a frantic pace, not stopping to consider where she was at or where she was going. It seemed a terrible paradox that one given so much should aim for so little. However, to a psychiatrist I knew, the problem was relatively simple.

"There's so many on drugs like her," he said, "all wrapped up in their own little mantle of intellectual arrogance."

The contradictions that puzzled me did not faze him. "She's not trying to please her mother," he said. "She's getting back at her, punishing her for those years of unlove and repression. But having been repressed so long, she is essentially shy, lacking confidence, with a low opinion of herelf, a reflection of her mother's attitude. To function with a semblance of normality, she must remove her inhibitions. Either alcohol or marijuana will do this, but with pot she gains acceptance in her set, and there's always the fiction that marijuana produces a spiritual experience."

What status was there in recklessly exposing herself to the loss of freedom?

"In revolts of this type, the authority figures are all mixed up. Since kids equate their parents with the law, this was still another challenge."

But how in her self-deprecation could she possibly be arrogant?

"She is essentially too narcissistically involved with herself to be open to change." The psychiatrist shrugged. "Nothing can be done until she is ready to face herself—and reality. She'll go on, until one day she runs out of steam."

And what then?

"The body and mind take so much, and then protest. For a few years, being young and healthy, she'll get by with drugs, and then one day her central nervous system will be affected and she'll be a setup for hepatitis, upper respiratory infections, and God knows what."

"But why take all this on?"

He laughed. "In their arrogance, they never believe it until it's too late."

This being the diagnosis, what then was the cure?

"The honesty to recognize the truth about oneself, and the intestinal fortitude to do something about it."

He smiled. "After all, she's old enough to drop Mother."

His words were still rattling through my brain when I responded to Gloria's invitation. I had assumed that she was having a small cocktail party, but the moment I stepped into her living room, I realized that Gloria had put one over. The air was filled with an acrid bluish smoke, and there were five or six young men and women sitting around carelessly, drawing in deeply on thin wisps of cigarettes.

Gloria greeted me with a raucous laugh. "I decided," she said, "that you needed an experience." She passed her cigarette, down to the nub, to a well-dressed youth sitting next to her. "We all agreed that you couldn't write about pot, without observing how it worked."

She giggled, touching off a wave of giggles around the room.

An old friend was sitting quietly at a small table, his hands busily occupied. It was Roger. I looked closer. He was fiddling with a small cigarette-rolling machine, some cigarette paper, and a bowl of green seeds.

"This is the best stuff available," he announced importantly.

His face was even pastier and puffier, and there were shadows under his eyes.

"Are you having an audition?" I asked.

His gaze held mine, then fell.

"I just turn on once in a while," he said suddenly. "I have appointments at the studios all week. My agent tells me we're on the verge of a contract."

One of the others laughed. "Roger's all set for the role of the little old pot-maker, he."

Roger frowned. "I'm doing all right. I don't have to smoke if I don't want to." He licked a cigarette together, and stuck it in his mouth.

"Then why do it?" I asked.

He sighed involuntarily. "Because I'm bored."

Gloria had been following the conversation. "So we bore you," she said, "what do you think you do for us?"

"Boredom," I said, sententiously, "may be confession of inadequacies."

Gloria grimaced. "So who's adequate?"

It was against the law to knowingly stay where marijuana was smoked.

As I checked my watch, she said, "Don't get up tight; we're leaving."

My eyes quickly scanned the room. The windows were shut tight, and the smoke moved in heavy layers toward the ceiling. It wasn't necessary, I commented, to smoke oneself in that atmosphere. Breathing in was all that was necessary.

Gloria gave me an apologetic smile. "I'll take you to a groovy place. The food is good, and you can see how the pot changes hands."

I looked at her closely. Her eyes were clear and she appeared in control of her movements. The same could not be said for her friends. A blond young man of twenty-two or -three, identified as a commercial artist, was sitting glassy-eyed, enthralled by the smoke from his cigarette. His hair hung over his face, and he sprawled dangerously in a hard-backed chair. His jaw was slack and his mouth open. He looked like the classic description of a "dope fiend."

Two young men were talking in a corner. They passed a cigarette back and forth, sniffing with obvious satisfaction. They seemed to inhale, without breathing out. I remember Gloria telling me, "You keep it in, and let it ooze out."

Another young man was staring moodily at the ceiling.

"He's in real estate," Gloria told me.

There was one other girl, Pat, in the party. She was tall, dark, and good-looking, despite the unevenness of her features. She had been appraising me good-naturedly.

"Oh, sit down and observe us," she said with a pleasant smile. She pinched off the last of her cigarette. "We're not very high, and should float down by dinnertime."

She was of a socially prominent family, and worked off and on as a fashion model.

"Do you do this every night?" I asked.

Her smile widened. "Oh, no, just when the pot is groovy."

Gloria was ready to go. "Now everybody finish up, open the windows, and get rid of the junk. I don't want to see myself in the papers."

"Then why not behave?" I asked.

She shook her head. "Stop being odious."

On this note, we finally left for dinner. It had seemed an eternity, but was barely ten minutes.

"You can relax now," Gloria said lightly, making for her car.

"You're not driving?" I exclaimed, suddenly remembering her description of another ride under pot.

"Don't be silly," she said, "I'm all right."

I took my car, and the others, Pat and Roger, reluctantly climbed in after me.

"You are reflecting on my judgment," Gloria said stiffly, nevertheless joining us.

In a few minutes we were at the restaurant.

It was certainly not very prepossessing—a hangout for unemployed actors, supported, as Gloria ironically pointed out, by the taxpayers in the form of unemployment checks.

As one might expect, it was dark and murky, as we filed into a booth, opposite a crowded bar. Everybody seemed to know Gloria and Pat.

A hulk of a man, obviously intoxicated, turned on his barstool. He apparently recognized Gloria. Then his eyes focused uncertainly on me. "Hey," he called roughly, "get up and let the lady come over here."

Gloria grimaced. "Don't mind him, he's stoned. He's a loser. His wife left him, he can't get a job, and his best friends won't tell him."

I looked at my little group curiously. It seemed incredible that they weren't turned off pot by the deterioration so apparent in the man at the bar.

It was Gloria's turn to be incredulous.

"Pot didn't make him that way—he was a jerk to begin with."

I had noticed many unescorted girls at the bar.

Gloria interpreted my glance. "They're trying to get it on."

"Get what on?"

She tossed her head. "You'll see."

Dinner was good, and reasonable. By the time coffee arrived, I had noticed a husky young man passing our booth a number of times. He headed for the bar, where he mingled a while whispering, and then made for the street, only to return and repeat his performance.

I drew Gloria's attention to his puzzling behavior.

"That fellow has passed this booth a dozen times."

At this point, the man again walked by with an air of vast unconcern, and approached the bar.

"Watch his hands," Gloria admonished.

In the midst of an apparently rapt conversation, I saw the man deftly pass a small flat packet to a girl closely behind him. Her purse opened, and claimed the object.

Gloria gave me a sardonic smile. "Well, Mr. Reporter," she said, "what do you think of that?"

"Pot or heroin?" I asked.

She yawned. "Nobody hip takes heroin anymore—that's for losers."

As we paid the check, the pusher again headed for the street—and a parked car—where he apparently replenished his supply.

Gloria gave the crowded barroom a last once-over. "It's been a dreary day," she said, "business should be good all over tonight."

She had decided to show me a hippie bar in the mountains overhanging Malibu. And so we traveled west from Hollywood to Santa Monica and the ocean, chatting meanwhile over the youthful trend to awareness with drugs.

"Why," I asked, "in your search for values, can't you develop inner resources through drugless meditation?"

"You mean 'à la Maharishi'?" Gloria said, referring to the East Indian guru currently having a vogue through his work with the Beatles and several Hollywood stars.

Roger suddenly seemed to wake up. "You have to know where you're at before you know where you're going," he said.

"You may be eighty or ninety before you find out," I said.

Roger was annoyed. "You haven't tried acid or pot," he said, "so how can you properly discuss it?"

"Gibbon," I said, "wrote about the Decline and Fall of Rome without even being a Roman."

Roger bristled. "Are you Gibbon?"

"I have the advantage," I pointed out, "of observing a contemporary scene with detachment."

Roger obviously considered my questioning of the hallucinogenics as criticism of him.

"I'm no hippie," he said, "but a serious actor, and I enjoy benefits and rewards as much as the next one."

In the tanginess of the moonlit night, it was difficult to visualize anything out of harmony with nature.

And then we came to the Spot.

The influence of the Establishment soon became apparent. There was a door charge, a dollar a person. It had no effect on the turnout, for the place was jammed. Young men in beards and strange garb were lounging at the tables, the bar, and dancing on a small patch of floor with hippie girls with radiant faces and raiment. Psychedelic lights played over the dancers, exciting them to greater efforts. The room was dark and dingy, and heavy with smoke, conversation, and rock 'n' roll.

Gloria was not impressed by the motley scene.

"They're stoned," she announced authoritatively.

They seemed lively enough.

"All functional," she reported, "they're going through their numbers."

From our jammed table, I surveyed the crawling room.

"Where are they getting on?" I asked.

"In their cars," she replied.

She caught Roger beaming at a teen-age naiad in a flowing robe. "You'd have to be stoned," she said, "this is VD Canyon."

The girls were all so beautiful and so young.

"Hell," Gloria said, "they're like rabbits."

Roger seemed to lose interest. "I really don't like hippies," he said, "they're all bombouts."

As Gloria and Roger took to the dance floor, a blonde girl, who had been watching us curiously, sidled over to our table.

"I," she announced, blinking long golden lashes, "am a Puritan hippie."

"And what," I asked, "is that?"

"I don't drink or smoke pot, but believe in love and sharing."

Pat gave her a sour look. "How old are you—twelve?"

The girl smiled brightly. "I am twenty—and very much aware of life."

She was a vision in a golden tunic, and matching mini skirt which revealed her shapely legs.

She spoke evenly, without animus, as though reciting. She had gathered, from overhearing our conversation, that I was a reporter. "I have an awareness," she said, "an awareness of whatever is opposed to love, and with this awareness, I resist the bombings in Vietnam, the slum Ghettos, and the hypocrisy of people cheating one another."

And how was this opposition expressed?

A smile lit up her angelic face. "Right now," she said, "we must work on your generation, then one day the decisions will be ours."

As dramatically as she had arrived, she now walked off, arm in arm with a young man with a ragged beard, matted hair, and a dirty sweater.

"There's a sharing for you," Pat sniffed.

By now, Gloria and Roger were back. Gloria was all for a late snack. And so we stopped at a little roadside inn. Roger studied Gloria across the table.

"Why," he asked accusingly, "have you never taken LSD?"

"I've never felt the need."

"How do you know?"

"How do I know I don't need a hole in my head?" she rejoined.

"That's no answer, as you would know with the insight from one trip."

Roger had been trying to convert Gloria since his own instant enlightenment with LSD.

Gloria showed her disgust. "Don't you read the papers?"

Roger shrugged. "What for?"

"Why, people are 'crashing' every day on bad trips, or getting their chromosomes all messed up."

Roger was unimpressed. "People are getting hit by cars every day but that doesn't affect your driving."

"I function very well without it," she said tartly, "and I'm working."

"There's more to life than working," he said stubbornly.

"Yes," she agreed, "there's also not working—and scrounging on friends."

He had the grace to blush.

I joined the conversation, remarking that just that afternoon, a physician who had taken LSD as part of a medical research project, had told me that from three to six months after each drug experience there had been a marked personality deterioration. It had taken him four or five days to make simple decisions, such as to buy flowers for his wife.

The doctor had reported that three apparently stable subjects had "crashed" on the project. "It knocks hell out of your judgment values," he said.

Roger heard me out in annoyance. "Oh, what does this fink doctor know?" he snorted.

Pat nodded assent. "Yes," she said, "we took it more times than he did."

Gloria shook her head. "But it was a supervised project, and they still crashed."

Roger was bristling. "Not working doesn't make me a loser. But," he conceded gruffly, "everybody has the right to decide for himself what experience he wants."

"That's white of you," Gloria said shortly.

The snack had turned out to be a hearty meal. Gloria and her friends were ravenously hungry, surprisingly so, considering their heavy dinner.

"I'm always famished on grass," Gloria explained with a yawn, "and sleepy, too."

A medical authority had attributed the marijuana hunger phenomenon to the increased energy demands imposed by the smoker's "high."

"The more they hallucinate, the more energy they use, and the more food they need."

Gloria agreed only partly.

"This was our first time with such strong stuff; 'ice-pack,' they call it—it leaves you a little numb."

"What comes after 'ice-pack'?" I inquired.

"Oh, stop being straight arrow," she said.

I wondered how long any system could take this abuse.

She shrugged. "I have to feel; otherwise, I might as well be dead."

The group broke up outside Gloria's house. I walked Gloria up a long winding lane to her door.

She was still angry with her friends. "Such jerks," she said, "sitting around stoned every day, not getting with anything."

They had been on pot regularly for the two years she had known them.

"You have something to look forward to," I said.

She regarded me coldly. "They blew their minds with LSD."

Their deterioration had none of the drama of an LSD "bummer," more the insidious loss of ambition cited by Miras.

Gloria looked me in the eye. "I never heard anything so ridiculous," she said. "Pot never hurt anybody."

The evening had a little afterlude. One night Gloria called, noticeably agitated. "It's horrible," she said, "horrible."

She seemed quite unstrung, and I wondered whether she was on drugs.

"Lord, no, and I don't think I'll ever touch another thing."

She became calm enough to tell me what had happened. She had gone away for the weekend, and loaned her house to Pat for a party. It was a shambles when she got back, and the party was still on.

"You should be used to potheads," I said.

"Pot nothing," she screamed, "they were all on the needle."

"Not heroin?" I said.

"Speed and Nembutal, jabbed right into the veins like a bunch of dope addicts."

"Why don't you throw them out?" I suggested.

She was almost incoherent. "Three of them passed out and are on the floor."

How about Pat, the staunch defender of LSD?

"She's wandering around the garden in the nude."

"What are you going to do?" I asked, not knowing what else to say.

She gave a grunt of disgust. I'll have to put up at a hotel, until they fall out or die."

There was a click at the other end of the line.

9

LSD KICK

The man sitting across the table was a famous playwright who had made a great success studying human motivations. He had been on a drug kick himself at times, taking barbiturates to get to sleep, amphetamines to get going in the morning. His personal life was stormy, beset with matrimonial difficulties. His childhood had been lived without God, his father being a confirmed atheist. He had been eight when his mother died, and shaken, childlike, by her passing, he had tremulously asked his stony-faced father, "Where has Mother gone—is she in heaven with the angels?"

The father had turned, replying with a harshness that perhaps masked his own emotion. "She has gone nowhere," he said. "There is no place to go."

For years thereafter the boy tossed and turned in bed, afraid that once he fell asleep he would not awake. The death specter had come early in his life, too early to be rationalized away by the conscious mind or to be eased and understood by psychiatry.

Success in the theater, instead of assuaging the anxieties that had grown with the years, seemed to bring new problems. Each succeeding creation had to surpass the previous hit, or he would be tormented by the haunting fear that he may have dried up. He would be no better than the man who sold tickets at the box office or the usher who led playgoers to their seats. He would be a nothing, with no distinction, a vegetable among vegetables.

Just as he was absorbed in the motivations of others, he became obsessed with his own. He had the money, time, and interest to explore the darkest corners of the mind. He had read somewhere that the Freudian concept of sex as the prime motivator was not borne out by methodical analysis. The playwright had no great sex drive himself, had never thought of himself as sexually oriented, nor as sublimating his sex impulse with creative work.

Under the watchful eye of a psychiatrist, he had taken LSD in the hope of opening the doors of self-perception. In the process, he had undergone a momentary, revealing glimpse of truth. The LSD had given him an ego release, permitting him, he felt, to understand his own motivations for the first time. In a dramatic, kaleidoscopic review of the highlights of his life, he saw now that he had been struggling ever since he could remember to achieve himself as an individual. That was it, of course, the fight to be different, to stand out from the crowd, not only because of what others thought, but because of the self-respect that he needed to give him the faith he had never had in himself—not since the day his father had shattered his dream of a benign God watching over him with sheltering care. "The Lord is my shepherd, I shall not want . . ." Suddenly, the magic had gone out of the Bible and its glorious psalms; the story of Jesus and the Apostles was all a giant fable, all meaningless.

Now, with the LSD, with a mind peculiarly analytic, he peered beyond the frontiers of the mind. In realizing self-fulfillment, he saw himself merging with the will of the universe, and just as the

universe had its cycles, its seasonal order, its upheavals, its predictable movement, so did his life have its own pattern, of which
his will was the conscious instrument. What could this universal
order be but the will of God? After the desire for self-approval,
came the need for the approval of others, beginning with the
infant's craving for the parental breast.

And then, only then, came the Freudian sex drive. He may
have had sex problems. Every sensitive person had some misgivings about his sexuality. At twelve or thirteen, in the years of
puberty, the sexual direction was in a fluid state. Hero worship
was prevalent, in furtive unsureness with the other sex, boys often
felt driven to the more familiar male figure. But this feeling had
passed in time, without misadventure. He had known other boys
who had not gone through this phase unscathed. Some eventually
became homosexuals, and developed a neurotic disapproval of
themselves and their associates. Others reverted to heterosexuality,
but still brooded darkly over the lapse, impairing their confidence
in their own integrity and self-image. These misgivings, these
doubts were almost as damaging to the ego as homosexuality itself.

And so, where deviated, where irretrievably wound up with the
subject's own conception of himself, sex then became a para-
mount factor in the individual's orientation. For as it worried and
fretted him, it narrowed the flow of individual expression, as the
individuality could only express itself free and untrammeled.

There was little doubt that LSD removed sexual inhibitions,
regardless of what insight it did—or didn't—give to individual
sexual problems. No less a buff than Timothy Leary once said that
it gloriously enhanced the whole sexual procedure, sufficiently hallucinatory to liken one's sexual partner to Cleopatra or Casanova.

However, much more has been claimed for LSD, by the acad-
emicians pushing it across the face of the nation for ten years.
They have claimed that the apparent facility LSD has of freeing
the ego, and dredging up the subconscious, has brought sufficient
insights to cure alcoholism, addiction, criminal recidivism, not to

mention opening wide the doors of perception to the brave new world of Aldous Huxley.

But even so, these were not unguided LSD experiences, and the guide often appeared as important as the drug. "Without the giver reassuring the subject and guiding his thoughts," a psychiatrist observed, "there is no gift."

Only the trained observer could clearly comprehend a subject's experience. Examining a thousand volunteers—normal and psychotic—over ten years, researchers of Boston Psychopathic Hospital found that LSD sharply affected the adrenalin output, reflecting varying emotional stages as the subject passed through them. Visible effects lasted six to eight hours, but within an hour, subjects manifested restlessness, tremors, sweating, hot and cold flashes. They became irritable, hostile, anxious, apprehensive. In the second hour, they experienced the sensation of not existing, feeling that various parts of their body had altered their form. One subject felt there was nothing between his hip and foot, though another corner of his mind, recognizing that he was under the drug, knew perfectly well that his leg was intact.

Time and space lost its meaning. Conscious thinking slowed down. A whole world appeared to have opened up visually, including an experience of being born, even of dying. Some men, oddly, had the hallucination of giving birth, indicating to some a remarkable clairvoyant experience.

The Boston medical group felt there had been some help in providing new insights into mental disorders. "We can see the various defenses a subject brings into use, one after another, to protect himself from stressful experiences," they reported in *Scientific American*. "We can detect distressful situations of which hospital staffs have not previously been aware. And we can determine what treatment and what experiences give the most support to a patient and are most effective in reducing his symptoms. We can telescope a severe psychotic reaction . . . and follow the emotional disintegration step by step."

The greater the disintegration, of course, the more successful the experiment. But any disorganization had to be carefully watched, or the results could be disastrous. Indeed, greater demands were often made of the guide than the drug. "In certain patients," advised Dr. Harold Abramson, Long Island, New York, pioneer of LSD therapy, "the defenses are disorganized to a point making it possible to reorganize them in a more healthy way afterward." However, there was a point of no return. Under LSD, an Abramson patient felt he had become so small he was in danger of being washed down a toilet bowl. Immediately recognizing this fantasy as normal ego depression, sparked by the drug, psychiatrist Abramson was able to restore the patient's confidence with a few reassuring words. But without his knowledgeable guidance, the patient might well wash down the drain—emotionally speaking.

Because of its provocative effect on the mind, professional savants—psychiatrists, educators, sociologists—have been enchanted by LSD. Many gave it to their students, and took it themselves, heedless of side effects, until, in some instances, they "crashed" themselves. Some studies were highly revealing, as they revealed the takers. Sociologist Robert M. Schwieder of California Polytechnic College, Pomona, had in depth examined over fifty young people on LSD. He was with some "coming down," others just after their trip, and in some instances he knew his subjects well enough to judge personality change. Schwieder saw the problem in its broadest social implications. Students of deviant behavior had observed that society gets the drug it needs. "Why then," Schwieder asked, "did our society need LSD when we have so many other drugs?"

Graphically, he summed up:

"Ten billion capsules and pills of dangerous drugs are legally produced each year. In addition, seventy million Americans use alcohol; five million or more are alcoholics. Americans take drugs to sleep, to stay awake, to feel better, to reduce tension, to solve psychosomatic problems, to escape reality, to lose weight. And there was always coffee, tobacco, even cocoa and tea.

"With all these drugs," he marveled anew, "why did our society need another—LSD?"

Schwieder found his average LSD user was essentially middle-class: his parents suburbanites, well-educated, with an active religious orientation. The father was a responsible citizen, with a responsible position. He drank some, but seldom became intoxicated. He was interested in his children, spent considerable time with them, at home and vacationing. There was no permissive coddling here. "He set up reasonable standards and expectations for his children, slightly stern for even his generation."

His relationship to his wife? "Tranquil was a word that seemed to fit."

Schwieder dealt with a significant cross section of young suburbia. And it was a stifling suburbia, with its syndrome of conformity, that the youthful venturer into LSD was reacting against, "Conformity-nonconformity seemed a major issue. Every subject commented upon it with some considered feeling."

A certain sameness ran through the Schwieder interviews with the young rebels:

"Almost all talked about the death of the ego, but what they apparently meant was the shattering of the defense system that protected them from their own fears of death, suicide, homosexuality and dependency, but prevented them from feeling much of anything while they were engaged in activities (suburbiana) that they now felt both pointless and meaningless."

They were not compulsive drug users. "Most were using LSD not as an escape from somewhere, but in order to get somewhere and would stop using the drug when they got there."

There was a prevailing lack of sophistication about the experience. "The LSD user was convinced that LSD was the answer to all mankind's problems, a way to break out of the mass conformity of the mass society."

Their own drug background was sketchy. Most had used marijuana, amphetamines, and barbiturates before LSD. But they had a very real contempt for alcohol, which they related to the country club culture they were resisting.

Like their parents, this LSD user typified the middle group of his society. "Originally, he was either ex-activist, or from the same pool from which the college activists drew their numbers." However, there were discernible changes after LSD. "An identifiable culture was being developed characterized by an anti-Establishment nonactivism." Even more consequential perhaps was the impact on friends, who did not use LSD or marijuana—at this time—but did not put down others for using it. It would be only a matter of time before intellectual curiosity got the better of them.

Considering the exciting unreality of the LSD experience, it was obvious why the bored and frustrated, particularly of the leisure classes, hugged to immature bosoms the electrifying excitement of their experiences, feeling they had encountered the meaning of life for the first time. Nowhere had I seen this illusory paradise so eloquently portrayed as by Dr. Oscar Janiger of the American College of Neurology and Psychiatry, who shared the experiences of his subjects:

"Clock time is irrelevant; you are involved in a larger cosmic time, which tells you that in a flash you can see all.

"Your mind may be flooded with all these vibrations, visions and flaming jewels, so that you may not be able to handle simple abstractions. The attendant asks you: 'If your sanity depends on it, tell me why a rolling stone gathers no moss.' The question seems hilarious, and you greet it with laughter. Or you frown in an attempt to stimulate deep thought. Suddenly, the meaning of the universe becomes completely clear—but you are not able to answer why a rolling stone gathers no moss. What a small insignificant question, when you are synthesizing all the great paradoxes of cosmology. You forget to answer, for you are listening to the voices that call you into Eden . . .

"Of all the big changes you notice, the change in self-concept and body image is the most immense. You feel at first no definite sharp location of yourself. 'I was being unglued from my earth

gravity . . . I was in space. I was standing on the rim of a planet.'
This 'you' which stands outside yourself shows no rigid shape
. . . 'I suddenly find myself about fifteen feet tall—looking down
at my feet, which seems a long way.' And you may take new
pleasure in your body, as if just discovering it: 'I became aware
of the almost unbearably good, painfully sweet disposition of my
physical self. I was aware of myself to the roots of my hair.'

"You may have a strange reaction to the mirror, as if seeing
a stranger. 'Someone showed me a mirror and I looked in to see
myself. The face I saw looked so beautiful. Then, in a tragic
burst of evil creativity, I composed my face into the way it normally is—and felt great sadness, that I could not see that beautiful
face all the time.'

"You feel able to step out of the rented costume of the self
you held rigidly within narrow bounds."

What a clarion call to the eyeless in the Gaza of suburbia?

And now compare this to the monotony of a dull, routine life
yawning grimly ahead:

"When transcendent feelings flow, you want to describe unity,
illumination, revelation, rebirth and exaltation. Then you are reduced to finding the most fantastic phrases to evoke the unevok-
able. It is as if you saw a new color, one outside the band of
the spectrum people normally see . . . 'At the height of the drug
I was really aware of only two things: my own existence and the
world of nature which seemed to me beautiful and right!' "

LSD meant understanding for some, despair for others, and so
high a degree of sensory perception was apparently attained that
words cannot describe the depth of understanding, the feeling of
exaltation, or the terror that may crop up any time. A "bummer"—bum trip—may strike without warning, and have been effectively interrupted with the tranquilizer thoriazine. However,
this only suppressed the terror, which recurred, inexplicably,
months later. At the free clinic at Haight-Ashbury, Dr. David
Smith, apprehending the danger of chemically aborting a "bummer," encouraged a talk-out instead.

Talk was apparently the key to LSD, for in the average experience, regardless of the insights, that was all that comes out, endless conversations about self. I sat with myriad artists, writers, doctors, educators, philosophers, who had taken it, and listened by the hour how their experience awakened them, only to discover there was no discernible change in the way they handled their lives. My playwright friend, for instance, after his own flash of insight, kept on marrying the wrong woman, when, actually, there was no right woman for him.

Again, one of the leading apostles of LSD, acclaimed by the cognoscenti as the architect of a new psychedelic world of universal infinity, couldn't manage his own home life. Despite all his New Thought he was left high and dry by his wife and children, outraged by his preoccupation with psychedelic indulgence, and his lack of occupation with them.

If anybody could profit through the visual expansion of LSD, one would certainly think it would be a painter. I knew such a painter. He was a modern, who had won much attention both at home and abroad. Early in his career he had won competitions for study in Europe, and many considered him the most promising of the younger American impressionists. He had been glad to tell me about his flights into fancy, supervised by a physician who felt, like Timothy Leary and his erstwhile associate, Richard Alpert, that everybody was bound to be better for the experience.

Under LSD, he saw his own paintings as never before. It was a thrilling experience. "Right there on the wall of my living room, they began to breathe in and out, pulsating slowly, evenly, with a definite rhythm." The colors also began to move, and he watched fascinated for thirty minutes, as they intensified in brilliance, yet retained their composition, even in movement. He studied a drawing, framed in glass. It began to writhe, merging with the glass in a kaleidoscopic-like flow. For twelve hours, until the LSD wore off, he wandered through an apparent maze of Rembrandts and El Grecos. Never before had he seen such color and symmetry, such purity of form. "I seemed able to peel the paint off my pictures, and though painting has only two dimensions, the third being an artistic illusion, I now saw not only three, but a fourth—motion."

Not only as an artist but as a sensitive human being, the painter had a soul-searching experience, as he lay there on the couch, steeped in the symphonic background of Beethoven. He had an almost Godlike awareness of Beethoven's power, sensing the force and will behind the music, as he began to merge insensibly with the music, first feeling he was Beethoven and then the music itself. What Beethoven had done with music, he realized in an access of exaltation he wanted to do with his art.

Meanwhile, he was at the mercy of his guide. The doctor appeared able to alter or modify his visual reception with a word. A reference to the sublimity of Beethoven touched off a reflection about the divinity of man. Suddenly, he felt a mystical presence in the room, and with the overwhelming impression that he, the artist, could will what he wanted of life.

Suddenly, sitting up, his eye was caught by an abstract painting, and his mood swiftly changed. He felt tired, chilled, his body drooped as though carrying a tremendous load. He was on the verge of the greatest mystical experience of his life. "Suddenly, an image formed of a man bent over, struggling and straining, carrying a huge, square-hewn log. With a jolt I realized this was Christ carrying the cross to Calvary."

At the same time, with the curious multiple-vision of LSD, he realized it was also himself. "This image then dissolved into a hazy Resurrection scene, and as Christ walked off, triumphant but sad, he looked at me with a tear in His eye and said, 'Thank you.' At that moment there was also a tear in my eye, as I experienced all the suffering that was His, and I could feel the tear trickling down my nose."

Although he was not especially religious, the blinding vision of Christ carrying the cross burned into his brain. The symbolism was obvious. His painting career had reached a new creative phase. He felt calmer, more introspective, at peace within, in tune without.

He had additional trips, and they only strengthened his conviction of new power. He had never felt so confident, so productive. So great was his enthusiasm, so deep his regeneration, that I was convinced his name would soon flash in meteoric flight through the museums of the world.

He did have some success, but not as I had anticipated. He opened a small restaurant, featuring his paintings as well as a flavorsome cuisine. The restaurant caught on instantly. He opened another restaurant, decorated it with more paintings. When I saw him last, he was considering a third restaurant. He hoped to have enough paintings to cover the walls.

With all the insights he had gained into the mystique of painting, with his new appreciation of dimensions he had never dreamed of before, with his new inner calm and unity, he was unable to create even as well as he had in the past. He was a successful restaurateur.

For millions of youthful users—and oldsters—LSD was drugdom's supreme status symbol. It transcended marijuana, speed, barbs, morning glory seeds, and was a yardstick of the user's intellectual interest. By inference (not implication), it even made an intellectual of some, who could now brag about an esoteric experience that none but an LSD user could possibly understand. Thus it became almost part of the LSD credo to patronize others who hadn't taken it. "You can't know anything about LSD," they would invariably say, "unless you have taken it yourself."

As to describing an experience, without sampling it, that was patently absurd. And so they were an exclusive fraternity, of from one to five million members, many of whom had crashed, winding up in hospitals, without, in their eyes, reflecting on LSD but the user. Some, with guidance, appeared to have learned something about themselves. The Hollywood star Cary Grant, taking LSD under professional supervision, saw his marriage Number Three so clearly that he got a divorce. And his actress wife, Betsy Drake, taking the drug too, welcomed the divorce.

"You learn to die under LSD," Miss Drake commented. "You face up to all the urges in you—love, sex, jealousy, the wish to kill."

On the other hand, the perennially youthful Grant, in LSD's moment of truth, discovered that all his life he had been running from what he wanted most—women who looked like his mother. The LSD, Grant felt, had a positive result. Because of his new insight, altering and freshening his personality, younger women started finding him attractive.

Grant's reaction was the usual one. The individual felt his whole life in flux before him, broad new horizons had opened wide, and truth was at last entering their lives. But invariably, despite the great moment of truth, investigation showed little progress in the user's life. "I suddenly knew what was wrong in all my human relationships," a disillusioned LSD user advised, "but I couldn't do anything about them, because *I* was still *me,* and *they* were still *them,* and the chemical hasn't been made that can bridge the action gap."

But hadn't it helped Cary Grant?

After LSD, he had attracted a much younger woman, Dyan Cannon, a little-known actress in her twenties, and they were married. At last report, they were where he was at with wife Number Three, divorced.

So what could be said positively of the great moment of truth?

Despite the "insider" fraternity feeling of many LSD users, it was obviously not necessary to take LSD to know how it worked, and affected people. The smallest effective dose was twenty or twenty-five micrograms, and some users, inadvertently perhaps, have taken seven or eight hundred. As described by Dr. Pierre Renault, a resident in psychiatry at the University of Chicago, LSD was absorbed rapidly and began to concentrate in the brain within minutes. Its action moved through distinct phases. The first stage was illusory, familiar objects seen as new. Next the dramatic hallucinatory phase where external reality was so distorted it wasn't distinguishable from fantasy or past experience. The third stage brought depersonalization, ego release. There was a loss of distinction, Renault reported, between self and nonself. In this stage an LSD subject might imagine himself a chair, a teacup, even a bird.

The fourth stage was pure delusion. In an effort to reintegrate the personality fragmented by LSD, the individual was often involved in a choice between mysticism or madness, frequently marked by the panicky feeling that either the self or the world around him would momentarily dissolve. If the anxiety state continued, he was on a bad trip.

At times, according to Dr. Richard Moy, director of the Chicago University's student health service, delusion was so overpowering the subject could not cope with the ugliness of what seemed raw reality. He mentioned a youth who had taken LSD shortly before having sexual relations. After the drug took effect, the youth mistakenly perceived his sex partner as his sister. It had a crushing result, psychologically.

LSD could also be euphoric. And while it was apparently not habit-forming, it was obvious that many in the intellectual fraternity were psychologically addicted to pleasurable escape from the demanding realism of the outer world. Some had taken LSD so often, they couldn't recall whether it was two or three, or four hundred times. They were acid-happy and the trip was all that mattered.

It spread rapidly on college campuses, where for years professors lent it prestige as an intellectual experiment of the highest order. In the interests of mind-expansion, LSD's hazardous side effects were unscientifically forgotten, and the fad of the moment indulged. Fortunately, there was a return to common sense. One-time LSD users, alerted to its risks, passed on their warnings. "It is hedonism, pure and simple," a user reported. "The people taking it regularly are only indulging themselves. Actually, they're all

Narcissus, so involved with themselves they can't see between their legs."

Many LSD regulars were suppressed personalities, who were seeking desperately to remove emotional inhibitions. They suffered a basic lack of communication, not only with others but with themselves. "Nobody can communicate," a pretty coed told me, waving vaguely toward the ivy-covered spires. "You've got to give them credit, though. They're trying."

I had met Dorothy through another student, a proud exponent of LSD and pot, who had advised that practically everybody at this famous old university had tried marijuana at one time or another. Dorothy was one of the few holdouts. "I'm a little 'chicken,'" she said, "but Pearl, my roommate, tells me I'll get to it yet."

The two girls were roommates and of an age, twenty-two, but of different backgrounds. Dorothy came from a strait-laced New England family, and had an indefinable look of refinement. Pearl was from a bustling metropolis, and rather aggressive.

"I value her immensely because she is the only person I can communicate with," Dorothy said softly. "I can talk about anything with her—love, ethics, philosophy, psychology, anthropology, we can go on for hours, communicating."

Sitting there, sipping her tea, looking up at me, she was as pretty as the proverbial picture. Her complexion had a smooth rosy tint, her hair was a rich golden brown, her teeth as even as matched pearls.

"Can you tell me why," she asked solemnly, "I find it so hard to communicate with other people?" She frowned a moment, "I never had anything to say to my family—that's why I went away to college. They were stifling me."

"You don't have any difficulty communicating with me," I smiled.

She laughed, "We're not communicating, we're talking." She knit her brow for a moment. "How can I explain it? Now when Pearl and I are talking, it's as though everything came alive.

Ideas I never had before come flooding into my head. I don't even know where they come from." She looked across the table with vaguely troubled eyes. "Now, why should only one person in the world do that for me?"

I was as naïve as the next man, and the Puritan simplicity of the girl, her wide-eyed innocence, led me to explore an uncertain area, her relations with the other sex.

She sniffed. "They don't do anything for me."

"Have you wondered why not?"

"It doesn't seem to matter anymore. I suppose if I could find somebody I reacted to I'd have it made."

I felt a twinge of sympathy for this apparent product of a Puritan culture.

"With your background, I suppose sex takes on all the hideousness of original sin."

She shrugged. "Fundamentally, I just don't find men as interesting as women. It's as simple as that."

"Perhaps you haven't given them a chance?"

She laughed. "How much chance?"

"Because of your family background, and your own moral sense, you quite properly have not expressed normally healthy impulses of a young woman your age."

Her gaze widened. "What impulses?"

"I assume," I said, "from what you have said that you are a virgin."

Her eyes widened even more. "You think that's my problem?"

"Only if you make it a problem," I said.

She cupped her dimpled chin in her hands and regarded me with a twinkle in her eye, "I'm as promiscuous as hell," she said, "and that's my problem."

I sighed, the sigh of the disenchanted middle-aged. She cut into my reflections. "Pearl keeps saying I should try it."

"Try what?" I said, coming back to life.

"LSD, what else?"

"How do they get it?"

She shrugged. "All you need is some lysergic acid and an elementary knowledge of chemistry. They make it in their labs, under the professor's nose."

"Why did Pearl take LSD?" I asked.

She considered me blandly. "I suppose she wanted the experience."

"Was there a problem?"

"Everybody has a problem."

"What was her problem?"

"Like myself, she had trouble communicating." Dorothy frowned. "She found it easier to communicate with girls than she did men." She picked up a paper napkin, folded and refolded it. "Funny," she said, "how people get themselves involved."

"Are you saying she has lesbian tendencies?"

"Every girl wonders about herself at one time or other. Pearl thinks of herself as a lesbian, but it's just a phase."

And her own attachment for Pearl?

"It has nothing to do with sex. I just feel happy and alive around her."

"Has she ever made an"—I hesitated—"overture?"

Her lips tightened. "We have a beautiful relationship. We talk about poetry, philosophy, and"—her arms waved airily—"life."

"Would it be possible," I asked, "to discuss Pearl's LSD experience with her?"

Dorothy's face lit up. "I don't know why not, she really has a beautiful mind."

Not surprisingly perhaps, I found it difficult to pin Pearl down. Besides attending classes, which she did whenever she felt like it, she maintained an artist's studio. Over the telephone she explained that she was trying to launch a career as a commercial artist. After she had broken two or three dates, she suddenly turned up one day, announcing she was there in response to Dorothy's bidding. "She'll be along after a while," she said.

I had not known what to expect. Had I pictured some dramatic young star out of a mod movie, notably *Juliet of the Spirits,*

Pearl might well have been it. She was boyishly slim in a thin jersey, her skin was fair, providing a striking contrast to her dark eyes. Straight black hair came down over her face in twin spears, adding a vaguely Mephistophelean appearance. Her lips were a thin smear of red conveying a mood of severity. She sat down primly, crossed her legs, and waited.

"Would you care for a drink?" I asked.

She considered a moment. "Maybe a little vodka."

She tasted her drink gingerly, then put it down, apparently satisfied. She appeared to be sizing me up, even as I was quietly appraising her.

"I suppose," she said finally, "that you already have it all figured out?"

"If that were true," I said, "there wouldn't be much point to your being here."

Her voice held a sharp edginess. "I don't know how much Dorothy has told you, but I have nothing to hide. At twenty-two I've done more with my life already than my parents have." She looked at me coolly. "I understand you're interested in what's motivating this generation, drug-wise." She lit a cigarette and inhaled deeply, whistling the smoke out through her nose. "It isn't just drugs. It's the whole outlook of a generation far more adventurous and introspective than your generation ever thought of being. They have thrown off the shackles of convention, and are taking a good hard look at themselves and the world around them. It's as simple as all that."

It didn't seem that simple to me. "Can't they do all that without marijuana and LSD?"

She wrinkled her nose. "I was afraid you wouldn't understand. Obviously, you've never had a drug experience."

"I don't have to be an animal," I said, "to visit a zoo."

She reacted sharply. "Are you implying that people who take drugs are animals?"

"That was an analogy, not a comparison."

She spoke carelessly. "I suppose Dorothy told you I am a lesbian."

"She mentioned that possibility."

She suddenly shifted tack. "I've been going out with a writer, a very gifted person. He's written two wonderful novels."

"What are they?" I asked.

"Oh, they haven't been published. They're beautiful, but they weren't written for money, so of course the Establishment doesn't want them."

She sat stiffly, rigidly erect, reflecting the inflexibility of her attitude.

"Would you explain," I said, "how one writes a book that will make money?"

"You take sensational material, and treat it sensationally."

"Some people might consider you sensational," I pointed out, "and yet you're a valid subject."

"Alan—my young man—has written beautifully of life, of people with heart, who want to live life to the fullest—and yet he got no recognition."

She was chain-smoking now, nervously lighting up one cigarette before the other was half finished.

"My problem is not lesbianism. I could be a lesbian, and still be reasonably satisfied with myself if I weren't such a perfectionist. That's my hangup." She reached for the vodka, and polished off the glass with a gulp. "I just need to start something and finish it properly, just once."

She was searching for the self-approval my friend the playwright had talked about. But how could a homosexual in a heterosexual society approve of herself?

She appeared to read my mind. "I was never able to relate to my mother, I always resented her, and I'm intelligent enough to know that this turned me away from the kind of relationship she had with my father. She was so damn domineering she was more like a man, anyway."

She had fought it for a while, and in her confusion had turned to drugs. "I took marijuana because I was searching, trying to know more about myself. And I took LSD for the same reason."

She looked up with a wry smile. "Funny thing, I was always looking for somebody to take care of me, and I always wound up taking care."

From the time she was eighteen she had many lesbian relationships, but only three or four that mattered—"where it seemed as if the world might end if the other person stopped looking at you."

At this point there was a ring at the door. It was Dorothy.

I looked at Pearl uncertainly.

She smiled bleakly. "Go right ahead, I have no secrets from Dorothy."

I was about to inquire about a possible connection between marijuana and her sexual problem.

She shook her head. "Not anymore than cigarettes. I noticed that I gravitated to older women. I had the feeling they were more stable, but the way it wound up they wanted to be taken care of, too, and there was no emotional satisfaction in this."

She would turn from women to men and, still dissatisfied, back to women, hoping for completion. But it never came. She always seemed to pick on the wrong person, not realizing it was she who was the wrong person.

Despite all warnings, she had taken LSD after recognizing the psychedelic limitations of pot. A psychiatrist had cautioned against it, pointing out that hidden mental aberrations might be disastrously brought to the surface.

What had finally decided her?

"My boyfriend, the writer, had taken it a number of times." She looked up at me slyly. "He says every writer should have the experience, it enhances the perceptive mechanism."

They had decided to try it together. Alone in her apartment, they downed the LSD with water. The dosage was large, about 450 micrograms, three times the normal dose for experimental purposes. The chemical soon took hold. The pictures on the wall began to vividly bleed in color. Strange geometric forms flashed across the room, an awesome blends of reds, purples, oranges and blues, as though a Gauguin had been turned loose with brush and palette. As an artist, she began to comprehend, like my painter friend, that there was a third and even a fourth dimension a painter could strive for—motion as well as depth.

Images passed by as though in orbit, reflecting any relationship of importance she had ever known. She kept seeing herself, her father, mother, Jim the boyfriend, her mother again, then just the two of them coming toward each other, always toward each other, but never meeting. "We would just barely touch and then go by, as we had all our lives. Then Jim would come by, and I couldn't meet with him. I just couldn't join with anybody, and I realized this was the story of my life—not belonging, not completing anything, not even the most superficial relationship. It was like a year in analysis, being on LSD."

If the experience had ended there, it might have been all to the good. For she even got an understanding of her mother, and why they had never been close. She saw herself in the womb, uncomfortably twisting and squirming, even there—unsafe, unprotected—and unwanted. That was it: her mother had never really wanted her and this she had known subconsciously even before birth!

Pearl had hoped for some sexual insight into herself, and her boyfriend. Like herself, he was homosexual, the masculine dominant in her apparently establishing a rapport with the feminine dominant in him.

She shrugged, "I don't know about all those genetics. But the first few times we tried together, nothing would happen to him." They tried both pot and LSD.

The LSD experience had been much more exciting together. As she looked across the room at him, she felt a deep yearning. She started to slip out of her clothes, without any of the self-consciousness she usually felt. Jim also slipped his clothes off and they fell into a tight embrace there on the rug. The LSD magnified everything. She looked into his eyes, seeing the veins behind the eyeballs, and then was occupied by his nose. She had not noticed his nose particularly before. It was a good nose, straight and well-formed, but it now appeared hard and swollen. It excited her strangely. She drew him closer, wanting him to love her, but he drew back almost imperceptibly, and then her gaze traveled over his body. He was physically unprepared for love, impotent, only his nose was swollen. Nothing could happen. He was a fraud. His nose had lied to her.

Suddenly, new images started to wheel before her. She saw herself floating by on her back, her legs crumpled under and her arms flapping weakly. She was dead—dead from LSD. She started to scream in terror, real screams, and hearing the sirens of passing fire engines rushed to an open window. She looked out into the street, and felt suddenly an urge to be free, free of all life's fetters, of the frustrations of not relating satisfactorily to another human being or herself. She would jump out of the window, and in jumping find the freedom she needed. She was thinking only of liberation. She climbed out onto the sill, ready to leap, and felt restraining hands on her. It was Jim. She struggled and screamed, but he finally pulled her back. She collapsed sobbing, and when she came to, the visions had disappeared. But she was still shaken and semi-hysterical.

That was the first and last she had ever tried LSD.

She looked up now and her eyes traveled to where Dorothy was sitting demurely, as though not even listening.

"I guess," Dorothy said, "we'd better stick to pot."

I regarded her questioningly.

"Yes," she said, "I finally turned on. Why not? It must have something, or they wouldn't all be doing it."

"You held out for a long while?"

She beamed across the room at Pearl. "I finally was convinced we could communicate even better with pot—contact high, they call it." She giggled.

And had the communication improved?

"Not really, they tell me I'm not breathing in deeply enough. But I'll catch on."

Pearl appeared a trifle annoyed. "You might explain that I haven't been polluting you."

Dorothy smiled brightly. "It was all my own idea. I just got tired of being the only 'virgin' in the house. I suppose it'll be LSD next, except that Pearl's experience scares me a bit."

Pearl shrugged. "Your experience might be entirely different." She regarded her friend speculatively. "You know, if we took it together, it might do something for us."

Dorothy smiled back warmly. "It's worth thinking about."

Pearl suddenly got up to leave, and Dorothy followed. As I took them to the door, I suddenly thought of something. "Whatever happened to Jim?" I asked.

Pearl grinned. "He saw the great truth, and went back to being a faggot."

The door closed on them.

I sat for a while and reflected. These were not hippies, but young people who were very much involved in a very involved world. They were typical, I suppose, of what Wisconsin's Dr. Halleck had called the alienated. Above all, they seemed to lack faith, and most of what they lacked faith in was themselves. God was only a phrase to them. "If there's a God, why does he allow our young to be destroyed in a senseless war?"

They prided themselves on an intellectual curiosity, which seemed a justification for everything, no matter how negative, but what passed for introspection, often seemed a morbid preoccupation with their own shallow sensuousness.

If there was a denominator in this group of the alienated, it lay in their passive response to the ordinary challenges of living, and a restless groping for an easy way—a pill or a pipe—to grapple with the philosophic problems which have stimulated man's genius from the beginning of time.

It was a terrible waste, so many had good minds, and could have done something with discipline and effort. One could only sympathize with the desire for a religious experience, even with a chemical, if that experience were sufficiently valid to leave a beneficial mark. But like other visions under LSD, these appeared as ephemeral and meaningless as the sexual experiences often released.

The LSD user was the last to understand his reasons for seeking recurring experiences which actually added nothing to his total comprehension. Nick, for instance, had been a brilliant scholarship student, headed for the ministry, when, like greater evangelists before him, he had his moments of dire misgiving. He not only questioned his church, but the very actuality of God. He talked over his doubts with other divinity students and his teachers and they pointed out that his was by no means a new dilemma. He could go on and study, as they had, and one day the truth would strike in its sublime glory.

It was all too vague for him. He looked around and saw nothing but injustice. The world seemed in a terrible state. It was obvious there was no orderly management, as one might expect with an onmiscient God at the helm.

He had lived a disciplined, moralistic existence, abstinence and restraint had been integral parts of his credo. But one day, deciding he was living a lie, he cut his ties with the school. He had been out only six months when I met him, yet was already a changed man. He was twenty-four, reasonably good-looking, with dark liquid eyes, and a charming white-toothed smile that illuminated his features.

He had a certain Latin appeal that some Nordic women found particularly fascinating. He was introduced to me by two attractive sisters, of wealthy parentage, who had mentioned that he had taken LSD a dozen or so times, and had smoked marijuana and hashish, doing what he could to find himself.

Both girls, in their early twenties were engaged in social work. They seemed of good intelligence, had traveled widely with their families, and had some knowledge of what an eligible young man should be like. Yet, they were fascinated by an idler who sponged off his friends, including them, and was on drugs most of the time. He had a flair for painting, but had sold nothing.

"You've got to understand him," Mamie said enthusiastically, "he's got a wonderful mind, but right now he's confused."

Nick was very much at ease during our meeting. He shook hands politely, but quickly jumped to the attack.

"Have you taken LSD?" he asked.

I shook my head.

"Marijuana?"

Again I answered negatively.

"How can you understand the action of these drugs, unless you take them?"

"I don't have to be a homosexual to understand homosexuality, nor a fish to understand its habits."

He gave me an indulgent smile. "But this is different. LSD uniquely opens all the thought processes, so that only with a subjective background of LSD can you understand another's LSD experience. Otherwise, it is like trying to describe the rainbow to a blind man."

"All you are trying to do, with these drugs," I rejoined, "is to broaden your horizons by opening your subconscious; I can do the same thing naturally with Yoga, with meditation and deep-breathing."

Nick nodded wisely. "Yes, I thought of yoga myself at one time; they say you can really get with it in time."

"The advantage is," I said, "that if a moment of illumination does come, you have gained it yourself, and it stays with you, a guide in future experiences. Besides, you don't expose yourself to dangerous side effects."

Nick yawned, and with a careless movement, reached over and dropped his hand in the lap of the pretty blonde sitting next to him on the davenport. She was Mamie's sister Ruth, a year or so older than Mamie. She responded with a bright smile.

"Shall we have some tea?" she asked.

Nick guffawed loudly.

As Ruth put on a kettle of water, I turned to Mamie curiously. "Have you ever smoked marijuana?"

"Only once," she said, "Nick brought over a cigarette. But it didn't do anything for me; it only made me a little sick."

Nick smiled. "Next time," he said, "you'll inhale properly, and it'll do something for you."

"How about LSD?" I asked.

"I've been playing with the idea," she said, "but I'm afraid a little. I know of a couple who took it and went off their rockers."

Nick gave her a pitying glance. "They had to be nuts to begin with." He gestured eloquently. "Look what it's done for me."

I turned to him. "What has it done for you?"

He regarded me pleasantly, drawing deeply on a cigarette. "This stuff is worse than anything we've mentioned," he tapped the cigarette lightly. "It can give you cancer."

"How do you know," I asked, "that marijuana won't do the same?"

His eyes measured me tolerantly. "I'll tell you what it's done for me, mister. It's given me peace of mind, and kept me from making a hash of my life."

Ruth had now returned and his hands again found her lap and started slowly caressing her thigh. She didn't seem to mind, occasionally patting his dark head fondly.

"I would have been the world's lousiest minister. It took some courage to quit, since I had a scholarship, but with the LSD I saw this was not a life for me."

"Have you done anything since you left the seminary?" I asked.

"It all depends on what you call anything," he said with heavy irony. "I have thought, I have examined myself, I have studied the world. These are all somethings."

"Have you done any work?"

His smile was relaxed. "That's what I thought you meant— the job, that is the important thing. It doesn't matter whether you believe or not, so long as you do something, anything, no matter how stupid." He frowned. "What difference does it make if you work hard if you work at the wrong thing for the wrong reasons?"

"How do you earn your living?" I persisted.

He shrugged. "I live with friends here and there." His hands were now exploring Ruth's lower back, and I could see Mamie trying not to see what stared her in the face.

"How did you pay for the LSD?" I asked.

He smacked his lips. "I've never had to pay. Friends give it to me, so we can go on together, or else I'd trade it for a picture or a piece of sculpture. All my friends in the Village have works of art piling up in their apartment."

Normally, the LSD came in a cube of sugar, wrapped in aluminum foil to avoid waste through evaporation. Sometimes a cube was five dollars, sometimes ten, sometimes less, depending on the law of supply and demand.

Before LSD, Nick had tried hashish, which he smoked in a pipe, and various grades of marijuana. At the suggestion of a friend, he had turned to the drug during the crisis over his faith. It had helped form his decision to leave.

"With marijuana," he explained, "you see everything more intensely." He pointed to a portrait on the wall, while still fondling the blonde. "Take that picture," he said, "you can see exactly what the artist was trying to do, you have contact high—you tune in to the painter's subconscious, into his very inspiration."

On pot, he had seen that he was not properly motivated for God's work.

"If marijuana did the job," I said, "why turn to LSD?"

He snorted. "That's what I meant by having to experience these drugs to know what they do for you. Then you wouldn't ask. With LSD you see all of creation, and its meaning for you."

"Does that meaning remain after the drug has worn off?"

"Once you understand something, you understand it. Take the society we live in. It's really a very negative place. That's why so many younger people are rebelling. Everything is in terms of defense, psychologically speaking and actually. The police, the courts, the Army, the fire departments—everything's defensive."

"What do you want, anarchy?" I asked.

"No, but not everything in society should be formed out of fear."

With marijuana his anxieties were dispelled, nerve came back, he found reason to laugh, or laughed without reason. "Life is pretty much orally motivated," he observed, "and with marijuana, all the substitutes are available. The weed takes the place of food; sex inhibitions disappear, and we talk and laugh. Things that once bothered you now strike you as funny." It had its serious side, too—he said. "The world comes together. Painters gain new perspective and perception, writers focus more clearly. Baudelaire, Dumas, Balzac, all used hemp. It gave them a new dimension."

The girls appeared fascinated by his eloquence. But while Ruth purred softly under his touch, Mamie frowned the least bit. "You know, Nick," she said finally, "your friend George brought some pot over one day, and we smoked for fifteen minutes. But all I felt was giddy."

Nick smiled. "That's all right. Keep it up, breathe deep and things start to happen."

He still hadn't explained why he had taken LSD.

"That's obvious," he said, a bit impatiently. "Marijuana only heightens senses you already know you have. LSD makes you aware of inner powers and outer dimensions you never knew about before."

He turned to Mamie. "Anytime you want it, just say the word. You don't know what you're missing."

Mamie looked at me mischievously. "Maybe you and I can take it together."

"You seem to be doing all right without it," I said.

"I get terribly bored. What I really need, I guess, is a good romance."

Nick laughed uproariously. Ruth was now almost on top of him, and his hand was groping under her sweater. She didn't seem at all self-conscious.

He turned to Mamie who was still trying hard not to notice.

"You got too many inhibitions, and LSD is probably just what you need. It releases the ego, and lets you move about free of your own self. For the first time, I understood what it meant to stand outside myself and see the truth in human action."

I was tired from listening.

"Truth is like love," I said, "neither word means anything out of a context where they can be pragmatically judged."

"All right," he said, "let's take love as an example. Not long ago I shared an LSD experience with a very attractive girl, whom I hardly knew. We both took LSD, and suddenly we communicated with each other. I became intensely aware of her, knowing she was similarly aware of me. If we had not turned on together, this communication would not have occurred. You can't talk to anybody intelligently unless they're on with you."

Perhaps an hour had passed, when lying on a mat next to the girl, he saw her rise to an elbow, and start kicking off her clothes. He helped her, only because he realized that she was trying to be free of her restricting raiment and he sympathized with her. They had now reached LSD's contact high—and he found himself removing his own clothes.

"Originally," he said, "a sexual relationship was the last thing on my mind and hers. But with the ego release, inhibitions were removed, and we seemed to melt together. Her expression changed as I looked at her. She took on the aspect of many people—now Marie Antoinette, now a harlot, now a religious. And in truth of course, she was all these different facets."

The joining bodies had seemed to merge for hours, though only minutes were consumed. There had never been a completely ecstatic moment like it—it was certainly a great moment of love.

My impression of this incident was considerably different from his. It occurred to me, even as he was reciting his experience, that sensuousness not love was the prime motif of this dramatic union. I wondered now, watching him poking around Ruth, what had happened to his LSD lady love.

He frowned. "How could I ever top that moment of love. Of course, I never saw her again. We had shared something beautiful that could never be duplicated without detracting from the original experience."

It was hardly my idea of a great love.

But then, as I was to discover, he was on pot even as we spoke, and pot, like LSD, was not considered an hallucinogenic without cause.

10

LSD—ELEPHANT KILLER

So the scientists had killed a bull elephant in a "scientific" experiment with LSD.

Dr. Edward Pinckney, nationally recognized authority in preventive medicine and public health, laughed incredulously.

"I knew they were killing people with it, but elephants?"

Actually, the poor elephant never had a chance.

Unlike virtually all other scientific subjects, he had neither volunteered for the project, nor had he been reassured by the Messers Leary, Alpert, Osmond, Cohen, and the rest of the scientific fraternity that LSD was just what the doctor ordered for the troubled mind.

Tusko, a seven thousand pounder, one of the few bull elephants in captivity in the United States, was resident in the Oklahoma City Zoo when he was chosen for this singular honor. It was all for science. Trying to reproduce symptoms of recurring elephantine temper tantrums, the men of science had decided to induce a behavior pattern simulating the elephant's going on such a tantrum. That's what they were doing with people, so why not do it with elephants?

With Drs. Louis Jolyon West and Chester M. Pierce of the Department of Psychiatry of the University of Oklahoma supervising in the interest of science, the three and a half ton behemoth was injected with a heavy charge of LSD shot from a high-powered rifle. As the shot pierced his thick hide, Tusko gave a startled rumble and began galloping aimlessly around his pen, snorting madly, and then, suddenly, with a last bewildered trumpet, he keeled over on his side. All restoratives failed, and in an hour and a half, mighty Tusko was no more. Death, an autopsy revealed, was due to a laryngeal spasm. The LSD had paralyzed his muscles before it could do anything about expanding his mind.

The scientific experiment apparently had not been scientific enough. Other psychiatrists subsequently reported that Tusko, even for his body weight, had been given a hundred-times overdose.

However, even with normal dosage, there was no certain way of knowing ahead of time, even in the two-legged family, when four-millionths of an ounce of LSD, an average dose for man, was enough at times to throw an emotionally unstable individual into a mental ward. Even the scientists were not immune. One psychologist, experimenting scientifically on himself, took his doses of LSD intramuscularly every day for ten days, and wound up in an institution. However, after a year or so, he eventually recovered, and was duly released.

Like myself, Dr. Pinckney had observed the passing LSD scene for years, and never without wonder that a drug or chemical, whose effects had been so little known in the beginning, should have been dosed out by the thousands to college students in the name of science and by teachers and college officials without the slightest knowledge of the physiological effects.

"And now," Pinckney scowled, "that they know how much

harm it is doing, they are still giving it to selective people, for selective reasons."

It was quite a collection that Pinckney had made. While so many scientists talked about expanding doors of perception, and of miraculous cures of alcoholism, addiction, schizophrenia, Pinckney spoke of brain damage, possible cancer, suicide, insanity, chromosomal changes affecting even the unborn, deformed babies, and a life style, even where there was no drastic damage, that was often slow death.

And while the positive claims were conjectural, Pinckney's information on LSD was all validated; at times, only too well validated. Cases of embryo malformations, caused when either the mother or father were on LSD at the time of conception, or the mother during her pregnancy, were pouring in. Brain defects were tied in with the deformities, occurring both experimentally in animals, and, tragically, in humans. The magazine *Science* carried this Wisconsin report: "Evidence continues to accumulate that the drug LSD, lysergic acid diethylamide, can cause serious developmental malformations when administered to pregnant animals. Zoologist Robert Auerbach and one of his students, James A. Rugowski, have found a 57 percent incidence of grossly abnormal embryos when mice are injected on the seventh day of pregnancy with LSD-25.

"All the malformed embryos exhibited characteristic brain defects. The midbrain was frequently enlarged or shifted, and the mid- and hindbrain regions showed improper closure. The fourth ventricle of the brain was correspondingly modified. Frequently associated with these defects were abnormalities of the lower jaw, shifts in eye position, and modifications of facial contour."

The time of pregnancy was significant. There was apparently a limited period when the brain was most sensitive to LSD. "Embryos of mice injected on day 6 of pregnancy showed brain abnormalities, but when mice were injected later than day 7 of pregnancy there were no gross observable defects in the embryos."

Pinckney now stressed from the report:

"Since the seventh day is the stage where neural structures are first being formed, it is a stage uniquely sensitive to induced abnormalities of the brain."

On the basis of body weight, the LSD dose used in the study was less than the average dosage rate for human subjects. And, even more significantly, and potentially more hazardous, was the fact that the time of pregnancy in mice found to be sensitive to LSD was equivalent to human pregnancy of sixteen to twenty-two days—a period when pregnancy was frequently unsuspected.

There were similar, confirmatory reports, with animals. From the Medical College of Georgia, Dr. William F. Geber reported comparable damage on fetal hamsters from mothers injected at various times with single doses of three different hallucinogenics— LSD, mescaline, which is infinitely weaker, and a monobromide derivative of LSD, known as BOL, 2-bromo-d-lysergic acid. Examinations of the dead fetuses, taken from the mothers on the twelfth day of gestation, showed an already rotated limb and an abnormality of the head, known as meningocele. "My results," said Geber, "indicate that LSD and BOL can induce a wide variety of congenital malformations in the hamster embryo."

All this was very interesting, but how about humans? Their experience would be far more relevant than mice, hamsters, or even elephants.

Pinckney agreed with a bland professional smile.

"Never fear, there are more humans taking LSD than there are animals." He riffled through his notes, and picked out a report from *Science News*. It was a case, reviewed in Iowa, and originally hurried into print in an English medical journal, which would get it before the scientific world before any American publication could:

"A pregnant woman who took four hallucinogenic trips on LSD has delivered a child with congenital defects, including a deformed right leg and foot.

"The woman took no other drugs during pregnancy, and pediatricians who report the case believed LSD is at fault.

"Dr. Hans Zellweger and associates at the University of Iowa reported in the Nov. 18 issue of the *Lancet,* a British journal, that neither parent had a family history of birth defects.

"The Iowa case is the first full report attributing birth defects to LSD use, though there have been other indications of such defects during the past few months.

"San Francisco General Hospital, for example, has noted cases of malformation among babies born to mothers who had taken LSD. Doctors, there, however, do not feel they have enough evidence to link the two definitely.

"Dr. Zellweger reports that both mother and father showed chromosomal breaks in blood cells. The blood cells generally reflect what is happening in other areas, such as reproductive cells, and high rates of breakage have recently been found among LSD users."

The Iowa case intrigued me, but there was a baffling absence of detail. There was no reference to the husband being on LSD, for instance, though he also had chromosomal damage. "If the husband didn't have a similar experience," I pointed out, "it breaks down the premise of LSD as the cause."

Pinckney agreed and soon I had a full report. Both parents had LSD. The mother, nineteen years old, took LSD on four occasions during her pregnancy. The crucial LSD experience had apparently taken place, University of Iowa pediatricians said, on the forty-fifth day of pregnancy. "During the thalidomide experiences of the early 1960s," Pinckney observed, "we discovered that when the drug was ingested between the forty-second and forty-seventh day of pregnancy, there was resulting limb deformity, as this is the period apparently when leg formation is taking place in the embryo, with limbs then most vulnerable to drugs taken by the mother."

The child's malformation was reminiscent of thalidomide damage. Every part of the right leg was shorter than the left, including the right foot, which had only three toes. The leg was joined to the hip at an odd angle.

There seemed little question that LSD was the culprit. It was the only drug the mother had taken, the father had similarly taken it. Even so, from the thalidomide experience, it had become apparent that chromosomal damage in the mother alone was enough to cause malformation.

There was no history of birth defects in the two families and the parents, aside from the chromosomal breaks, were otherwise healthy. Moreover, these were not isolated cases. Dr. Zellweger, rated a most conservative pediatrician, had found chromosome breaks in twelve other patients who had taken LSD. However, he had rushed his article into *Lancet,* the British medical journal, because he didn't want to wait for the report in preparation on all twelve cases. *"Lancet,"* Pinckney pointed out, "has a reputation for getting articles into print faster than American medical publications, and Zellweger obviously thought it important that he get his warning message in print."

Dr. Zellweger had worked with associates, Dr. John S. McDonald and Gisela Abbo. And their report came only a week after the *New England Journal of Medicine* reported chromosome breaks among LSD users, together with evidence—not of malformation itself, but that such breaks can be transmitted to the progeny.

This report had stirred Pinckney even more than the dramatic news out of Iowa. "Don't you see what this suggests?" he exclaimed.

I shook my head.

He smiled. "We will be producing an entirely new breed of cat, if chromosomal damage is widespread enough, since this damage, like nerve pathway damage, is not reversible."

I still didn't understand fully.

"Physiologically," he said patiently, "it is not the LSD causing the malformation, but the chromosomal breaks due to LSD. So if the breaks are passed along genetically, succeeding generations that had nothing to do with LSD can still give birth to malformed embryo."

If this was so, then perhaps the *New England Journal of Medi-*

cine, itself a most conservative publication, was right when it reported that evidence of such transfer was a potential threat to the future of the human race as we know it.

Pinckney gravely nodded agreement, "Medically, I would say they were not understating the problem."

Pinckney was particularly concerned by a study of LSD users at Northwestern University, where he had once been a professor of medicine. There, an assistant professor of neurology and psychiatry, working with a control group of twenty hippies of both sexes, had come up with "pretty solid evidence" of brain damage. The hippies were tested with electroencephalographs. Their brainwaves, said Dr. Howard D. Kurland, showed significant increase in electrical activity, blocking in time perceptions of certain things, dulling—functionally—response to some environmental stimuli.

"In other words," Pinckney commented, "if they take enough LSD long enough, the doors of perception close in their faces, and they become dopes."

The Northwestern study, in collaboration with Dr. Charles Yeager of the Langley Porter Neuro-Psychiatric Institute in San Francisco, dealt with San Francisco hippies aged fifteen to twenty-eight, who had taken LSD fifteen to four hundred times. And brain damage, Kurland suggested, could be, as the New England report had also shown, irreversibly final.

Pinckney picked up an article from the Annals of Internal Medicine, titled the Nonpsychic Effects of Lysergic Acid Diethylamide. He adjusted his glasses. "Recent investigations have demonstrated that small doses of LSD yielded a two to threefold increase of chromosomal damage in comparison with untreated control cells. A similar *in vivo* [in a person] effect was predicted by finding of increased chromosomal abnormalities in one patient receiving LSD therapy for a psychiatric disorder.

"This observation was borne out in a study of eight users of LSD, six of whom manifested considerable chromosomal damage of their lymphocytes . . . and have also examined the chromosomes of cultured lymphocytes from seventeen individuals who repeatedly ingested LSD, four children who were exposed to the drug in the utero, and twelve drug-free controls.

"Fourteen of the seventeen young adults in this study demonstrated rates of chromosome breakage that were two to six times as great as those observed in the controls, with a threefold mean increase.

"In this series of subjects, as in the cells treated *in vitro*, [in a laboratory test] we observed structural chromosomal rearrangements (dicentrics and exchange figures) that were absent in the controls. Of the four children exposed in the utero, two, born to mothers taking the usual dose (300 to 600 micrograms) of LSD, showed three- and fivefold increases in chromosome damage, while the remaining two, born to a mother taking only 50 to 100 microgram doses, did not demonstrate a significant increase. It may be important that one of the children with a high frequency of chromosome damages was two and a half years old at the time of study and had not been exposed to the drug since birth.

"Although evidence in man is not yet available, two studies with experimental animals have clearly demonstrated the teratogenic (monster-forming) potential of LSD. When injected into rats early in pregnancy (day four), the resultant litters were decreased in size, with a high proportion of stillborn fetuses and over-all stunting in some of the animals. In addition, some of the liveborn rats failed to develop properly. Injections late in pregnancy had no apparent teratogenic effect. Similar techniques used in mice produced severe malformations of the central nervous system as well as other morphological anomalies.

"In addition to the potential danger of teratogenesis already demonstrated by the animal studies and the likelihood of similar effects in man due to transplacental transport [direct passage from mother to embryo] as evidenced by the children exposed to LSD in utero, other possible risks must be considered."

The frequent user of LSD, and/or the infrequent user as well, was laying himself open to leukemia and cancer. The reasoning was quite clear medically. "Chromosome aberrations, similar to those induced by LSD, have been noted to occur spontaneously in three autosomal [induced chromosomal breakdown] recessive diseases—Bloom's syndrome, Fanconi's anemia, and ataxiatelangiectasia. Patients with these syndromes also show a high propensity to develop leukemia and other neoplasms [new tumor masses]. In this context cells of neoplastic origin quite frequently illustrate a variety of chromosomal aberration, many of which are not unlike those seen after LSD exposures. Additionally, many agents known to produce similar chromosome aberration [for example, radiation in man and other species, viruses in experimental animals] are known carcinogens. One of the obvious potential dangers, therefore, of exposure to agents such as LSD is the possible future increase in the incidence of leukemia and other neoplasms in the exposed individuals."

The recurring, or delayed effect of the drug had already been established in other disorders with similar chromosome damage. "These studies in which chromosome damage of long duration has been observed, demonstrate the long inter-mitotic [cell-dividing] life span [over two years] of the circulating lymphocyte and again emphasize the association of such chromosome damage with the later appearance of an increased prevalence.

"Since LSD appears in the circulation, it presumably has free access to germ cells . . . another agent, streptonigrin, known to cause chromosomal damage in human leukocytes and teratogenic effects in rats has recently been shown to inflict damage on the mitotic (dividing phase) chromosomes of the ova of the mouse."

The deformed, malformed, unformed and retarded can directly result from these breaks. "Chromosome rearrangements produced by breaks and subsequent incorrect healing [as in diathalidimide] result in structural anomalies including balanced reciprocal translocations. Ample evidence already exists that segregation of such translocations results in chromosomal imbalance leading to fetal wastage and a significant percentage of offspring with congenital anomalies and mental retardation. Since the carrier of such balanced translocations is clinically normal, as are many of his offspring, the consequences of the chromosomal imbalance may not appear for several generations. The total damage caused by LSD to the human population, both genetically and psychologically, therefore may not be assessable for some time to come."

An apparent lack of damage for the present was no guarantee of the future. *Nobody* who had ever taken LSD could proliferate with assurance. "The fact that many normal children have been born to women ingesting LSD in pregnancy does not diminish the danger," observed Dr. M. M. Cohen. "In many instances the carriers as well as the offspring of LSD chromosomal damage may be normal; the consequences may not become apparent for several generations."

Although the language was sometimes technical, the meaning was plain. LSD, as already noted frequently had a delaying action, resulting in panic reactions, even nervous breakdowns, months after the last ingestion. Obviously, this delay had a corresponding physiological impact not discernible for months, years, even unto the next generation. LSD was indeed the miracle drug, but not as arch-proponents, Timothy Leary and Richard Alpert, had so often and so glibly suggested.

The revealing paper on chromosomes, which should have given scientific pause to any scientist, was the product of painstaking research by Dr. Kurt Hirschhorn, division of medical genetics, Mt. Sinai School of Medicine, and of course, Dr. Cohen, of the division of human genetics, Buffalo (N.Y.) School of Medicine.

But one center of learning, regardless of the evidence, was totally unimpressed by the adverse genetic reports on LSD. That was the University of California, at Berkeley, which had frittered away its once formidable academic prestige in a climate of permissiveness yielding indiscriminate undergraduate use of pot and LSD. A Berkeley report—by Dr. Thornton W. Sargent, Dr. David M. Israelstam and William D. Loughman—challenged the validity of earlier research indicating that LSD damages the genetic substance of human beings. In their Berkeley tests leukocytes, white blood cells, were obtained from eight clients of a San Francisco welfare agency, who had been taking large doses of LSD regularly. The Berkeley scientists reported abnormalities not significantly greater than those in people with no history of drug use.

Their report was apparently a rebuttal of an Oregon report showing high rates of chromosome abnormality. The findings of the Oregon scientists, Dr. Samuel Irwin, professor of pharmacology, University of Oregon Medical School, and Dr. José Egozcue, Oregon Regional Primate Research Center, coincided with everybody's research but Berkeley's.

The Berkeley challenge appeared in *Science,* journal of the American Association for the Advancement of Science, and won the immediate acclaim of LSD users. It was suggested humorously that the LSD in Portland might vary from the LSD in San Francisco. "Not as much," rejoined an observer of the Berkeley scene, "as the outlook of the researchers."

Geneticist Egozcue had found unusual genetic damage in the blood cells, supporting an earlier report that LSD induced genetic disruptions in human cells grown in laboratory flasks.

In one case, spontaneous disruptions were significantly found six months after the subject last took LSD. Similar changes were found in only one of nine persons who had not taken LSD, and that person had received extensive X-ray therapy, capable of causing permanent genetic disruptions. The disruptions, Egozcue said, consisted of breaks in the chromosomes, and of wrong chromosomal combinations, adversely affecting the bearers of hereditary factors.

The observed blood cells, Dr. Pinckney pointed out, were lymphocytes, a type of white cell that plays an important role in the body's defense against disease. Besides disfiguring unknown generations of progeny, the genetic damage to the lymphocytes might one day seriously impair the body's ability to fight disease.

The full importance of the chromosomes, and the corollary

danger from their derangement, was clarified by one of Pinckney's colleagues, the eminent medical journalist, Dr. Walter Alvarez of Chicago, formerly of the Mayo Clinic in Rochester, Minnesota. "Some men have found," he wrote, "that the additions of LSD to cultures in a test-tube of human white blood cells causes a marked increase in the frequency of chromosomal breaks and rearrangements—as compared with what happens to the chromosomes of white blood cells not treated with LSD."

He explained: "The chromosomes are forty-six tiny particles in the nucleus or growing center of our body cells—particles that are the most important bits of tissue that we have. They determine what a just conceived embryo is going to be: white- or black-skinned, blonde or brunette, male or female, well-sexed or a sexual deviate, intelligent or feeble-minded, sane or psychotic, and so on."

A tendency to homosexuality, as an aspect of temperament, could be inherited as any other susceptibility was inherited, though circumstances might oppose its development. "It is very important," Alvarez pointed out, "that the chromosomes as they come together, half from the mother and half from the father, be arranged properly. For instance, a normal female has two X sex chromosomes, and hence is denoted as XX, while a male has an X and Y chromosome, and is denoted as XY. A person who is XXY, is usually mixed up sexually, and sometimes is not sure whether he is more female than male.

"Similarly a person who is XO is usually a woman who is mixed-up in her sex characteristics. A child who is born with three little chromosomes stuck together, where there should have been only two, is what is called a mongoloid—a short, chubby, feeble-minded and good-natured child. From all this we can see that to be well-born a person must have forty-six chromosomes —properly arranged.

"Hence, it is now alarming to read that LSD in large doses can mess up the arrangements of the chromosomes. Exactly what this production of many abnormal chromosomes will do to the children of an occasional LSD tripper or acidhead can as yet only be speculated on.

"One hunch that I would have is that some of the embryos conceived by users of LSD, if markedly defective, will die in the womb, and will be lost in miscarriage.

"If the sticking-together of just three chromosomes can cause such severe mental retardation and bodily defects as one finds in a mongoloid child, what will many chromosomal misarrangements cause?

"A student of teratology, the science that deals with the malformations of fetuses (like those made by the drug thalidomide —babies born with no arms and legs) might well say that a wise person will quit playing with LSD until experts find out if the taking of the drug can ever lead to the birth of malformed or idiotic children."

And of course that was just what Dr. Zellweger's research at Iowa had established.

Oddly enough, the lone dissenting report, from Berkeley, was seen by a distinguished zoologist, Herman M. Slatis of Michigan State University, as confirming rather than denying chromosomal damage. Quoting from the Loughman, Sargent, Israelstam paper, Slatis said the Berkeley researchers had incorrectly evaluated their own findings. "Loughman, Sargent, and Israelstam," Slatis reported in *Science,* "have confirmed earlier reports that LSD consumption is correlated with chromosomal damage in vivo. However, the authors misconstrued their results and interpreted them as indicating no evidence of damage.

"Their paper," he stressed, "mentions three distinct types of changes that are indicative of chromosome damage.

"1. They found that only 12 of the 112 cells of the control (10.7 percent) did not have the normal chromosome number of 46, but that 45 of 245 cells of LSD users (18.4 percent) had other than 46 chromosomes.

"2. Loughman *et al.* occasionally . . . found large cells with multiple micronuclei in cultures from LSD users, but not in cultures from the non-LSD control.

"3. Chromosome aberrations were seen three times in 697 cells of LSD users, but not in any of 112 cells of the control. This is the expected result if LSD is associated with chromosomal damage."

He concluded:

"Thus Loughman *et al.* observed three types of abnormalities associated with chromosome damage, and each was more severe among LSD users than in the control . . ."

While Berkeley was finding what it apparently wanted to find, the Medical Society of the County of New York, in the January 1968, issue of *New York Medicine* concluded from studies at Manhattan's Bellevue Hospital that "the specter of genetically induced damage in the users or their progeny is raised." The studies involving scores of youthful LSD users, revealed that approximately 80 percent of the number "manifested both an unusually high incidence of chromosomal breaks and chromosomal rearrangements."

In apprising doctors of these "convincing" findings, the Medical Society pointed out that some 135 young people, average age twenty-two, had been admitted to Bellevue Hospital suffering acute mental disturbance from LSD in an eighteen-month period from 1965 to 1967. In 16 percent of the cases, phychoses persisted and the patients were referred elsewhere—for long-term hospitalization.

Dr. Pinckney had the statistics, and the damage reports, thoroughly broken down.

In 13 percent, the prevailing symptom was overwhelming fear, and 12 percent had "uncontrolled violent urges," in which some attempted murder or suicide, and others were sufficiently disoriented to travel about nude in the streets. No user was safe. "Normal, well-adjusted persons," the Medical Society warned, "apparently can undergo an acute psychotic break under the influence of

LSD, while those with unstable personalities are likely to experience prolonged LSD psychoses."

Every day almost there was a display of LSD's bizarre mind-expanding qualities. At UCLA, where so much research had been done with LSD, a twenty-four-year-old coed had been brutally slain by a graduate student, unanimously acclaimed by his professors as brilliant, charming, gentle; the last to commit a heinous crime. He had killed the girl he loved, he told police, to liberate the spirit of his mother which he saw cooped up inside her. It seemed a senseless tragedy. But Pinckney offered a possible clue. "If you check into the case, you'll probably find this young man had an LSD history." The very next day, in the newspapers, I read where the alleged killer had taken LSD. It was by no means a scientific correlation, but Pinckney's suspicion at least made an incredible murder credible.

LSD's casualty list was impressive.

"In Brooklyn, U.S.A.," Pinckney elaborated, "Dr. Doris H. Milman, a professor of pediatrics, had a five-year-old patient who found a sugar cube in the family refrigerator and swallowed it. Within twenty minutes, she was transformed into a raving psychotic." She had taken LSD. The child saw her body cut off at the waist, had severe burning sensations, and sobbingly related how "they stole my Mommy and tried to cut her in half." She was taken, screaming and glassy-eyed to the county hospital. The hallucinations passed, but the melody lingered on. With acute visual distortions had come a sharp drop in intellectual functioning. "Within days the most florid evidences of disturbances had disappeared," Dr. Milman reported, "but the thinking disorder, distortion of body image, and depression of intelligence quotient persisted for several months."

Originally, the girl's IQ was 125. One day after her mishap, it was 108, and four days later 94. Five months later it had resumed a near normal 121, and four months thereafter was back to 125. Equally significantly perhaps, five months after the accident, with the IQ 121, the child's brainwaves were still slightly abnormal. But after nine months, coincidental with the return to the original 125 IQ, the brainwaves were back to normal.

Ironically, there were reports by LSD buffs that the child's IQ had improved with LSD.

Dr. Milman had a one-word commentary:

"Preposterous."

To Pinckney's way of thinking, this experience was as revealing as any experiment, for the simple reason that the child's reaction was clearly objective. Nothing of the impressionable subjective could have been possibly involved. "She didn't know what she was taking," he said, "so the IQ drop was virtually a reflex action."

Many psychiatrists, particularly with wide pragmatic experience, believed hallucinogenic drugs were vastly more dangerous than any narcotic. "Your ego or central control mechanism falls apart," reported Dr. Nathan S. Kline of New York's mental hospital, Rockland State. "It's not that the drugs themselves induce anger or violent behavior, but loosen the controls over impulsive behavior." Perhaps that explained so many who felt they could walk in space or the fifteen-year-old Philadelphia boy who fell from a sixth-floor window after telling his mother, "I took LSD, I'm going to bed." His body was found on the sidewalk minutes later.

Dr. Dana L. Farnsworth, director of health services at Harvard, had unparalleled opportunities to observe at close range the multitude of students Professors Leary and Alpert had turned on with hallucinogenics before they were in turn turned off.

In the *West Virginia Medical Journal,* Farnsworth preambled there was nothing new about taking drugs. "For thousands of years, alcohol, peyote, marijuana, hashish, opium and other substances which produce similar effects (such as laughing gas—nitrous oxide—ether, and glue solvents) have been used to alter human consciousness and distort the ordinary sense of, and responses to reality."

Was this then the same old thing, history repeating itself? Not so, said Farnsworth. There was something startlingly new. "What is new, however, is the high incidence of young people participating in the drug scene and the extent of acceptance or encouragement of it by influential members of the literary and academic worlds."

And these "influentials" had given the drug trend impetus in the face of contrary evidence. Even with professional supervision Farnsworth questioned the therapy value of an LSD experience. "As yet, research has not established LSD as an effective treatment for any disorder." There were not only psychological but physiological changes. "The chief objection to the use of LSD arises from the growing body of evidence that it produces irreversible changes in the life style and personality of those who use it. Physiological changes are suggested in Cohen's work on chromosomal disruption." Farnsworth spelled out the changes.

"Psychological changes usually include impairment of the subject's ability to make realistic judgments. An individual who is under the influence of LSD can ignore facts previously held to be valid and construct new beliefs, no matter how irrational. Such forms of thinking bear much similarity to psychosis. A person may feel that he has powers which he did not previously have, or that certain laws of the environment (such as vulnerability) are not operative in his case. For example, feeling omnipotent, he believes that he can jump out a window without being hurt. Wishful thinking becomes prominent. Preoccupation with isolated aspects of sensory experiences may replace all other sensations."

In Dr. Farnsworth's backyard, in Harvard Square in Cambridge, a student on LSD decided he could walk through a moving vehicle. The vehicle decided otherwise, and he was taken to a hospital, critically hurt.

The Pied Pipers of LSD, hailing it as a cure-all and end-all, had cruelly duped and hurt the innocent. "When research was begun with it, following its accidental discovery in 1943," Farnsworth pointed out, "it was hoped that studying its effects on volunteer subjects would enable research workers to understand more fully the causes of mental illnesses, particularly the psychoses. But responsible investigators have been seriously handicapped by the irresponsible experimentation of those of whom we have all heard so much, who are motivated by other factors than the curiosity of the scientist.

"LSD differs from most other drugs because its effects occur at varying periods after the ingestion of the drug. What it does, in effect, is to start in motion processes, as yet not understood, which produce effects after the drug itself has left the blood stream. There may be severe depressions lasting for several months, psychotic reaction, or at other times both pleasant and frightening episodes. If an individual goes into an LSD experience expecting a pleasant effect, he is more likely to have one. If he is fearful, he is more likely to have an unpleasant effect, such as visions of menacing animals and other threatening and ugly fantasies. In general, the use of this kind of drug is encouraged by persons who almost willfully disregard such evidence. There are some theologians and philosophers who think we can experiment with LSD, but they disregard or underestimate the adverse effects. Unfortunately, in some areas, the drug has become social currency. In several urban centers we are confronted, not with professional entrepreneurs in the sense that heroin pushers are, but with social pushers. Their approach is: 'Let's take it! You have to take one of these sugar pills with me as a part of your total experience. You really haven't grown up until you take them.' "

But the contrary was only too often the case. "One of the central concerns about those who take drugs of their own volition is that the practice tends to reduce the responsibility of the individual. We might define responsibility as an inner discipline which directs the activities of the self toward attainable and idealistic goals. As each person develops, his range of responsibility keeps on increasing year by year. Only when responsible people around him consider him to be unfit to accept further responsibility does the pressure to expand the areas of his responsibility decrease . . . The responsible person is one who knows when to accept pleasure and when to postpone it, either because of a certain risk or because of later gains, or, in some instances, because of the advantage to other persons.

"The evasions of the young usually take the form of pursuing the most pleasurable paths and staying away from those which are found to be unpleasant or painful. As one develops, and has many experiences, pleasure can be postponed for a greater good at a subsequent time. The responsible person is one who knows when to accept pleasure and when to postpone it, either because of a certain risk or because of later gains, or, in some instances, because of the advantage to other persons.

"It is the opinion of many of us, both within the medical profession and outside it, that the chief effect of taking drugs such as LSD is a reduction in responsibility—that is, the individual judgment is impaired. One of my colleagues in charge of a very large student health service says that it is inadvisable for an individual who takes even one dose of LSD to make a major decision about himself for at least three months." As Farnsworth saw it, an LSD society might predictably lead to chaos: "Society can operate because most of its people have basic beliefs which are consistent with the actions they pursue. When one takes LSD, these basic beliefs may be profoundly changed or new ones may develop that were hitherto unknown. Those who are enthusiastic about LSD are often given to wishful thinking. They see in their experiences only what they wish to be true above all other truths. They are told that the drug promises great expansion into inner space, comparable to the work being done in exploring outer space. Others think that great religious insight is going to be obtained. Some have said that for the first time they understood the true relation between man and God. Others welcome the idea of having a psychotic experience. Most of those who are prone to taking the drug are young, mainly between seventeen and twenty-five, but a great many older persons also take it, or are enamored of the idea, especially if they have some personality conflict.

"The LSD state differs from ordinary daydreaming and wishful thinking, particularly in the brilliance and intensity of the projected visual images and in the intensity of the aroused feelings coupled with these images, sights and sounds. It is as if one's feelings were fed through an amplifier which gives one the subjective impression of increased powers of control over one's own thinking processes. One may not have such control, but one has the impression that one has. This LSD effect may be caused by the turning inward of one's self away from the external reality and paying more attention to one's own inner processes."

Ironically, even as widespread reports of chromosomal damage spread a note of caution among college students curbing indiscriminate use on the campus, the LSD habit caught on with the so-called underprivileged, who, it would appear, had more reasons for trying to alter the reality of their lives. The changing social pattern became apparent with a new class of LSD users turning up in the psychiatric section of the Los Angeles County Hospital. Some fifty of these LSD "bombouts" were studied by Dr. Walter Tietz, of the department of psychiatry, University of Southern California School of Medicine. They were young, from a lower socio-economic order, and in 57 percent, as a direct result of LSD, an extended psychosis developed, although there was no previous psychotic behavior. They were so affected that even after their hospital discharge three months later they made poor social adjustments.

They all wanted to be helped, and were admitted only if their symptoms were so severe that they had expressed a desire to be hospitalized. They were a reasonable cross section. Of forty-nine patients, thirty-seven were male and twelve female. Forty-three were Caucasian, five Negro, and one Mexican-American. The majority were under twenty-five, the largest single group between eighteen and twenty-five.

Most patients had taken other drugs—the amphetamines, marijuana and heroin, but generally not with the LSD. They were given psychological testing, similar to that given schizophrenic patients. There were three types of symptoms; panic reactions, reappearance of drug symptoms without reingestion of the drug, and overt psychosis. "Acute panic reactions," Tietz reported, "were seen at first in all the patients. This was an acute anxiety reaction in which the patients essentially relived the horrors experienced during the psychedelic experience. During this period, the patients usually needed large doses of phenothiazines and often needed to be secluded as well. The acute panic reaction lasted a few days, and if the patient seemed to recover completely after this, he was considered to have had only an acute panic reaction. Other patients remained in this state, which then could not be differentiated from psychosis."

And how did the doctor define a psychosis?

"Patients in a panic state often became quite paranoid, and the paranoid delusions were often expressed as fears of homosexual attack."

Symptom recurrence suggested inescapably that LSD left an indelible mark. "Patients would say that a particular light or sound would remind them of the total LSD trip, and they relived the entire psychedelic experience," Tietz declared. "One patient could, by looking at a map at a particular angle, recall and relive his entire LSD experience at will."

LSD obviously played a role in the human revolution.

Pinckney thought it no accident that LSD—and pot—had become virtual symbols of the youthful flare-up. As psychiatrist Humphrey Osmond of the New Jersey Neuro-Psychiatric Institute, had observed, "Every age produces the thing it requires." But the quest for enlightenment was also marked by an obvious euphoric desire for escape. While many actually sought to broaden themselves with a drug experience, ill-starred or otherwise, others clearly turned to drugs as a cover for their own inadequacies. "It gives many hippies the excuse they apparently require to live the disgusting way they do," Pinckney said, "since the drugs obviously block out common sense and the proprieties."

On the other hand, one of the Pied Pipers of the LSD set, novelist Aldous Huxley, had apparently had a helpful mystical experience with a psychedelic administered by Dr. Osmond. The experience with mescaline, a derivative of the peyote plant, had led to *The Doors of Perception,* in which Huxley reported seeing with Adam on the morning of creation—"the miracle of naked existence." But there were admittedly few Huxleys to respond adequately—and predictably—to the Osmond homily that "this age requires ways of learning to develop its inner qualities."

LSD was powerful "medicine," as almost any qualified researcher would admit. It was infinitely stronger than any other hallucinogen. Colorless, tasteless, odorless, barely perceptible in single doses, one ounce of the drug was enough for three hundred thousand excursions into "naked existence."

Pinckney was thoroughly familiar with its properties, having conducted research experiments with the drug in his practice. It was developed synthetically by the Swiss, Dr. Albert Hofmann, from ergot, a fungus growing on rye, and also the source of an abortive. Hofmann had stumbled on his find, accidentally hallucinating through merely breathing in the substance he had been experimenting with. At first used only experimentally, it was not popularized until Leary and Alpert took to the podium, television and the printed media to sing its praises for all and sundry. Subsequently, on a broad black market, it was supplied in saturated sugar cubes or animal crackers, small ampules of liquid, crystalline powder in capsules or spoonfuls, and tiny white pills. It was usually taken orally, the powder dissolved in water or in sweetened fruit or cola drinks. As a liquid, it was sometimes injected, intramuscularly or intravenously. It had become part of the youthful jargon, known variously as: the beast, the hawk, the chief, the ghost, twenty-five, crackers—and of course acid. Other hallucinogens were psilocin and psilocybin, out of the sacred Mexican mushroom, or synthesized, DMT [dimethyltryptamine], particularly effective with marijuana, and mescaline. But LSD was easily the most potent, reacting eight to twelve hours, or considerably longer, as so many hospital cases had shown.

On the credit side, I pondered the therapeutic claims of many who had used it to relieve such social ills as alcoholism, and addiction. After thirteen years of research, Dr. Abraham Hoffer of Saskatchewan's public health department reported improvement in two-thirds of the chronic alcoholics given guided LSD therapy. There were many similar claims, as Pinckney pointed out. At a Princeton conference, sponsored by the Josiah Macy Junior Foundation, Dr. T. T. Peck, Jr., of San Jacinto Memorial Hospital in Texas, held that LSD could be useful during difficult pregnancies. He gave it to an expectant mother, twenty-four and neurotic, who had been under psychiatric care with the "screaming meemies." She was five and a half months pregnant. "She was pathetic," Peck reported, "wanted to die, wanted to kill the baby. She had been taking barbiturates by the handful. She was given about 175 micrograms of LSD, and actually saw the problem: She was afraid that with each succeeding pregnancy, she would only have that much more to worry about, in addition to the fear of losing her husband." All this was before subsequent disclosures of the hazards of chromosomal changes from LSD. LSD, Peck felt, made the subject susceptible to hypnotic suggestion and was responsible, he thought, for unusually easy delivery in three other difficult maternity cases. "While they were under the influence of LSD, we suggested that delivery would be very pleasant and easy, and in all three cases it was."

Other doctors reported successful LSD therapy with ailing children. An eight-year-old child, treated unsuccessfully for bedwetting, staged a dramatic recovery with the aid of LSD, according to Dr. Robert C. Murphy, Jr., of Waverly, Pennsylvania. "She was an enuretic child," he stated, "with deep sexual conflicts, whom I had in unsuccessful psychotherapy for a year before she started LSD. I was getting absolutely nowhere with her." He gave her doses up to 300 micrograms regularly, once weekly.

Murphy described the progress stages. "Her enuresis, which had been with her every day for several years, stopped after the second session, a very violent one, in which she became disoriented and called continually for her mother." Her personality began to change noticeably. Before LSD, Murphy observed, she had been a "thoroughly dull and boring person, a narrowly moralistic, unimaginative child." The deep sexual conflicts in an eight-year-old child were not explained. However, Murphy was gratified by the changes. "She changed so that everyone, relatives and friends, as well as her mother and herself, noticed it. It wasn't so much spectacular, as it was profound and convincing. She was by no means free of problems, but became so free and creative, and so much more outgoing and generous that it was clear her behavior was springing from something spontaneous within herself." Her progress was so remarkable that she wound up virtually treating herself. "Like the adults who have done well in treatment," the psychiatrist reported, "she participated in every decision to increase her dosage, and it was she who decided when she was through."

Through LSD, she had apparently become a practicing physician at eight.

Despite the enthusiastic claims, LSD has been dismissed as therapeutically unreliable by Dr. Sidney Malitz, research chief at the New York State Psychiatric Institute, after experimenting elaborately with the various hallucinogens. "It's like nail soup," he said, "you throw in a lot of meat and vegetables and then you call it nail soup." LSD, of course, was the nail soup and the attending psychotherapist the meat and the vegetables. "As long as the psychotherapist has to do the work anyway," Malitz observed, "why bother with an agent as unpredictable as LSD?"

As other drugs, the impact of LSD varied with the vulnerability of the subject. Some, given LSD as a prank, became temporarily deranged, others had no reaction. For this reason, Dr. Pinckney felt that the most spectacular results were often the result of psychological pre-conditioning. In cases, for instance, where researchers reported triumphantly that impotent males had become dramatically potent, Pinckney considered this may have been so much "nail soup" too. Actually, as Pinckney pointed out, no one knew exactly how LSD worked; there were only theories:

"Some things known about LSD would seem to indicate that it produced a chemical reaction on certain cells of the brain. Surprisingly, some people could take large doses of LSD with no effect at all. It was felt these people had a built-in antidote that destroyed the LSD as soon as it entered the blood stream. Curiously, these same people also manifested the lowest problem rate of mental illness or emotional instability."

Ironically, the most unstable were ordinarily those who tried LSD and crashed with it. "There is more than a reasonable coincidence between the people who react violently to LSD," Pinckney stressed, "and those who show overt signs of being unable to cope with the everyday problems of life. It might be assumed that such people do not have or do not produce sufficient anti-LSD chemicals within themselves. An interesting analogy has been shown to exist in people who have what are called schizophrenic symptoms. [Schizophrenia is not really a specific disease, but a term to describe unusual emotional behavior much the same way headache is not a disease but a descriptive term.] By giving certain chemicals to some individuals who have schizophrenic symptoms, it seems possible to bring them back to reality."

Although LSD's most positive results have been reported therapeutically with alcoholics, drug addicts, chronic lawbreakers, Pinckney stressed anew that the person about to take LSD was often brainwashed into expecting certain reactions. "What was rarely brought out," he said, "was the fact that after similar pre-conditioning, many people reported the same weird results even if a completely innocuous substitute was ingested instead."

While the Pinckneys had their misgivings, hallucinogens did appear to have worked wonders with chronic prisoners, recidivists, at the Massachusetts Correctional Institution at Concord, Massachusetts. In this instance, the chemical was not LSD but psilocybin, a sister drug, not anywhere as potent as LSD, but having similar impact with larger doses. The project was initiated by Harvard's Timothy Leary, before his dismissal, and supervised closely by Dr. W. Madison Presnell, a psychiatrist on the Harvard faculty. The record was apparently impressive. Thirty-six prisoners were given the psilocybin, and two years later not one had been convicted of a new crime.

How was it done?

Leary expressed the view that even the most hardened prisoners had transforming religious experiences which softened their hostilities. He reported the prisoners gaining fresh insight into self-motivations, while awed by budding feelings of being at one with a universe that was suddenly as much a part of them as they of it. "I wanted to murder you guys who did it to me," said one prisoner of his captors, "and then I realized that it was my mind which had created enemies where there were none, and which had always done this."

The project ended when Leary insisted on administering the hallucinogenic to himself at the same time he gave it to the prisoners. Though this may perhaps have given Leary closer empathy with his subjects, Presnell felt it was an indulgence which deprived Leary of the delicate judgment the experience demanded of its guide.

Not all were impressed by the results. Pinckney thought it mostly "nail soup." "It was obviously more psychotherapy than anything else," he said. "For the first time in these prisoners lives, another human being showed a profound interest in them, and it had the salubrious effect of easing their hostilities and having them take stock of themselves."

Why, with all the disastrous trips, and the bad publicity, did so many keep taking LSD?

Pinckney had one answer. "People never think disaster will overtake *them*. The highway accident always happens to somebody else, the bullet always hits another soldier, the other fellow always get VD, or 'blows his mind.' It is never you, until it happens."

Larry, a "crashee," had another answer. "Even when you crash, you somehow are left with the idea you were given fresh insight into your own world, and the world around."

And the "crashee" usually discounted his crash by attributing it to his own special weakness, or vulnerability.

I had met Larry at a spiritual center for ex-druggies, and we had become friendly. Though no longer on drugs, he had volunteered to take me to a hip, if not hippie, party in the untrammeled wildness of the Hollywood Hills. "There won't be anybody there," he said, "who hasn't been on LSD or pot."

The party was in full swing when we arrived. A young man and a pretty girl were doing a duet on the guitar, highlighted by the parody: "We don't need no pot or LSD nomore, nomore . . ."

Larry introduced me to the young man with the guitar.

"Frank," he said, "crashed on his second trip."

Frank grimaced slightly. "Don't remind me," he said, "I still see myself sitting in the fountain, and diddling in the water like a three-year-old kid."

I asked, "How did you wind up in a pool?"

He laughed. "I guess I just got so frightened that I reverted to childhood." He mused a moment, hunching his heavy shoulders. "It might not have happened if there had been somebody to talk it out with." He had felt inexplicably panicky, unable to sit or stand still.

"Did you take a solo flight?" I asked.

"Oh, no, there was somebody with me but he bombedout first."

As the drug first took effect, they climbed into their car, and drove to Sunset Strip, searching about for where it was all at. Miraculously, they avoided an accident, barely missing pedestrians and motorists alike. Attracted by the lights, the friend brought the car into a filling station, and got out to go to the washroom. It seemed an eternity to Frank. He looked around for his friend and saw some people staring down at the pavement. And there was his friend, Gordon, on his back on the concrete near one of the pumps. His eyes were closed, and he seemed perfectly relaxed.

Frank got excited. "Get up, man," he said, "before the 'fuzz' get here. We've got to go home."

An expression of beatific serenity came over the prone man's face. "I am home," he said, "home at last."

With the help of station attendants, Frank got his friend back into the car, and took the wheel. They arrived home in surprisingly good order, but the friend soon wandered out into the night. Being alone terrified Frank. Horrible images kept crowding through his mind. He needed someone to talk it out with. He telephoned one friend after another, but could find nobody in. Meanwhile, he was seeing ogres and monsters in livid color. He saw himself writhing into birth, and he saw himself dead, the lid of the coffin pressing down on his face. It was too much. He had to talk to somebody, or something, even if it was only the rippling water.

He drifted out into a patio, stepped into a shallow pool created by a feeble geyser, and sank his head in it. He sat for hours, in twelve inches of water, without any notion of time or place. Gordon finally wandered back, and solemnly helped him out of the pool. The experience was ten hours along now, and the images were beginning to fade. Frank was given a "downer," a barbiturate, and put to bed. In the morning, he awakened feeling as if he had been through an edifying experience. Oddly, he seemed to notice things unnoticed before: seams in the sidewalks, the wrinkles on people's faces. He felt more aware, alert, a new power surging within. He had always wanted to be a writer, and now felt he could do anything he wanted with words—plays, novels, short stories, essays, anything. And so he began writing feverishly.

He kept reading and rereading aloud what he had written. He was captivated with it. His thoughts moved so fluidly that his typewriter was hard-pressed to keep up. His output was prodigious, and all due to LSD.

It seemed a rather remarkable transformation. And I interrupted to ask where his work had been published.

He laughed good-naturedly. "That's the whole point of it. I was doing all this writing, and how was I earning my living? Parking cars on the Strip."

"But your writing?"

He shrugged. "All tripe, reflecting my own state of hallucination at the time."

"But you weren't on LSD then?"

He smiled thinly. "I guess the melody lingered on." Subsequently, he had moods of black depression, and paranoia. He imagined people watching and following him, and several times turned sharply, only to find nobody there. He had violent impulses, and feared what he might do. In desperation, finally, he signed himself into a state institution. He came out several weeks later, apparently cured. He had vowed never to take LSD again, nor pot. "One bad trip," he shuddered, "is all I need."

Out six months now, he was working fairly regularly as a writer, director and actor. "I have no delusions of grandeur," he said, "it'll be a tough uphill fight, and I have a chance as long as I try to make it myself. I'm learning to look honestly into myself without being overly critical. Why be all that hard on yourself?"

He was tolerant of friends on hallucinogenics. "They'll pay soon enough."

Why, I asked, didn't experiences like his dissuade others?

He laughed. "Like it did me?" He pointed to a small gray mouse of a man. "George there had a tough deal, and it didn't stop anyone."

George hardly looked up when Frank introduced us.

"I was telling him about your bum trip," Frank said.

George still didn't look interested.

"Tell him about it," Frank coaxed, "it's something special."

George mulled this over. "I suppose it was rather unusual," he conceded finally.

He suffered from a mild epilepsy, and had taken LSD in the hope of straightening himself out. "I wasn't satisfied with the kind of person I was, and everybody was saying how LSD made them see where it was at for the first time."

The first trip had been a pleasant, rewarding ride. "It was the greatest thing that ever happened to me. I could see clearly not only all my early relationships, but every relationship I ever had. It was astounding." He felt it had put his work in a new dimension. He was a director, and not terribly successful. Now he began to visualize vivid scenes with great originality, he felt new power, he could do anything. It all seemed so clear and so easy. What a fool not to take LSD before! Gratefully, he thanked the friend who had supplied the LSD for that first trip. Eagerly, he took a second LSD trip, and a third, and a fourth. Nothing new or exciting occurred. However, his subconscious did seem to gradually open, yielding sharper awareness of people, paintings, moving objects, landscapes. He felt he understood the delicate balance of creation, but he could not put it in words. "You have to take LSD yourself to know."

He seemed to understand his own motivations better now, and he didn't hate himself as much for being what he was. As for his epilepsy, it seemed to have disappeared. He wouldn't have believed it, and neither could his doctor, who had appeared concerned when he told him of taking LSD.

"Epileptics," the doctor said, "shouldn't trifle with drugs like that."

George had smiled secretly, feeling the doctor was understandably jealous of LSD's instant cure.

Two months passed. He was driving to his office, when a sudden tremor racked him from head to toe. Gasping for breath it was all he could do to get his car to the curb. He sat there for what seemed an interminable period, then lumbered off uncertainly to a nearby telephone booth. He managed to call his doctor, then fainted dead away. An ambulance carted him off to a hospital, more dead than alive. He was unconscious for hours. When he revived, knowing of his LSD experience, they strapped an encephalograph on his head, and measured his brainwaves. They were about as abnormal as they could get. There were also indications of pressure on the brain. Instead of mild seizures, he now had great incapacitating ones.

Fortunately, there was a new miracle drug, which actually worked miracles—Dilantin.

"I take Dilantin three times a day," he told me, "and live the life of a monk." He couldn't ever smoke or drink. "It puts extra pressure on the brain."

There was one other restriction. "One more trip with LSD, they tell me, and it'll be my last trip with anything."

What had possibly triggered his bad reaction so long after an uneventful trip?

He scowled. "It was my birthday."

The connection escaped me.

He shook his head impatiently. "Birthdays have a way of reminding us of intimate phases of our lives, I presume my subconscious was busily kicking up all the horrid things that had happened to me in childhood."

What could these horrid things have been?

A look of pain momentarily dulled his eyes. "It doesn't matter," he said, "just some childhood associations, which helped make me the kind of person I am."

It sounded rather mysterious.

"Why," I persisted, "after experiences like yours, do apparently intelligent people still try LSD?"

He smiled tightly. "Everybody thinks he's a little special."

Shortly after his crash, a young married couple had asked him to guide their LSD experience. The husband was a brilliant professor of thirty, his wife, five years younger, was studying for her doctorate at the same school. They were considered an ideal pair, but had had some slight problems, and had thought, with all the talk of mind-expansion at their college, that they should try it. They had looked off-campus for guidance, however, as they didn't want associates to know of their problems.

George, mentioning his own bad time, had refused to have anything to do with it. "They felt my bad reaction had come only because of my epilepsy, and they may have been right."

Turned down by George, they went to a hippie, barely twenty, but bearded, with the soulful eyes and the poetic pallor of novelist Stephen Crane. He was agreeable enough. "Just happen to have some acid on me," he quipped.

The wife took the LSD first, on Christmas Eve, the hippie holding her hand and playing soft music in the background. When she became panicky, he calmly reassured her, stroking her head and body gently. She found herself admiring his gentleness, his wisdom, his assurance, his maturity. He seemed to have every quality the LSD was telling her that her husband didn't have.

She was still in a daze days later, when her husband took his LSD trip. Like others on LSD, she was inordinately impressed by the guide. He was masterful as before, patient, kind, wonderfully mature.

It was still not clear to me why they had taken the drug in the first place.

George's brow knit. "Though brilliant intellectually, the professor was emotionally immature, and she was tired of the mother role." He smiled grimly. "A mother finds it rather difficult to enjoy her son."

Behind the scenes, a new romance was taking shape. Indeed, even as the husband moped about under LSD, the couple made plans, rashly initiated by the older woman, who now felt she was madly in love with the hippie.

"What do you think did it?" I asked.

George grinned. "It might have been his beard."

"Seriously," I said.

He frowned. "You're rather impressionable under LSD, and she wasn't the first to lose her head to her guide. And he may have been interested in an ego adventure, taking a professor's wife away from him under his very nose."

That was really a bum trip.

George laughed. "And she took all their money with her, too." His eyes gleamed with pleasure. "Under LSD, she fantasied that the hippie was everything her husband wasn't, and she was pretty much under his thumb. With LSD, as I said, people are remarkably suggestible, and she was no exception."

Before taking off they had gone together to the Establishment bank. George pictured the long-haired, bearded hippie in his beads, bells and sandals, dawdling in the lobby, as the mind-expanding candidate for a PhD. drew out her savings for their high adventure together.

They immediately flew to San Francisco, where they did the Haight-Ashbury bit, and then, without warning or ceremony, the sworn foe of materiality deserted with enough lucre to make his going worthwhile.

His recent disciple was inconsolable, and it was not readily apparent whether it was from unrequited love, an LSD hang-over, or both. She was taken to a mental ward in the San Francisco Bay area, where she was put under intensive care, but was expected to be discharged shortly.

There was only one remaining problem. "She wants to go back to the hippie," George said, "and he couldn't care less."

The husband was surely filing for divorce?

"Oh no," said George, "he's delighted. With the insight gained through LSD, he now feels that his marriage will be on sounder ground than ever, if she will only give him another chance."

It seemed to me as if the world had gone topsy-turvy. "I don't follow his reasoning at all," I said.

George smiled. "LSD made him realize that it was healthy for his wife to express the resentment that obviously festered below the surface. Now with the air clear, they can start all over, without prejudice."

It still got no better, but my curiosity was piqued. "What," I asked, "did she ever see in the hippie?"

George thought a moment. "The hippie had a certain superficial resemblance to her husband. They both had similar mustaches, and the hippie a beard besides. She felt her husband was weak, and she was tired of weakness, so here was a young man like the one she had first married, with none of his weaknesses as yet evident."

I was appalled by the terrible transformation that had shaken the lives of these apparently secure people in a few brief days.

George didn't seem at all affected. "In a way," he said, "the LSD may have been a lifesaver."

How in the world did he figure that? I recalled what Frank and Larry had said earlier. "What LSD—or pot—changes most is the individual's value system or life style."

Was it also because of this distorted perspective, that with all the disastrous reports, they still took LSD?

George shook his head. "LSD," he said, "was the greatest thing that ever happened to me—even though I crashed." He paused for a moment. "It made me realize for the first time that being a homosexual was not all that bad."

11

HEROIN FOR THE DISINHERITED . . .

In the Ghetto, there was no hope or aspiration, no pride, no purpose. There was resentment, rancor, bitterness, fed by the apostles of hate who spoke glibly of equal rights. Over all, there was a desperate feeling of frustration, frustration at the empty words of the politicians and the social reformers, frustration at the black man's realization of his own incapacities. And in the frustration, the young who had not yet succumbed to sloth, seething with hostility, turned to aggression, violence and drugs. "Every time I take a fix," a youngster told me, "the garbage cans disappear."

In the Ghetto, there was little discipline, little family or neighborhood structure. Where it did exist, life was more even, violence and drugs less common.

In the Ghetto, there was little tradition.

While the politicians, particularly of the "liberal" stripe, promised ever more welfare funds, this same largesse was emotionally crippling its very beneficiaries. Many were now the third generation on relief, beginning with the Depression of the thirties, and to them relief had become a way of life—degrading them internally, while accomplishing little of lasting value.

Relief was a statistic to the earnest liberal, prattling of helping people who couldn't help themselves, but to the youngsters living off it, it was a stigma and shame. For, unlike the politicians, they had to live with it, as well as off it.

Families with four, five, six, seven—even a dozen illegitimate children—were commonplace, with as many different fathers. Youngsters grew up to the creak and groan of the bedsprings, blushing inwardly at the thought of half-siblings whom they euphemistically described as cousins, nieces or nephews, as another brawling infant added to the family relief allotment.

In the Ghetto, for the most part, they did not fuss about integration and school bussing of the young. Unlike the demagogues with a panacea for every ill, they realized there would be no miraculous improvement in bussed Negro children, even granting the dubious implication that White children were superior.

"What the so-called White liberals and politicians don't realize," a representative Negro workingman reflected, "is that the average Negro wants what he does—a chance for equal education, housing, jobs. How can he think seriously of social equality, when he sees the White prejudiced against even other Whites?"

In the Ghetto, the White was the adversary. He was Whitie, Ofay (Pig Latin for the Foe). He was the Have, the Negro the Have-Not. They grumbled about the Whites having the jobs, the power, the money, ignoring the fact that the majority of Whites had none of these, and that money or power was seldom acquired without sweat, tears, toil and discipline.

In the Ghetto one typical addict came from a family of four full siblings and three half siblings. The original father abandoned five children and the mother shortly after Philip was born. His mother subsequently found a lover, an alcoholic. The father figure was a contemptible one. The "stepfather" relinquished financial control, did the laundry and prepared the meals, even though like the mother he had a menial job outside the home.

In the Ghetto, someone in the family usually had a record. One of Philip's older brothers served seven years for homicide. Philip, off the hard stuff—heroin—drank cough medicine.

The Ghetto, ironically, was more North than South. It was not only Harlem in New York, and Bedford-Stuyvesant in Brooklyn, but Chicago, Detroit, Pittsburgh, Watts in Los Angeles, Cleveland, Akron, Rochester, Newark, Philadelphia—all seething with frustrating hatred, all ready to explode into a misspent violence.

Characteristically, the black man did not profit even financially from the corrupting plague of drugs sweeping the crowded squalor of his streets. Even in his misery, he was exploited by Whites who cynically drew on the wretchedness of the Ghetto's *Les Misérables* for their tainted dollars. Nor did the entrepreneur of heroin—a Ghetto staple—try H himself, or keep a lieutenant who had, for that lieutenant could no longer be trusted. He had traded masters, and his new master was heroin.

In the Ghetto, as elsewhere, there was no way of knowing how many heroin users there were, law enforcement agencies, unable to cope with the problem, tended to minimize it. The Reverend Oberia A. Dempsey, a dedicated Negro pastor, who has run a Halfway house for addicts in New York's Harlem for over twenty years, estimated a half million addicts in New York City alone, some 100,000 in Harlem itself, and sixty thousand of these on heroin. The rest were on morphine, codeine, opium, amphetamines, goof balls; marijuana didn't count. In five years, the Harlem pastor had registered some 37,000 addicts—inveterate users —a total greater than was officially conceded for the entire city of New York.

"Drugs," Dempsey observed, "are about as easy to get as candy. And there isn't any place in New York where you can't get it. There aren't enough law men on all the streets of New York for even one block in Harlem."

Without heroin's availability, the plague would necessarily diminish. As it was, Ghetto youngsters grew up with Horse, at ten or eleven starting with glue, pot, or cough medicine, before going on to the biggest status symbol of all—Big H. "In my neighborhood," one Ghetto youngster said, "we had a group of about twenty guys, and out of the twenty, eighteen were on stuff." The compulsion was strong. For in the Ghetto, where there was little else to gain status with, marijuana was kid stuff, H for men.

The New York City Youth Board, working with problem youth, found that the typical known addict had mainlined at fifteen, and at seventeen was "busted," arrested, for the first time. And despite the risks, he kept shooting. "I don't know why really," one teen-ager reflected, "it's just around." He had started off many youngsters himself, giving them money to buy the stuff. "It made me feel like I was some sort of big guy, and they were looking up to me."

His best friend was his "connection," the pusher who never failed him, and whom he never failed, regardless of how much he had to steal to pay for his ever-increasing habit. Occasionally, with a big seizure, the heat would be on, drugs in short supply, and the pusher would lay low. But the traffic was too profitable to be long discontinued, its overlords too greedy.

There were many suppliers. The Reverend Dempsey did not put all the blame on the Mafia, the White crime syndicate which ran the rackets. "More than fifty percent of illegal narcotics are brought in by United Nations officials from other nations with underworld connections," he said. "Let's face it, we don't grow poppy plants here, the stuff has to come from some other country." There was apparently no way of stopping it. It rolled over the Canadian and Mexican borders in the tubes of rubber tires, too numerous to be searched, in precious packets concealed by innocent-appearing airline passengers, by persons bearing diplomatic immunity, hidden in seagoing cargoes. Ingeniously, a fifty million dollar cache of pure heroin was secreted in the fenders of a car shipped from France, and discovered only through belatedly checking the weight of the docking vehicle with the ship's manifest. There was a fifty pound difference.

Some saw a plot in Communist China as the largest producer of the opiates and the synthetic heroin originally produced as a harmless substitute for the opiates. Had they planned it, the Chinese could not have done better off dope. "Through the spread of narcotics addiction," observed crusading television commentator George Putnam, "the Red Chinese obtain funds for political enlargement. More than five million acres in starving Red China are now devoted exclusively to the intensive cultivations of narcotics poppies. It provides tremendous dollar exchange pools all over the world, and it provides a fiendish weapon of sabotage against this free world. For every new dope addict impairs the total productive power of the victim nation."

The profits in the drug traffic were colossal. A kilo of heroin, 90 percent pure, weighing about two and a quarter pounds, brought eight thousand dollars on the wholesale market, and diluted for the retail trade, yielded a million dollars on the street. The dilution, with kalsomine, chalk, milk powder, even roach powder, was often so weak that the potential addict was spared addiction despite himself.

But once hooked, he was a slave to the drug. New York City had its own costly monument to the inadequacy of therapy for young addicts, a teen-age treatment center, Riverside Hospital, opened so ambitiously and closed so ignominiously a few years later. The "cured" wasted little time getting uncured the moment they got back to the street. "Until they're hooked, the problem is psychological," a Riverside psychiatrist reported sadly, "after that, it's physical as well." The body had developed an agonizing need for the opiate its cells had become used to, and only the drug would soothe the pangs of denial. But some lessons were learned. "We now know," a social worker observed, "that incarceration of an experimenting teen-ager for any extended period, whether in a hospital or jail, only aggravates the problem, especially if the addict is isolated from the normal nonaddict teen-ager. In too many cases we provided him with an informal school for learning new tricks of the trade."

Like others toiling in this thankless trough, the Reverend Dempsey was often discouraged. He felt that a spiritual renascence, providing the will power to kick the drug and stay off, was required. But how did one impart faith to a depressed people, slogging along in a rut that was a heritage of their own bondaged past—victims of a stereotyped image they all too often accepted themselves?

Dempsey, himself, did not know where and how the solution would arise. "Why do addicts turn to drugs?" he echoed. "They all tell you something different. I've preached at funerals of addicts, with their brothers and sisters out in the congregation sobbing, and six months later one of them is using drugs. Everybody is out for kicks, and heroin kicks harder than any horse."

To his House of Hope, streamed the hopeless, referrals from hospitals, jails, welfare, and he gave them food and a bed. This was about all he could give. "They have no place to sleep, no food, nobody to talk to, except maybe another addict or pusher on the street." They were helpless derelicts by the time they got to him, often no longer physically able to rob for the drugs they needed. It was a two-way scourge. "The addicts rob the poor, who can afford it hardly anymore than they can," the minister said ruefully. "They rob their own mothers, when they aren't home, taking everything portable. They know when the welfare check is coming to the neighbors, and they get to it first."

Not all became addicted, even though users, spared by the peculiar social pressures of the Ghetto. "This is a strange community by middle-class standards," a street worker from the New

York City Youth Board observed. "Its mores, motives and moralities were often incomprehensible to outsiders. A girlfriend, for example, might object to the lack of sexual vigor in the youngster because of his drug usage and withdraw all sexual favors until he stops. His peer group (gang buddies) was likely to object to his decreased aggression and 'work him over' in order to get him to return to bopping. There were even cases of a primary objection of the parent stemming from the fact that drug use jeopardized the youngster's chances of getting into the numbers racket." This was pressure he understood. "These kinds of rationales were more meaningful to the slum kid than talk of the illegality of drug usage or possible reprisals."

Many of the addicts were school dropouts. Some, truant, were just waiting for their sixteenth birthday so they could drop out officially. They lacked basic reading skills, but were not up to admitting deficiencies or correcting them. "It was truly sad," the Social Worker noted, "to get a youngster finally to admit that he cannot read or write, get him interested in doing something, and find there is nothing he can do."

Drugs helped idle away the empty hours. "When we were high, we'd buy comic books," a young addict related. "One book would do for all of us for hours. Your eyes get the size of pins so you can't read. But pictures look great and you can see the same picture over and over." They didn't buy their picture matter. "We'd go to a drugstore, get a table, and just 'read' the comic books and feel so good." Sometimes they would venture to Chinatown, in lower Manhattan. "In one of the windows there was a dragon I loved to stare at for hours at a time."

There were distinctions in the Ghetto, particularly in the Harlem fringe areas, inhabited by Italians and Puerto Ricans. "The Italian boys regarded sex as 'dirty' and believed that intercourse should only be had with prostitutes and pick-ups and never with girlfriends of similar family background," the Worker found. "The Puerto Rican boys regarded sex more objectively and tended to believe that it was something that was normal to do

with their girlfriends. The Italian boys also had a negative attitude toward drugs. They regarded addiction as an evil and
addicts in the Italian community had a low status. The Puerto
Rican addicts, however, did not have this same self-critical attitude and were not ostracized within the community."

Ghetto youngsters were frequently overdependent because they
felt inadequate. One youth, aged eighteen, could not travel downtown by bus or subway without getting lost. Most did not know
how to go about getting a job. All felt cowed and uneasy in
restaurants having linen on the table. Others had never left the
immediate neighborhood on a social occasion. Many expressed
unrealistic expectations from life, possibly overcompensating for
the feeling of inadequacy. The youngster, too frightened to apply
for any job, rationalized his not looking for work by insisting
on an impossible starting salary—one hundred dollars a week.
Their unrealistic expectations, present in most teen-agers, were
highly intensified in these addict-prone youngsters. Living in a
world of euphoria, abetted by drugs, they never gained the experience necessary for adult living. But the longer they avoided
the problems of living, the more inadequate they felt—and the
more inadequate they felt, the more drugs they took.

One kid, typically, explained that he had not worked for a
long time because he was afraid that if he had money he would
only spend it on narcotics.

In consorting with a neighborhood group of some twenty
youngsters on drugs, the Worker learned to know the Ghetto, and
its victims, as few outsiders could, but only after months of
arduously gaining their confidence. To discuss narcotics easily
with kids reluctant to discuss anything that threatened to expose
their frightened feelings, the Worker used the gimmick of Friday
night card games. He learned quite a bit playing cards. He observed emotional patterns through the manner of betting—cau-
tious, reckless, erratic; the rate of education or intelligence, the
inability to add numbers (such as seven plus eight), types of
scapegoating, means of avoiding or provoking arguments.

One boy, sixteen, had been to a "headshrinker," the first time he was found with narcotics. "I couldn't think straight then, my mother was catching on, but I couldn't get off the stuff. Still, you got to hide things from parents and people."

On one occasion, the Worker had brought along a file of newspaper clippings on narcotics. Most of the youngsters had been following the series closely. One boy, Sheik, mentioned an article dealing with a middle-aged addict, saying, "Can you fancy 'taking off' with some old buzzard like that?"

Whitey had gone through the clippings carefully. "There was one thing I didn't know about," he said with a smile. "They say we're all queers."

In the resulting silence, the Worker explained, "That isn't quite right. One of the theories on narcotics users is that addicts may have homosexual tendencies. This could only mean they are more comfortable around guys than girls."

The boys sneering and hooting, began boasting of their sexual prowess. They all insisted they liked girls. "You know," one said, "only guys who ever kick it, coming to think of it, do it by getting a girlfriend."

The others talked about boys who had gotten girlfriends and moved away from narcotics. They next discussed how each had got on to the habit. Nearly all started with marijuana, a few mainlined from the beginning. They had taken it in schoolyards, schools, hallways, roofs and streets, wherever the Ghetto smart set gathered.

With heroin, the youngsters would often dwell on specific problems, particularly as the euphoric effects wore off. Torpedo wanted to get off junk, but something upsetting would happen at home and he was off again. "I can understand why so many are messing around with junk, they're from broken homes like me. A kid doesn't have a chance growing up without a father." He scratched his head. "It ain't the same when a big brother or uncle beats you up."

The uncle Torpedo referred to was actually a common-law

stepfather, who was spawning a brood of illegitimate kids in sight and sound of the boy. He felt "stupid," having everyone know his "nieces" and "nephews" were really half-sisters and half-brothers.

The Worker had gradually become the solid father figure so many of the group lacked, though of a different social and ethnic background (Irish Catholic). Through his card games and coffee klatches, he nearly always knew who was on H, who was trying to get off, how it all started, and who would be a help. A youngster trying to stay away from heroin could be paired with another who had been off junk for a while, serving to strengthen his resolve through example. Heavily addicted youngsters were not invited to participate in group activities.

Where the parent was trying to get the youngster off, the Worker usually had access to the home. But the parents themselves were rarely helpful. One mother confined her addict son to the house, without realizing he was rebelliously turning on under her nose, "snorting" three or four times a day.

Without giving the boy away, the Worker induced the mother to lift the house arrest. The youngster, to show his appreciation, made a determined effort to stop using heroin. But it was an uphill battle. The use of heroin in the Ghetto was beyond one man's control.

The Worker soon learned as others had that the addicts' only boss was the drug. He had taken six youngsters to the movies. One by one, they went to the lavatory and came back. Then as the picture reached an exciting climax, they slouched back in their seats, nodding. He looked at the boy next to him, and squinting in the dim light could make out the dilated pupils and the droopy posture of the addict on stuff. They were all stoned.

The Worker was a good journeyman psychologist. A heavy addict, Apache, had complained of the difficulties of kicking the habit.

He threw up his arms. "I keep trying, but it's no good."

"There's got to be something you can do," the Worker frowned.

"I suppose I could cut my throat," Apache grinned.

"That's one possibility. What else?"

"I could rat on the pushers and put them all out of business."

"What else?"

"I could get out of town."

The Worker jotted down the possibilities, as the boy kept mentioning new alternatives. "I could lock myself in my room. Or, better still, I could tell my old man and he would lock me up. I could steal something and get myself busted. I could start standing, hanging around corners and hallways, with different guys."

The Worker handed the boy a slip of paper with the suggestions he had just made.

"Now scratch off those that just wouldn't work," he said.

The boy carefully ran a pencil through all but two proposals: "Committing suicide and telling the family."

The Worker shrugged. "Committing suicide is what you're doing now, only slow-like."

Only one alternative remained. And so, Apache did the impossible, voluntarily surrendering to his family.

The Worker spent more time with his charges than the average parent. His day might begin with an employment interview at eight in the morning or a call from the police precinct at two at night. Each boy knew that if he needed help, he had someone to turn to—at last.

Under his guidance, the group began to become socialized. On their first outing, they chose an isolated spot so they would not have to watch their language—ostensibly. Actually, they feared being regarded as freaks. And they did attract attention at first. But eventually, they were able to visit museums without the critical scrutiny that prompted one to say uncomfortably, "More people look at us than at the exhibits."

Concerned about latent homosexual tendencies, the Worker had introduced girls into many of the activities. Off drugs for several months, going with girls, the group was no longer passive.

They roughhoused on the buses and in the streets. The Worker had to forcibly pull them apart. And when he remonstrated, one of the boys rebutted wryly, "We never gave you this trouble, stoned."

As between the environment and the Worker, there had to be an inevitable victor, and it wasn't always the Worker. One night he ran into Torpedo in a Harlem schoolyard stamping his feet to keep warm.

Torpedo pleaded, "Stay with me. I don't want to go home yet." There was an urgency in his voice. He had been on drugs for four years, only recently getting off.

The Worker pulled back the boy's sleeves, and saw the telltale needle marks. "You've got tracks a mile long," he said. "What's got into you?"

Torpedo shook his head disconcertedly. "I was doing great. Even had a girl. Now I got to 'shoot up' at work, besides the shot in the morning and the one when I get home." He shivered: "I've been trying to cut back. I haven't had anything since this morning. That's why I don't want to go home now. I got enough there for one more shot and I know I'll take off the minute I walk through the door." He shivered again, pointed to a passing youngster of thirteen or fourteen. "Look at me, I'm almost eighteen and that kid has more on the ball than me."

He looked appealingly at the Worker "How do I get back those four years?"

The Worker shrugged. "You don't, but you don't throw cheese down a rathole. You plug up the hole and start over." He laughed. "Besides, what makes you think eighteen-year-olds have that much on the ball?"

The Worker never took a holier-than-thou attitude, never lectured about the immorality of drugs, never raked over the raw gaping wounds of guilt. The use of narcotics was presented as an inadequate problem-solving device. "Horse may help you forget your problems for a while, but it doesn't do anything to change them, except make them worse."

A crucial problem during dry-out period was the reorientation of the youngsters to the neighborhood—and the neighborhood to the youngsters. Shortly after the group had registered at a community recreation center, one boy became involved in a fist fight with another youngster from a rival group and a brawl resulted.

The group, banned from the center, threatened to vandalize the building. But the center's director sternly advised they were being punished not for the fight itself, but for the subsequent mass attack on one youngster. Properly behaved, they would be permitted back in a month.

They returned a month later minus the boy who had started the rumpus.

The Worker, unlike so many social workers, had established the principle of responsibility for individual action. With this reestablishment of pride, many were ready to test themselves. Some returned to school. Others went out and got jobs through Youth Board referrals.

In the neighborhood they began to get respect as "clean." With the new freedom and pride stemming from their earning abilities, many formed an easier relationship with their parents. They had lost the junkie stigma completely, and avoided anyone using narcotics. For the first time in years, the local street corner was without a junkie. For the most part the youngsters were now able to furnish the support for each other that the Worker formerly supplied. Although several had moved out of the neighborhood, they still reserved a night for group bowling, movies or cards.

Of the fifteen original core members, two were in the Army, nine were respectably employed, one ran numbers, two were in jail, and one dead of hepatitis. Of eight peripheral members, six were working, one was in school, and the other's whereabouts unknown.

The record was impressive as far as it went, but cures could vanish overnight. It was an addict who once said wearily, "Drugs don't care who takes them." Drugs were no respecter of personalities. To users the opiates were G.O.M.—God's Own Medicine. And virtually everybody could be addicted in time, on G.O.M., as the Youth Board authoritatively defined addiction: "The individual develops an emotional dependence on the drug. Tensions and conflicts become resolved and one has a feeling of great 'normalcy,' euphoria and pleasure. There comes a time when tolerance for the drug is developed. To regain the original effect one must take the drug in ever-increasing doses and at more frequent intervals. The person who develops a physical dependence will become addicted, but not everybody becomes addictable, and potential addicts know this; they feel they can control it."

Only a handful were nonaddictive, and the rest wound up slaves to the drug, physically and emotionally dependent: "The body mechanism alters the stability of the body's balance, so that an addiction-prone individual will develop withdrawal or abstinence, if he should no longer have access to the drug. The addict then experiences, in addition to his fears, anxieties and depressions, physical torture. The organisms become dependent on the drug. He not only has an emotional dependence but a physical dependence, a tolerance and craving for the drug." Only too late did this become apparent. "There is no single symptom or personality trait which will definitely identify one as an addict until he is withdrawn from the drug and the abstinence syndrome appears. Needle marks, abscesses, warts are presumptive signs but the one and only positive symptom of addiction is the abstinence syndrome."

In estimating the spread of addiction, police claimed they caught up to nearly every young addict within five years. Actually they only knew what they caught up with, and had no way of knowing what got away.

Riverside, closed because it cured nobody, nevertheless provided some interesting statistics. In Ghetto gangs, kids were smoking marijuana before they started smoking tobacco. The average age of some two thousand admissions was eighteen, many were users since fifteen. Some 15 percent had relatives who used narcotics, and three-quarters had been arrested numerous times prior to hospitalization.

It was often a hundred-dollar-a-week habit, and most were forced into criminal activity to support it, the boys committing all manner of thievery, from rifling mailboxes to breaking and entering homes, the girls taking to the streets.

One could not get a standarized dose, and so never knew what he was taking. There was always the danger of an over-dose, as in the fatality of Big Daddy Lipscomb, the professional football player. There was always the threat of blood poisoning and hepatitis and the compulsion to live a life built about drugs, thinking of nothing but how to maintain the supply. "Heroin," as an addict once remarked wryly, "has a way of getting under your skin."

In the Ghetto, as elsewhere, parents of addicts often didn't suspect the worst until they began to miss clothing and furniture. "You've got to remember," a Ghetto youth said, "that parents really don't want to know, as they don't want to acknowledge their responsibility." In his case he had certainly provided ample clues. "My room was down to the bare essentials of bed and chairs—everything else was sold to get stuff. Records, TV set, pictures, sheets, even pillows began to disappear. There were fences all over town, and they would take anything and sell it."

Ironically, some addicts showed more enterprise raising money for drugs than they ever had in legitimate effort. "I soon learned to case a neighborhood to see which stores were wired (with burglar alarms) and which weren't, and which were the best to get into. Then you get together a bunch of guys and go at it.

"I remember one really funny time, during a transportation strike. I'd cased out this hardware store and we'd brought a truck to load stuff into. Everything was going fine until we ran out of gas. And no one had any money to get gas, and there were no cabs or buses to get away with, so we decided to siphon gas from the cars parked on the street." It was like Bonnie and

Clyde. "We made it finally, but I don't know how, we were all laughing so hard. You just don't know how easy it was."

As sturdy symbols of the Establishment, department stores were obviously fair game. "You go into a department store, take something off the rack and take it to the complaint department, saying you want to return it and get a refund but you left the sales ticket at home."

And what if it didn't work?

"You just return it to the rack and walk out of the store, and try again some other time."

After a while, drugs and plunder became a way of life, and the retreat from reality was complete, the addict finding what status he could in being a social pariah on the wrong side of the law. He could go nowhere but down without outside help. But the "cure" was an arduous one, indivisible from whatever genetic factors or environment had induced the habit in the first place. The family, with its weaknesses, was still the same, the flavor of the street had certainly not changed while the addict was in Lexington or Riverside, and the drug was as available as ever.

In the Ghetto, the problem was particularly hopeless, because it was the Ghetto. "If 85 percent or more of the known addicts weren't Puerto Rican or Negro, something would have been done about it," the Reverend Dempsey reflected the prevailing Ghetto feeling. "But as long as they are Negroes, who cares?"

Nevertheless, while heroin didn't have the middle-class status of LSD and marijuana, it was demonstrably interracial, filtering into White neighborhoods where pot was usually a prelude. Only rarely did an addict begin directly with H. "The trail," a narcotics officer observed, "began with glue sniffing, goof balls, cough medicine and marijuana. Marijuana made the smoker highly susceptible to suggestion and at a marijuana party it was not uncommon for a mainliner to suggest something stronger."

There was no question of the relationship of marijuana smoking to subsequent heroin use in a certain type of passive per-

sonality. In the State of California, some one hundred heroin
habituates interviewed at the California Rehabilitation Center at
Corona, without exception acknowledged going from pot to heroin. "One hundred consecutive parole applicants interviewed
successively, one after another," reported Dr. Victor H. Vogel,
chairman of the California Narcotic Addict Evaluation Authority,
"indicated they used marijuana prior to their use of heroin."

And the two drugs had a direct link, which could not be
speciously explained away. The heroin addict had a particularly
—and peculiarly—passive, addictable, personality. "When an alcoholic gets high," somebody once quipped, "he goes home and
beats up his wife; but when an addict gets high, his wife beats
him up."

"The addict," according to a Youth Board report, "was unmo-
tivated, passive, lethargic, sensitive, dependent, frustrated, impa-
tient and self-defeating. His behavior was impulsive, unpredictable,
infantile, stubborn and demanding. His constant companion was
fear. He was afraid of his aggression, afraid of his hostilities,
afraid of responsibilities and afraid of success. His social world
became narrower and eventually his only concern was himself. If
he should have an interest in another, it was only to the degree
that the relationship served his material gains. The here and now
was his essential point of view. Nothing else mattered. Social behavior, dress, companionship and family ties were of neither concern nor interest. There was no desire to maintain himself through
socially productive work. It was much easier to fall to the bottom
where he need not worry about struggling and getting ahead."

For every result there was a cause, and the causes could have
applied to any of the rebellious young on any drug, addictive or
otherwise:

"Failure of normal identification patterns during childhood and
an ensuing inability to initiate or maintain relationships with other
individuals.

"Strong dependency needs often reflected in extreme symbiotic (parasitic to the disadvantage of one organism) relationships with the mother.

"A lack of moral sense. These individuals judged a given act as right or wrong or as socially approved or disapproved, but didn't themselves really believe it.

"Confusion with regard to sex roles. There was a high incidence of homosexual traits among addicts.

"A bleak, hopeless defiant outlook on life which pictured oneself and the world as no good. Life was only real and worthwhile when they were pursuing the thrills, chance and pleasure of the moment. A drug like heroin was a specific remedy against this kind of an impossible outcome with regard to one's self and society.

"Aspiration to goals which cannot be achieved. Eventually one gave up striving and shut himself off from the realities which created the frustration and conflicts. The addict was unable to handle these feelings and turned to drugs as a solution."

Feeling secretly guilty, he wanted others to share his guilt, just as so many were trying to get others on pot and LSD. "With the increase in the experimental type of drug use, the need for rationalizing their own habits and conformity pressures operating within adolescent peer groups seem to induce addicted individuals to encourage others to try."

The rate of addiction among the young concerned about their own sexuality was notably high. Some authorities, interviewing hundreds of addicts yearly, insisted that fully 80 percent of those examined, treated or analyzed have a homosexual problem— overt, latent or merely obsessively involved.

Inwardly, and outwardly as they dared, Ghetto and middle-class heroin addicts, like the drug users, felt clearly apart from society, resenting the dull Babbitry in which the average person lived. They scorned as sheep those who went about everyday lives, making a living, and had only disdain for the young ambitious for marriage and a home.

"Your greatest enemy is your mother," they told one another, "she brought you into this stupid existence."

One group of young addicts, at a treatment center, was told at a Fourth of July celebration: "Now is the time to light a cannon, and put it under your mother. She made you what you are today."

Mother, Momism, was generally the chief culprit cited for the upsurge of homosexuality, and often for addiction. The deeper the studies, the more Momism entered the addictive picture. A study with nearly one thousand addict graduates of the U. S. Public Health Service Hospital in Lexington, Kentucky, traced a definite correlation between the domineering mother and her druggie son. It was the all too familiar modern story of alternate family coddling and tryanny.

"Overprotection to the point of infantilization was common," the study found. "There was a remarkable insensitivity to the addict's own needs and a lack of respect for his preferences in vocational, social or other areas, even when these were positive. The mothers often seemed less concerned that their son was unemployed, miserable and wasting his life than about the possibility of his getting into trouble and disgracing the family.

"A symbiotic (or parasitical) relationship with the addict, strongly tinged with seductiveness, was also frequent, the mother viewing the patient as a husband substitute. In one case, extreme to be sure, this took the form of having a twenty-eight-year-old patient sleep in a twin bed next to the mother, a practice beginning with the death of her husband eight years earlier."

Another mother, aware of her son's pressing need to discuss his problems with her, permitted him to do so only at bedtime while she was disrobing.

Mothers frequently sided with addicts against husbands, heightening the hostility in father-son relationships. One gave her son money for drugs without his dad's knowledge. "He cried and pleaded with me and I have no heart to refuse him," she explained.

Another mother confessed forging medical prescriptions for her son, practically coddling him to death.

A carefully nurtured self-image of a sacrificing, conscientious mother selflessly concerned with the addict's welfare was predominant among these mothers. They would have been the last to acknowledge that they were anything but devoted figures who had done all anybody could, and without proper appreciation from any source.

Regardless of the reason for the homosexuality swimming suggestively in the addicts' background, there was no questioning its authenticity. I had sat with Dr. Robert W. Baird in his East Harlem treatment center as he interviewed hundreds of addicts, and heard stumbling acknowledgments of misgivings of their own sexuality from 80 percent of his patients. The doctor's questions were skillfully probing, and the patients did their best to "level," for in leveling lay their only hope of his help in getting off drugs. The doctor, to effect addict withdrawal, gave massive doses of rehabilitating vitamins and hormones, non-narcotic sedatives to calm, and muscle relaxants to keep legs from twitching convulsively during "cold turkey." But most of what he gave them was himself, a strong male figure to identify with, where all too often there was only a dominant female.

But even granting a connection between homosexuality and addiction, it was difficult to assess its nature. Did doubts of virility eventually lead to drugs, which got rid of conflicts by making the user sexually passive? Or were there other, common causes for both addiction and homosexuality?

In this connection, I had been a curious observer at a meeting of a homosexual group, the Daughters of Bilitis, in which the subject for the evening was: The Influence of, or the Association of, Homosexuality and Addiction.

It was a memorable meeting. As I looked around, there were fourteen or fifteen acknowledged lesbians in the meeting room, together with a White case worker, who appeared a bit uncomfortable, and a Negro social worker, who seemed much more at ease, perhaps because she was of a minority herself.

All eyes were on the speaker, a pleasant-faced social worker of forty or so, with the least trace of an English accent. "We are living in a world," she said, "where it sometimes appears as though everybody is looking for escape from confusion and responsibility—either through heroin, morphine, barbiturates, tobacco, alcohol or television. Everybody seems to be trying to get away from what is staring them in the face."

She sketched the origin of drug use in the United States. "It wasn't until the Civil War that the problem became noticeable in this country. It was probably the first war in modern times where there were so many grievously wounded people, and morphine was used in large doses to ease the pain of surgery and the battle wounds themselves. Many of the returning soldiers became addicts and the Chinese working on the railroads in the West contributed to the problem with the use of opium. There were some four hundred thousand addicts at this time."

The problem gradually waned, then after World War I the Harrison Act provided that addicts be clinically given what narcotics they needed, but that didn't work as it was abused and the number of addicts only increased.

In time, the speaker came to the subject of the evening's discourse. Like Dr. Baird, and others probing this area, she, too, came up with an 80 percent figure, compounded thrice over. As a social worker serving the Women's Home of Detention, in New York's Greenwich Village, she had noted that 80 percent of the inmates were lesbians, 80 percent drug addicts, and 80 percent prostitutes.

"Wherever we go," she said, "we seem to run into that 80 percent figure."

There was immediate interest in the audience. One girl, a male-type lesbian, wondered whether that didn't suggest that homosexuality and drug addiction were neatly tied together.

"Not necessarily," the speaker replied, "because I don't know how many of the girls who were lesbians became that way in prison."

That brought another question. "Are prostitutes prostitutes because they're lesbians or are they lesbians because they're prostitutes?"

The speaker didn't have the answer, but some in the audience seemed to have given the problem serious thought.

"Practically every prostitute is a lesbian," one girl observed, "but not every lesbian is a prostitute."

A stocky girl with a close-crop haircut and heavy horn-rimmed glasses, seemed to know a good deal abut the drug problem. She was a nurse.

"Goof balls," she announced, "are just as bad as heroin."

"Actually," the social worker commented, "a nice clean shot of heroin is preferable to the barbiturates, as it doesn't affect the body so adversely." She smiled, "Not that I'm advocating heroin, but it doesn't have the toxic effects that Seconal, Doridin, and some of the tranquilizers have."

The nurse nodded. "The barbs," she said, "knock off the detoxifying function of the liver—that's why alcohol and barbiturates together often kill people who had no intention of killing themselves."

She had heard of drugs being smuggled out of hospitals. "But I don't think there are as many medical addicts as claimed, even though doctors do put people on tranquilizers and barbs to the point where they are eventually hooked. The withdrawals are just as rough on barbs, if not rougher, particularly if they've been 'shooting.'"

Another girl observed that in the maturing out of the habit drugs did seem reflective of a waning sexual problem. "There don't seem to be any old addicts," she pointed out.

"That's probably because they die off," another said, "either from malnutrition or OD—an overdose."

The social worker smiled. "As a matter of fact, we have reason to believe that there are comparatively few old addicts because the need for dope seems to disappear as they grow older."

"Sure," one girl put in, "when sex choice is no longer a problem."

Another nodded. "Kids usually start skin-popping or mainlining when they're fourteen or fifteen, just beginning to react to sex, and trying to resolve what they are sexually."

Addicts on heroin and other hard drugs showed definite signs of "maturing out" in their forties with the decline of normal sexual powers. Some explained they no longer had the strength to go through the travail of getting money for their habit, getting "busted" by police, and finding themselves in a constant hassle with authorities. But it was still a hassle they grappled with until aging glands began to dry up, turning academic any misgivings they had about sex.

The Lexington graduate study, directed by Leon Brill, centered on 912 addicts, many from middle-class families, with 791 male and 121 female. There was an equal distribution of Negro and White, chiefly from twenty-one to thirty. At one point, the study focused on a random fifty-four cases, twenty-nine White. It was obvious that many lived in a dreamworld of their own making. "Patients vacillated between wanting to have an ideal, tension-free life (the immediate drug reaction), or find a person with magical powers to keep them from using narcotics, or frankly admitting that narcotics are good and necessary, indeed indispensable, and should be legalized." None had ever been achievers. "Although there was among these young male patients an over-all verbal acceptance of the need to work, there was in fact tremendous resistance against it. This seemed related to strong dependency needs, self-doubts, difficulties in accepting authority and fear of independence and success. The various components of the addict's personality—his extreme immaturity, narcissism, difficulty with authority, feelings of omnipotence and poor reality perception—conspired to create problems in placing him in employment."

Addiction had magnified the basic problem. "Most addicts had left school prematurely, lived for years waiting only for the next shot, developed no work skills, had little work experience and poor work habits, with the result they had little to offer in a competitive labor market."

The dream world carried over to their pursuit of a vocation. "Unreal, even grandiose expectations, were very common. They spoke of starting at the top as a public relations man, or with an interesting and well-paying job, a clean one, where 'I won't have to take orders from anyone.'"

A job, perhaps as a sign of the times, was expected to yield tremendous returns with minimum effort and to meet psychological needs of all kinds.

Obviously, the addict was an adolescent personality, seeking to submerge his own sense of inadequacy with a job entailing contact with people of recognized status. And when he didn't find such a job he would turn away, disgusted. "He frequently reacted to normal rules and regulations with outrage and feelings of deprivation. The narcissistic and hedonistic concern with pleasure made it difficult for him to surrender one thing for another, to tolerate frustration, to realize that he could not have everything. One job pattern was to accept everything passively, allowing resentment to accumulate, then to walk out impulsively, without even waiting for a check, and not return."

The youthful addict was apparently addicted to his own sex problems. "In regard to heterosexual relationships, the young male's preoccupation with sexual functioning and his anxieties in the area were tremendous, hardly unexpected in view of his lack of male identification on one hand and confusion as to personal identity and social role on the other. The more deteriorated a patient, the more he discussed his sexual problems in clinical detail, and it was with difficulty that he was steered away from overemphasis of these problems and made to concentrate on immediate issues."

The usual complaint was that it was only by using drugs that a premature ejaculation could be avoided. However, this only appeared to sidetrack the main problem. "The fact that the sexual 'athleticism' thus gained offset by an inability to achieve orgasm at all may or may not be a source of concern. This problem may be used as an additional rationalization for resorting to drugs."

In retreat from reality, the addict made it clear his habit was but an extension of normally passive attitudes. "The young addict engaged in a good deal of fantasying about being cared for, catered to with food, money and sex by what is essentially a mother figure, while he remained totally passive and dependent," the study found. "He frequently dreamed of marrying a rich girl, seeing this as the solution for all problems. In one case where opportunity knocked in the form of a wealthy but very disturbed girl, persistent attempts were made to realize the fantasy.

"There was a good deal of bragging about being sought after by girls, or about drugs not having lessened the need for sex. It was suspected that in some of the latter cases it was a matter of 'protesting too much.'

"The patient may seek advice on how to act with a (nice) girl, usually with the comment that he is used only to prostitutes. This may reflect not only his lack of socialization and ignorance of the world and its ways, but also his deep fear of being challenged sexually ('Does she expect me to make a pass at her?'), as well as his rebellion against society, the latter aggravated by the confusion and double standards which confronted him in his home and community.

"Although there was much latent homosexuality evident in the patient's preoccupations and fantasies, cases of overt homosexuality were not often discussed. It was suspected that such activities (as in the case of the addict earning money by prostituting for men) may be more common than ordinarily reported.

"On the whole there was a strong impression that the addict's striving, at least on the conscious level, was in the direction of proving his masculinity, however distorted his concept of it and however futile, directionless or infantile his efforts may be."

In tracing the origin of these sexual misgivings was clearly outlined the many facets underlying the prevailing generation gap.
"In the vast majority of cases, the addict's relationship with his
father was a frankly negative one, that with his mother much
more complex and ambivalent. Male patients seemed to have
more difficulty expressing their feeling toward the mother, with
whom there was so much libidinal involvement, than toward the
father. In the latter case, feelings were expressed often with remarkably accurate comment. "My mother is the boss and walks
all over him . . . He thinks money is the answer to everything."

What the youthful alienated complained of, so did the addict
—a definite fostering of dependency by the family. "This interaction appeared to result from longtime family pattern of infantil-
izing the patient and keeping him helpless, due to the mother's
own needs. Also, indications were that the young addict often
acted out the unconscious desires of his mother, or in some cases,
of his father, and the whole complex of events and sequences
associated with drug use may be used as a family drama in which
each member has a role."

Discounting the squalor, there was as much insecurity out of the
Ghetto as in it. So many of the middle-class addicts were caught
up in a double-bind emotionally. "They were doted on, indulged,
shielded from responsibility, yet at the same time controlled,
nagged, deprecated and subjected to the conflicting influences of
two immature, confused and ambivalent parents."

And the result?

"A confused, spoiled, deeply insecure young man (or woman)
with no ethical values or standards of his own, seething with
hostility, acutely aware of his lack of identity, and able to anchor
himself only by identifying with big-time evaders of the law who
epitomized manliness and success to him." This was all too often
what he saw glorified about him.

The motivation behind heroin was obviously the same for marijuana and LSD—only the geography was different. Bridling at the
mother's domination, the potential addict rebelliously struck back.

"An oldest child in a fatherless home strove to be a big-shot in order to compensate for his feelings of failure in relation to the unreal expectations of an ambitious and status-obsessed mother. His repetitious failures served a number of purposes, including defeating his mother's wishes."

Mother was everywhere—background, foreground, middle ground. "A situation commonly encountered was that of the addict's mother, who having remarried, was caught helplessly between her continued symbiotic attachment to her son and the demands of her new husband." Again, youth was expendable. "The son was caught in a maelstrom of jealousy, anger and resentment which fed his need for drugs."

The Brill study, showing six males for every female, reflected not so much greater male addiction, as the peculiarly greater female ability to support her drug habit while still young and attractive.

"Case workers generally felt that the female addict seemed 'sicker' than the male. They came in with vague requests usually involving some faint striving toward a different and better way of life heavily tinged with hopelessness." Basic personality traits and adjustment failures were similar to the male's. "The father was essentially out of the picture," but not the mother. She was very much there, "totally rejecting, cruel, a bitch of a woman." Yet the alienated young woman was deeply involved with the mother in a dependent, guilt-ridden relationship, often acting out against her, and perversely unable to cut the maternal cord.

It reminded me somehow of my friend Gloria, in Hollywood, who was only on pot, and still couldn't get away from her mother.

Curiously, homosexuality was more prevalent among female addicts. "Overt homosexuality appeared more frequently than in the male, even in the small group of females seen by the Center, an impression confirmed by cases in the Followup Study." There were apparently social as well as psychological reasons. "This may perhaps be attributed to the fact that society was not quite so harsh in its condemnation of the female homosexual, as it was of the male. As with the male, homosexuality appeared related to infantilism and a lack of sexual identity. In at least a few cases, an element of defiance and rebellion against all adult figures and against society seemed to play a large part in the homosexuality."

The contemporary drug scene, regardless of the particular drug, was obviously an expression of the same defiance, rejection and disenchantment. Somehow, it was all inextricably woven together.

12

. . . AND THE DISENCHANTED

There was a sad haunting quality about her. Her eyes were a liquid black and strained. She was rather dark, slight and petite. She looked at me with the bold sweeping look of a woman accustomed to seeing men react to her beauty.

She was casually dressed in a blouse and skirt, but though it was a rather warm day, she wore black lisle stockings and gloves.

I studied her as unobtrusively as possible. Yet my eyes must have stopped momentarily at her hands, for she looked down at her gloves and said with a bleak smile, "Would you like to see what I am hiding?"

I had met her through a psychologist, who had warned, "One false word and she will run out on you."

"As you like," I now said cautiously.

"All right," she said, "I'll take them off."

She removed her gloves, tugging at them with a frown, and then held her hands under my nose.

They were not the hands I would have expected from her face. The fingers were swollen and misshapen, as were the tops of her hands. They were discolored, a reddish purple and blue. I had never seen hands quite like them before. The veins seemed to have collapsed.

She laughed harshly. "Let me really show you something."

She reached forward and peeled back the sleeves of her blouse.

Above the left wrist, I saw a raw, ugly scar. The flesh looked seared and congealed, as though a white-hot poker had been burned into the skin. There was a deep indentation I could have put a half-dollar in.

She held up both forearms now. There was a matching scar on the right arm, below the elbow. "Pretty, aren't they?" she said.

I watched with morbid fascination. It was my first look at the disfiguring abscesses caused by an overdose of heroin and dirty hypodermic needles.

She pulled down her stockings. There were similar abscesses on each otherwise shapely leg.

She sat back now and gave me a slow, mocking smile.

"You know, of course, that I am a prostitute?"

She seemed intent on giving herself the worst of it.

"Not I," she replied with an air of indifference, "my mother, life, everybody. They all want to use you, they keep after you, pressuring you, always pressuring you, until you do what they want you to."

Her feelings about being interviewed were ambivalent. She had expressed resentment at being regarded as a case history, yet she still had pent-up frustrations and hostilities that she wanted to get rid of. As an impersonal observer, I suppose I was a "poor man's psychiatrist."

"You're only interested in a story," she said resentfully.

She looked down and ticked off on her fingers. "One: How did a girl like me become a junkie? Two: How did a girl like me become a prostitute? Three: How did a girl like me wind up at twenty-five, wishing she was dead?"

Her dark eyes suddenly flared. "Dead? I'm worse than dead. Who'd want me the way I am, just some broken down pimp who thinks he can squeeze a few dollars out of me? But I'm not even good for that anymore."

She had sunk her head in her arms, apparently overwhelmed by her own misfortunes.

"Did you always feel sorry for yourself?" I asked.

Her head came up and she looked at me with a flash of contempt. "What do you know about it?" she said. "You're a man, and men run this stinking world."

"How did it all start?" I asked, trying to get her unwound. "Knowing might help somebody else, even you."

Her eyes turned hard. "And it'll help you, won't it?"

"It may help me understand the problem," I said.

"How much money will you make off me?" she said. "Everybody makes money off me."

She misread my hesitation. "Don't worry," she said. "I don't want anything—and if you did give me any money, it wouldn't go for a fix."

Above all, I did want to know how a girl—beautiful, intelligent, from a comfortable home—could have exchanged a life of apparent ease for a nightmare of horror.

"All right," she said grimly, "I'll tell you—my own way."

She had started with drugs at nineteen, and three times already, in six years, had tried suicide. As with nearly everything else, she had failed.

She laughed.

"I slashed my wrists, and couldn't find the right vein. Wasn't that a howl, considering how many veins I have shot with the stuff."

There was hardly a patch of skin on her arms and legs that didn't show the tracks of the needle. She had begun above the knee, to conceal the marks, then gone to her arms, and eventually the calves. She was running out of needle space.

As she warmed up to her story she gave me a friendly, almost confidential smile. "My psychologist," she said, "thinks I have a sex problem, and I couldn't care less about sex. Isn't that funny?"

The psychologist, exploring her childhood, discovered a significant lack of rapport with her mother. They were always at odds. There had been other children—two sons—and even before the father's premature death, the mother had ruled the roost. "Almost the first thing I can remember is Mom giving orders; she was always giving orders."

Her brothers were older, and the mother tried to exert greater influence over Jean as the sons drew away and left home. The mother was a devout Catholic. "I got to dislike church because she made me go with her," Jean said. "She kept telling me that she didn't want me like the other girls. She kept warning me about boys all the time, and wouldn't let me date them. She told me they were only interested in one thing."

Jean was precocious for her years, and attracted considerable masculine attention, both at school and after school at a neighborhood shop where she had taken a job just for a chance to get away from home.

She was little more than fifteen, working at the shop, when she met a boy three or four years older than herself who hung around just to talk to her when she wasn't busy. The owner didn't seem to mind; it was his son.

The boy was everything she wasn't, everything her mother would abhor. He was of a different faith and racial origin. He had a reputation for being fast but this only intrigued her.

The relationship—what there was of it—was not confined to the store. She didn't dare bring him home or let him call, but they did manage to sneak off to a dark movie every now and then. She was too innocent, or fearful, for anything else, thinking of all the things she had heard—pregnancy (the pill was just coming on the market), venereal disease, and her own reputation.

Her resistance only served to goad him on. She was just sixteen when he suggested they elope and get married.

She accepted.

"I was tired of living with my mother, and I convinced myself I loved him, otherwise I couldn't have done it."

The wedding night was a memorable one. She grimaced now even thinking of it. If he had been tender and patient, understanding, things might have been different. "I didn't even know what to expect. He forced me. I just lay there like an animal, trembling, and he kept forcing me. He raped his own wife."

She lay sobbing most of the night, while he snored noisily beside her.

They came back the next day, and moved in with his family. Her mother wouldn't speak to her. The marriage didn't improve with time. Jean shrank under his touch, and every night was a repetition of the first. He was furious and took to beating her. As impetuously as she had run off before, she now went back to her mother's. The marriage was quickly annulled. It had lasted three weeks.

Why had she married this young man, feeling sexually the way she had?

She shrugged. "I didn't know anything about sex."

"You must have had an idea of what it would be like?"

She smiled bleakly. "It's like grass or heroin, you never know until you try it."

It was not a satisfactory explanation.

"Have you ever had a good sexual relationship?" I asked.

"Lots," she said, "there's nothing wrong with me, not that way."

What had suddenly made sex less abhorrent?

She frowned. "The idea that it was all tied up emotionally with a lot of other things was what really bothered me. But if it was only sex, I could take it or leave it."

Jean was not yet ready for prostitution. She was too young, had not yet taken the dope that made her doubly vulnerable, and still had not discovered that she was basically indifferent to the predatory male.

She finished school and got herself a job modeling in the garment district. She had a flair, and worked part-time as a stylist. The boss took a fancy to her, and she moved up fast. "There was a buyer's job open and I wanted it. It meant a chance to make enough money to be independent and get out on my own, have my own apartment and make my own rules."

She got the job.

How had she managed?

She smiled wryly. "It was a fair exchange."

It was obvious what she meant.

"How about all those inhibitions?" I asked.

She shrugged. "I still had them. It was almost like I was somebody else, and he could have been anybody. I gave him nothing, though I went through the motions just so he wouldn't think he was being cheated."

She had an affair or two after that, with older men, like her boss. She didn't seem to relate with men her own age. "It was almost as if I didn't want anything to happen to me, and I knew I wouldn't get involved with these older men emotionally."

She had her own apartment then, and a good job. She was young, beautiful, sought after. Yet, she was miserable. Deep down she knew she had not really attained anything. She had no confidence in her ability, even her beauty seemed apart, something, actually, that she had nothing to do with.

She often took a drink or two, generally a martini, before going out on a date, or she would find herself tightening up. But alcohol left her headachey and tired. At a party, somebody offered her a marijuana cigarette. She was told it could do her no harm, and she smoked it. It didn't do anything, good or bad. She was told later she should have breathed deeply, sucking the smoke down to the diaphragm.

She tried it again, breathing properly, and it was groovy. And she liked the atmosphere it came in. There was always a crowd, always gay, and her inhibitions disappeared in a cloud of Acapulco Gold and Panama Red. She now looked forward with a thrill of excitement to the grass parties. They became a regular event, and though finding herself listless and lethargic the next day, she felt pleasurably relaxed and composed. Still, none of her problems were getting solved, merely pushed back into a dark corner of her mind. And even pot, after a few months, started to pall; she had to smoke more and more to maintain the same "high." She went through black depressions, particularly when she realized her only communication with others came with pot, and of course she couldn't smoke it all the time. She would never get any work done, and her job was important for more reasons than one. It provided all the things she wanted, which were yet so meaningless in attainment. Still, it was better than being poor and dependent.

She tried analyzing herself on pot and off. The problem had to be inside her. Off pot, she felt nervous and uneasy, not knowing why. She had no sense of belonging with anybody; perhaps because she had never felt that she belonged at home. She had never felt secure. She often wondered if other people, especially girls her own age, felt like her. But she was too self-conscious to discuss her misgivings with anybody. She didn't make friends easily, too introspective. She was tired of thinking of herself.

In this frame of mind, already receptive to the drug concept, she was introduced to junk—dope, the hard stuff. In this case it was opium. She was nineteen and vacationing in Miami Beach. She got a call from a friend that there was a party on, and feeling lonely, she dropped by. Only her friend, a young professional gambler was there. The others had gone on. The young man pulled out a pipe. It was a peculiar contraption made out of a four ounce baby bottle and a crochet needle.

I couldn't quite visualize it.

She explained. "He didn't use a regular opium pipe or a corncob or clay pipe; they might have served as evidence if the police broke in. No matter how you washed the pipe, there were bound to be scrapings under a microscope."

Despite her experience with pot, I was surprised that she had so readily accepted an invitation to an addictable drug.

"Oh, who thinks of that?" she said rather impatiently. "He pulled out this wild-looking pipe, got out the opium and started to smoke. It seemed like fun, putting the pipe together, and fixing the stuff in it. It reminded me of our soap bubble kits as kids."

She watched Jack closely. It apparently had no bad effect on him. He seemed in complete charge of himself. He assured her that it wasn't habit forming, if it was only done every now and then, and it would make everything seem warm and wonderful.

It was remarkable what the word warm connoted to her troubled mind. It suggested safety, security, being wanted. Normally, she lived in a cold world—distant, disinterested, hostile. Warmth was what she lacked, inside and outside of her.

She took a drag off his pipe, and inhaled deeply, remembering her marijuana. She didn't feel the full effect right away, but a drowsy euphoria crept over her, numbing her sensitivity to painful inner awareness, while apparently making her more aware of things about her. It gave her a feeling of crawling outside herself and viewing herself with detachment. She didn't seem so bad then, and her inhibitions, her fear of expressing herself—her fear of disapproval—seemed to diminish and leave.

"The first few times I smoked the pipe," she recalled, "everything seemed so much easier. The things you thought about but couldn't express were now easy to say." It was a pleasant ritual, as time went by, to fix the pipe, while others fixed theirs, and sit around in a congenial group and communicate. "We talked about books, philosophy, life, sex. It all seemed possible somehow. Even sex seemed less forbidding."

She laughed rather sardonically. "Sometimes we'd pass the same pipe from person to person. It was all so cozy, as though we were sharing a great adventure together."

She had no idea of getting hooked. Nobody ever has. However, she was made urgently aware of a growing need for the drug. In three weeks, it had become her best and only friend. She knew now why they called it G.O.M.—God's Own Medicine. And it had pot beat a mile. It was like comparing champagne and beer. There was no comparison.

Like an infatuation, it had built up its own neurotic need for itself. When she didn't have it, she was more frightened than ever. The vacation in Miami came to an end, but she took another week off, for fear she wouldn't be able to get G.O.M. back in New York.

But when Jean went back she had the names of several dealers.

It was easy to make a connection, though the price was a little higher than she expected. A $5 bag was good for only one session, and she needed two or three a day; otherwise the dreamy state passed, and she became nervous and edgy.

She discovered one day with a jolt that she was no longer just a user. "One afternoon I couldn't get hold of the man who sold the stuff and almost went out of my mind. I didn't show up for the job in the morning, and I didn't show up in the evening either. My boss had been sharing me with my customers, and since it helped my business, I didn't mind. But now all I could think of was the drug, getting it, smoking it, feeling warm and safe inside for a precious few hours. I didn't even call. The boss came over late that night, took a look at me, smelled around the place, and guessed what was up. "I got no time for hopheads," he said.

She wasn't out of work long. Her pusher didn't want to lose a hundred-dollar-a-week customer. He set out to get her a job. But his influence was restricted to the tenderloin and its fringes. Jean gratefully wound up as a shill for a clique of crooked gamblers. It was easy. "I would go out with some rich sucker they had lined up for me. There would be dinner at some smart restaurant, a few drinks, a bit of a tease, and then over to the gambling club. The 'boys' didn't require I have a relationship with the sucker. In fact, they discouraged it, since it was time away from the tables."

Her smoking continued apace. However, there were problems. Opium wasn't as plentiful as heroin, morphine, even cocaine, and one day when her pusher was picked up by police, she had lost her only opium connection. She also had lost her job as a shill. She wasn't feeling well enough to face up to the dates, and the pawing she got in cabs and doorways somehow bothered her more than just having an affair. It simulated the antics of romance, and the thought of romance nauseated her.

It struck me as odd that the supreme intimacy didn't affect her as strongly as petting.

"I didn't have to really respond the other way, and"—she smiled bleakly—"I guess I got a secret kick out of cheating the Johns." She held up a hand. "So long as he was paying for it—and the price was always at least fifty dollars, at first."

Cut off from opium, she went through the hell of "cold turkey" withdrawal. "I twitched and ached all over, and was scared out of my skin. At times, I felt like throwing myself out a window. The goose pimples came out all over me—little bumps. I guess that's why they call straight withdrawal cold turkey—you're like a plucked turkey ready for the oven."

On the second day, she was nauseous, she couldn't eat, and her joints and muscles ached. She writhed and twisted in her bed, trying to find comfort, and there was no comfort.

She looked up coolly as she came to this point in her recital. "Nobody but an addict knows what an addict goes through when he tries to kick cold. On top of the physical distress, you're just completely overcome with terror."

She bent her head down, searched through her tangled tresses with her fingers, and exposed a portion of her scalp. I noticed a sizable white scar. "That," she said, "is where I banged my head against the wall."

She was still suffering the agonies of withdrawal, when a girl-friend arrived from the West Coast.

"Don't be a fool," she said, "I have something that will fix you up."

And so Jean had her first shot of morphine. It worked quicker, more effectively than the opium, injected directly into the vein, her first mainline job. The friend provided her with morphine for two weeks, before returning to the Coast, and gave her a list of new suppliers.

She was now in the mood for almost anything. She heard the pusher extol the virtues of C-cocaine—and H-heroin. But the thought of heroin filled her with dread. Every hopeless addict she had heard or read about had been on H.

One day the pusher was short of morphine, and she tried C at his suggestion. It was not for her. "It didn't suit me at all. It was like drinking a martini or a couple of Scotch highballs. It made me want to get up and do things. I didn't get the dreamy escape of opium or even pot. It didn't make me gloss happily over everything unpleasant. It even gave me a sexy sensation at first, which only bothered me. Feeling sexy was the last thing I wanted."

By now her best friend was the pusher. She would pick up the phone and call, and he would arrive, just like the laundryman and the dry cleaner. He looked just as nondescript and innocuous, too. And was more friendly, and influential. "Occasionally," she said with a wry smile, "he threw in a little extra because I was such a good customer—like he did one Christmas."

She finally came to heroin. Everything else was in short supply at the moment and she couldn't wait, no matter what she had heard about H. It was easier to get for the average pusher. "But the trouble with heroin," she pointed out, "is that you have to keep increasing the shots, as it keeps doing less and less for you. I had to take stronger doses, more often. After a few months, I hardly had any veins left in my arms and my hands were running out of veins too."

Again she tried to get off, and repeated "cold turkey." "I was running out of money and I couldn't work. I just didn't have any energy; it all went into the drugs. I was beginning to worry a little about the future. I was still young but I couldn't count on that forever."

She looked up at me with a softness in her eyes, and a faraway look. "At this time," she said, "I fell in love, for the first and only time in my life. There was something sweet and gentle about him, without being feminine. He didn't make me constantly aware of sex like other men did, and he never pressed for anything. We had a nice, easy relationship. Then something went wrong, one of those quarrels that people in love sometimes have, and he walked out. I didn't hear from him for a couple of days, and I couldn't stand it. I had to have a shot. That started me off again, and things were never the same, because I felt then that the drug was the only thing I could count on."

I had watched her narrowly as she described her romance with a male as passive as herself. "Isn't it rather obvious that you picked the quarrel just so the relationship would break up, and give you the excuse you wanted to get back on drugs?"

She laughed harshly. "You sound like the 'shrinker.' But it wasn't so. If he had called the next day, instead of a week later, it would never have happened that way."

"You could always have called him."

She regarded me coldly. "It's not the woman's place to call the man."

Upset at her going back to drugs, he broke off the relationship for good.

"When he said goodby," she recalled, "I just couldn't take it. I couldn't see any reason for staying around. My existence was important to nobody, myself included. I'd been on stuff for four years now. My apartments had been getting shabbier and shabbier, and my friends seedier and seedier. I got together enough money for an extra shot of Horse. That night I filled the hypo needle, and shot it into my left arm. It was a big enough dose to kill a cow. Nothing happened. I put another jolt in the other arm. It didn't even make me sick. Either the stuff had been diluted or my tolerance had built up amazingly, or both. All I got was a couple of abscesses. Later, I tried sleeping pills. Maybe, I didn't really want to die, because I recovered from this, too."

Still desperately craving drugs, she got the money for drugs the way most women without money do.

"It was kind of funny," she said, "that somebody who disliked sex as much as I should wind up earning her living with it." She thought of herself as a prostitute for the first time.

We had talked for hours, and she seemed tired. We made a date, for a week later, and she didn't turn up.

A month passed and I had almost forgotten her when the phone rang one day, and a low, almost inaudible voice said, "This is Jean, remember?"

"Of course," I said.

She hesitated. "You said you wanted to talk to me again?"

"That was weeks ago," I said.

There was a slight crack in her voice.

"Could you meet me anyway?"

I was curious at her insistence. "Is there any particular reason you want to see me?"

She hesitated. "I need twenty dollars—can you loan it to me?"

I was in a dilemma. If I gave her the twenty, I was reasonably sure she would spend it on drugs—and that would make me an accessory before the fact, morally.

"It's not for what you think," she said.

"All right," I decided, "call me tomorrow, and if you still need the twenty it's yours."

The next day Jean did not call, nor did I ever hear from her again. I could only speculate what had happened to her.

Despite the middle-class emphasis on LSD and pot, heroin had lost none of its customary market—the acutely passive addictable personalities forming the roughly 30 percent passing predictably from marijuana to heroin. Over the years, I had observed the H-prone in the streets, clinics and prisons, in an endless revolving door from which only a tremendous effort of will, with even the best of outside help, offered a corrective.

I had spent countless hours at Dr. Baird's free clinic in East Harlem, the heart of the drug world, as he counseled desperate addicts of all social stratas until he was so weary himself that he could hardly keep his eyes open.

There was an almost unbroken procession of them—youngsters on drugs, since they were eleven or twelve, smoking pot they were assured wouldn't ever harm them; young couples, married and otherwise, who had put each other on; clerks and stenographers, and talented young singers and actors, their careers haunted by the habit they couldn't shake. None, actually, was a public menace, unless, of course, he was out trying to get money to fill his desperate craving. Dr. Baird felt that his addict patients, doubly susceptible perhaps because of their own vulnerable natures, were by-products of their environment, family, school and street. Since so many had never received the family vote of confidence once direly needed, he now insisted the family encourage the addict they had helped create by accompanying him to the treatment center, and getting families with his problem.

While many of Baird's patients were from the surrounding Ghetto, the majority were from the middle-class White districts. But the pattern was similar. They were largely passive and retiring, hardly able to face themselves, not to mention the rude aggression of a brusque world. They seemed more weak than anything else, controlled by the women in their lives, because their very weakness invited this control. As in the Ghetto, their mothers were so often the dominant family personalities, and curiously, in their own lives, they seemed to unconsciously seek out the same sweetheart type, as if to perpetuate a neurotic need they secretly relished even while bristling under it. In this way, they often surrendered the very essence of manhood before final surrender to drugs. Once married, they turned ever more gratefully to drugs, glossing over private guilts, and justifying, inevitably, their own inevitable failure to come to grips with the reality of their lives and their twisted relationships.

The incongruity of these marital relationships was not always apparent. For the women, often addicts themselves, were outwardly feminine and attractive. I had seen many such couples go through Dr. Baird's Haven Clinic, which served as a laboratory for the study of a problem as complex as the people who made it so. But there was no telling some books by the cover. How, looking at Marge, could one have suspected what she was? I first noticed her leaning against the doorframe, a seductive figure in slacks and blouse, looking into the room where addicts and their families were listening intently as Dr. Baird called on each to tell how long he had been clean of drugs. The name Johnnie K. was called off and Marge smiled as a tall, good-looking, heavily muscled young man announced that he had been off heroin for three months.

"He is one of a husband and wife team," Dr. Baird said proudly. "They're doing great."

As the doctor spoke, I looked at the young woman in slacks. Her face had lighted up briefly, and with her well-bred good looks she reminded me very much of a genteel governess or social worker. I assumed she had dropped in, like myself, to see how the addicts were doing.

As each addict rose and was introduced and gave his testimonial, she smiled and appeared pleased. But she remained strangely aloof.

After the meeting broke up, she stood motionless, still smiling enigmatically, until approached by the young man introduced as Johnnie K. "Let's go," he said in a friendly voice, and they walked off together.

"Who was that attractive girl," I asked the doctor, "a social worker?"

He appeared amused. "That's Johnnie's wife."

I visited the clinic a week later, and Johnnie was there alone. He recognized me from previous visits, and we got to talking.

His voice was modulated and soft and he had obviously had a good education. He was twenty-eight years old, his face ruggedly square and ruddy, his hair sandy, his shoulders broad and sloping, a pronounced Anglo-Saxon type.

He was a late starter at drugs. He had not started taking heroin until he was twenty-three, and was not hooked for two years thereafter. He had smoked pot from time to time, in his teens, and about the only effect it had at the time was to make him confident he could control drugs.

He was an anomaly, since most of Baird's patients had become hooked in their teens, generally after an introductory course with marijuana, and were addicts, physically as well as psychologically, a few weeks after the first warming shot of Horse.

He had not touched hard drugs until he was married, and, ironically, related his problem to the very person he depended on most—his wife.

"I don't think I would have ever taken the stuff if I hadn't been married," he said in a matter-of-fact voice.

I pointed out that he had been using pot long before his marriage.

He chewed reflectively on his lip. "That didn't have much to do with it," he decided. "I could take pot or leave it, and I suppose I had the same feeling about heroin. You never feel you're going to lose control when you start—that always happens to some jerk around the corner, not you."

He looked up quizzically. "Did you meet my wife?"

I shook my head. "I couldn't help noticing her. She's quite attractive."

His voice was edged with pride. "She's a beautiful girl and intellectual, too, reading all the time—when she's not on stuff."

He smiled. "That's how I happened to go on. She'd been skin-popping for years."

"But neither of you look the type," I said fatuously.

"There's no such thing as a type."

Had he known his wife was an addict when he married her?

"She wasn't an addict then. She was taking the stuff only once or twice a month, she wasn't hooked."

"How did she know, if she didn't try stopping?"

He shrugged. "It didn't become an important part of our life until after we were married. You know you're hooked when drugs suddenly replace everything you had, the places you went to, the theater, the concert, the dinner you didn't go out to, the friends you didn't play bridge with."

Again as I surveyed his broad open face, with its fresh ruddy color, I wondered what deep-seated cause had turned this normal-seeming young man to the plague of heroin. There had to be more reason than a wife who was on it; he could always have left her.

"Have you ever wondered basically why you took drugs?" I asked.

"Oh, yes," he said, "I had enough college to make me wonder what I was doing to myself, and I don't think I would ever have touched the stuff if I hadn't been married."

"She didn't force you, did she?"

He smiled. "Not really, but there's no such thing as one addict in a marriage; you turn on, too, or the marriage breaks off."

Couldn't he have reformed her?

He smiled. "My wife made no secret of taking the stuff before we were married; her first husband had introduced her to the habit. She was only fifteen when they married, so she did pretty much what he said. Anyway, it's difficult to stay outside when your partner is going through the most terrific sensation—and there's no way of describing it except by doing it."

He laughed. "So one day, as she was skin-popping, knowing she liked the idea of my sharing, I went along, too." This reflected an adolescent passivity I wouldn't have suspected looking at his stalwart frame and manly visage. How deceptive looks were!

It soon became evident, from his own testimony, that the introductory heroin experience was anything but distasteful to him. Actually, it was quite heartwarming, as he described it. All the problems that had vaguely troubled him seemed to vanish, and he felt he could do anything—anything. He had a secret desire to write, and he could fantasy himself turning out plays, he could see himself rising beyond the people he had to cope with everyday, he even fantasied his marriage. "Nothing can bother you when you're on, somebody could come and tell you that your mother had died, and it wouldn't bother you. You would think it was too bad—sure, it was your mother—but you would only shrug and go on fantasizing."

At first, they skin-popped together about once a month, jabbing the needle into the muscle, then twice a month, and then once a week. After a while, it was every day, and they were mainlining into the vein for quicker effect. Drugs had become a life-style, and they were hard-pressed to get on with their jobs, and get money for the obsessive habit. "Between us that first year, we made something like $16,000, and wound up in debt," he recalled ruefully.

It was their only expensive habit, but it was all-consuming, dictating every phase of their lives. They sold their car, pawned their jewelry and personal effects, sold furniture piece by piece until they were sitting on bare floors. Yet, they kept fighting tenaciously to stay working, and still had enough money—and pride— not to stoop to "boosting," rifling mailboxes.

More and more, heroin made procrastinators of them. "When the rent bill came, we said we'd take care of it tomorrow, and the next day we'd be on again, grabbing a 'bag' after work, and we'd say tomorrow, and pretty soon it would be the end of the month and the pusher would have the rent money, the grocery money, and the money we used to lay away for savings." They had no life that didn't revolve around the drug, either turning it on, looking for the pusher, or kicking it. "You just can't do anything else and be a drug addict, not unless you're a millionaire or just spend all your time boosting."

I marveled that their marriage had borne up so well.

"Would you mind a personal question?" I asked.

He smiled. "They haven't seemed impersonal."

As tactfully as possible I mentioned reports of underlying sexual problems with so many habitual drug users.

"I had no sexual problem," he said. "And I love Marge very

much, but after you're hooked, and are on stuff, the last thing you're interested in is sex. You feel affectionate toward your partner, but the thought of making love is not prominent." He smiled. "In fact, I don't think I could if I wanted to, as it affects you physically as well as emotionally. Nothing would probably happen if you tried, even though you might think you were capable at first."

I wondered if friends or relatives knew about their habit.

He was horrified. "Oh, no, I'd lose my job in a second. I'm with an engineering outfit, mostly Irishmen, and they'd knock me out in a second, as if I were a leper. That's why we only skin-popped at first. Marge popped into her legs, as her arms were so delicate that even the skin-popping might show." All their mainlining was in the upper leg. "When the stuff goes right into your veins, you get a rush for ten or fifteen seconds that is something like an orgasm, from what I can gather." He had never experienced this feeling himself, and yet he had brought it up.

I studied the clean-cut jaw line, the manly slope of the shoulders, the clear eyes. "Did you ever have any difficulty relating to women?" I asked.

He shook his head. "Not that I know of."

"Did you ever have any other type of relationship?"

"I don't understand." He seemed genuinely puzzled.

"Some authorities," I said, again as tactfully as possible, "have the idea that addiction is tied in somehow with homosexuality."

He laughed. "I did have my doubts at one time. When I was in school out West, somebody always seemed to be making a proposition of some sort, until I began to wonder whether they saw something in me that I didn't."

After he left the college campus, and began working with a rugged construction crew, the attentiveness of his own sex seemed to pass. And then he met Marge. She had already been married and divorced and she had a child.

"Knowing that she was on drugs," I said, "weren't you leery about marrying her?"

"Actually, I thought she had control. She didn't use it that often, maybe two or three times a month. She really didn't become addicted until afterward, when I started to use it along with her."

There had been an air of adventure about the whole experience. "I thought it would be like taking pot, but with more kick."

"Did it do anything tangible for you?"

He hesitated. "Well, I think the two of us taking it together was the big thing. The other way I felt left out."

"Did your wife coax you?"

"Not really." He considered a second. "She'd just look at me and smile, with the needle in her hand, and say, 'See what you're missing?'"

Since she seemed so cut off from him at these times, he suddenly resolved to take it and see what happened.

And what happened?

He was more specific this time. "There was a pleasant, zinging sensation, and then I saw myself as though I were another person. My problems suddenly seemed outside me and far away. Marge seemed more beautiful and a little hazy, and I could sentimentalize about our relationship. Actually, nothing in the whole world could bother me. I was beyond feeling bad about anything." And then one day he was hooked. "I hadn't had a shot for a couple of days, which wasn't unusual, but this time, I suddenly started to get restless without knowing why; my hands trembled, the muscles in my legs twitched, and I had cramps. I wanted that shot like I had never wanted anything before."

From that day a special "togetherness" was theirs.

I thought it would be interesting to get Marge's side of the story.

"You'll find Marge a lot more knowledgeable than I am," he said.

About ten days later we all met in a Manhattan restaurant

rather on the casual side. Marge was in a trim motor jacket, with big buttons, and underneath a button-down blouse, revealing the slightest swell of her breast. She wore narrow, sharply creased slacks and masculine footgear.

Johnnie looked around at the well-dressed couples chatting at the nearby tables. "I told her to put on a skirt or dress," he said, "but," he held up his arms expressively.

Marge smiled, that faintly enigmatic smile I had observed in the doctor's office.

"I believe in being comfortable," she said. Her voice was low and sultry; it had a definite character.

We had some wine and toyed with the food for a while. She seemed curious about my book, *The Grapevine,* a report on the rising aggressiveness of women together with a commensurate rise in lesbian activity.

"How did you happen to do a book like that?" she asked.

I explained that I had previously done a book on male homosexuality, *The Sixth Man,* and lesbianism had seemed at least as prevalent.

She nodded, as though satisfied.

As we turned to our coffee, I asked how it felt to be kicking the drug.

She sighed. "Three months is a long time," and then looking at Johnnie, "I suppose it's worth it."

He nodded vigorously, and shook a good-natured fist under her nose. "You better."

"It's rough on weekends," she said, "with Johnnie not there; there's not much to do, and I get bored."

But why wasn't Johnnie there?

She hesitated and Johnnie said, "The doctor thought we'd be better apart for a while. We were apart for that first week, and now it's only weekends."

It seemed rather drastic therapy, for I was sure they missed each other terribly.

He shrugged. "She's over with a girlfriend, and has nothing but gay boys for friends. So I guess I don't have to worry."

"And how about you?" I asked.

He smiled. "I haven't taken off with any girl yet."

She regarded him coolly. "You know you can do anything you like."

He looked at her sharply. "Do you really mean that?"

"Why not?" she said. "As long as it didn't mean anything, I wouldn't care what you did."

He looked up quickly. "I don't know what all the fuss is about, when sex is the last thing you think of when you're on stuff."

"Speak for yourself, John," she said.

"What do you mean by that?" he said crossly.

She smiled, that mysterious smile of hers. "A man doesn't think of sex at that time because he couldn't do anything about it anyway, but a woman's different."

He gave her a piercing look, and said lightly, "Just don't get carried away with yourself."

She looked at him fondly. "There's nothing for you to get excited about."

"There better not be," he said good-naturedly.

I suddenly remembered that she had a child, almost six, by her earlier marriage.

"What do you do with your little girl?" I asked.

"Oh, she's no problem," she said, "Mother's got her."

Wasn't this a bit unusual?

"Oh, she's better off with Mother."

"But doesn't the child think it strange that you don't keep her?"

"Not really. After all, she's Mother's baby in a way."

She explained:

"I was fifteen when she was born, that's too young to have a child, and be married."

"Then why get married?"

"That was Mother for you." Her voice rose slightly. "I didn't want to get married, and I didn't want the baby. I was too young for all that responsibility."

"Then why get married?" I repeated.

She smiled. "Must I draw you a picture? My parents were old-fashioned, and so I wound up marrying somebody I didn't care about."

"You cared enough to produce a child with him," I pointed out.

"Not really," she said. "It was just kidlike curiosity, and I discovered it didn't mean anything." She turned to Johnnie. "Sex never meant anything to me until I met Johnnie." She paused. "And my first husband was an addict, so it didn't matter to him, either."

"Do you see the child?" I asked.

"Oh yes," she said vaguely. "She visits us, and we see her at Mother's. Mother keeps telling me how inhuman I am, but she's glad to keep the kid. It gives her somebody else to boss around."

"You're not very fond of your mother?"

"Why should I be? She was forever trying to run my life."

"How about your father?"

She grimaced. "He kept the peace by staying out of things."

I hesitated, then said finally. "You know, your attitudes strike me as being similar to many of the girls in *The Grapevine*."

I noticed Johnnie looking at me curiously.

She smiled, not at all embarrassed. "Here I thought I was a great individualist, a non-conformer, and you pick me out because I'm like so many others. It's rather unnerving." She laughed. "But it can be pleasant being with girls like myself."

She seemed to enjoy my surprise. "With a man," she went on, "you always have the idea he's trying to make a conquest, and all that jazz. Whereas, with a girl, there's a basic equality, nobody is imposing on you, and you can exchange roles."

I looked at Johnnie, but he only shrugged. "So long as there's nothing like that now. She's had her problems, and that's probably why she went to drugs."

Marge laughed. "Don't be such a psychiatrist, I enjoyed shooting. If it didn't cost so much, and wasn't so hard to get, what would be the problem?"

Johnnie threw up his arms. "You know, it becomes your whole life."

She shrugged. "I wish I could say I was sorry."

Had she a feeling it was a sexual substitute?

"Not really," she said, "it occurs to you at times that you might even have sex, but"—she laughed—"Johnnie of course isn't capable at that time."

Her early association with drugs had left only pleasant memories. Afraid at first that she might become an addict like her first husband, she had used Horse with restraint, and immediately after the breakup of her marriage had turned to pot, reversing the usual order of drug use. There had been a good reason. Girls at the school had formed a pot club, which met regularly at the various homes, as a bridge club or sewing circle might—except that each girl had her own partner.

Marge had looked forward to the regular get-togethers. "You have no idea how much fun it was, just the girls."

"How did you manage it?" I asked, "without your mothers ever being the wiser?"

"Oh, the mothers joined in, and we'd sit and talk about men and what jerks they were." After a while, they stopped talking.

After quitting school and having her baby, she had worked as a receptionist in a publishing office, subsequently becoming a secretary, and reading scripts in her spare time.

"I suppose Johnnie told you I have to be careful." She held out her arms proudly. There was not a single mark on them. "Generally," she said, "I take it in the thigh."

She looked over at Johnnie fondly. "He makes it all so grim, but it can be fun." Her eyes lighted up whimsically. "Remember the time we almost got caught in the doorway."

He shuddered. "That's as close as we ever came to getting busted; that would have been the end."

I looked at them curiously. "You mean, you took a chance in the street."

He snorted. "The chance you take is walking around with the stuff, and so the quicker you shoot up after getting it, the less chance of being caught with it on. Besides, we hadn't had a 'bag' for a couple days, and it was hard to wait knowing we could slip into any hall."

With a junkie friend, they had been cooking the heroin in a spoon when a plain-clothesman barged in. "The junkie took off up the stairs, headed for the roof, and the cop followed. Another cop barged in, and asked us what we were doing there. He was an Irish cop and we're Irish, so he didn't figure us for junkies—just a couple of smooching kids. He didn't even bother to search us. We explained the junkie had stopped us for a match. Fortunately, they never caught him."

After this narrow brush, they took stock of their situation and decided they had better try a cure. "But all your resolution vanishes," Johnnie said, "when you start getting nauseated, and have the shakes. You tell yourself then that you need it so that you can function, and the next thing you know you're out in the street looking for a couple of three-dollar 'bags.'"

13

THE SAVERS

"Can you imagine that horrible man telling kids to smoke pot?"

She slid a San Francisco paper across the desk, and pointed to a column by "Our Fearless Correspondent," entitled "Why I Rap Pot Laws." The Fearless Correspondent was indeed that. After attacking a local narcotic official—"the State's ace narco boy"—the Fearless Correspondent vigorously punched out, "That I am certainly aging (are not we all?) and probably an eccentric, and a toper by some standards, has nothing whatever to do with the insane California laws against the use of pot. An aging, eccentric toper and a youthful sober college prof can reach the same conclusion. Thousands of college profs, I may add, have reached that same conclusion."

I looked up. "I really don't see where he's advocating pot," I said mildly.

The woman's jaw hardened.

348 THE SEEKERS

"He's saying there's nothing harmful about it, which is the same thing."

"And I suppose it's that much more effective because it's a cry from the Establishment."

She nodded. "Just read on."

The Fearless Correspondent had a candid confession, considering pot was outside the law, even the laws governing Fearless Correspondents.

"My own experience with pot is negative," I read. "During my life I've used it maybe ten times, but I've never turned on. I am not an advocate of change in pot laws because of any pleasure I've ever derived from the weed.

"My knowledge, such as it is, comes from users. I've talked to and heard from hundreds of these.

"Allowing for an element of self-justification, and a tendency to exaggerate . . . their pleasures, these people have totally convinced me. They have convinced me that their pleasure in pot is real, that it is something they can do without if need be, and that it makes them less dangerous socially than if they were without it (with the important exception of driving a car under its influence)."

I looked up in some surprise. "How," I asked, "does it improve their behavior?"

The woman, a hotel executive, pulled in her chin. "He'll be comparing it with mother's milk next."

The Fearless Correspondent was warming up. "The weed does make most of them other-worldly, to be sure. They sometimes smoke with girls, surely a terrible thing, and sometimes with girls of a different color, even worse. But they were bright, intelligent, well-mannered kids before they used the stuff, and just the same when they were using it, and after they stopped."

She frowned as I put down the article. "Some people—particularly Fearless Correspondents—relate everything to themselves, overlooking the fact that thousands of others may have opposite experiences."

She eyed me rather grimly. "I happen to know of a whole family ruined by marijuana, simple, ordinary, fun-making pot."

I conjured up a picture of Mama, Papa, and their little potheads blowing up a tranquilizing storm of blue smoke.

She laughed mirthlessly. "This was a real American-type family, until the girl, a real beauty with blue eyes and long blonde hair, took off on a marijuana kick."

"A lot must have happened in that family before she turned to pot," I said.

She shrugged. "Not necessarily. Practically all the kids smoke, but some react differently—just as there are individual idiosyncrasies with all drugs, including aspirin."

This seemed reasonable, though neither the Fearless Correspondent and his pot-smoking professors seemed to consider human variabilities in their enthusiasm for the weed.

It was a familiar story she told me.

At fifteen, the girl had started smoking pot because "everybody" else was.

The family noted she was getting listless; her studies suffered, and her friends changed. They were the way-outs now, the plastic hippies, the long-hairs with the sideburns. She became sloppy about her person, not scrubbing as vigorously, not brushing teeth as often, no longer grooming her hair till it glistened.

Suddenly, the mother was uneasily aware of a gulf. She couldn't get through. She tried gently at first to find out what was happening, and finally one day, having read about the rash of drugs in the schools, she asked her daughter if she was taking any. Receiving an affirmative answer, she looked at her fifteen-year-old in stunned silence.

"I don't believe it," she said.

The daughter yawned. "You better believe it," she said.

When the mother remained incredulous, the girl took umbrage.

"Why so shocked?" she sneered. "You take alcohol and amphetamines, and call them cocktails and diet pills."

There was a family gathering that night and the threat of

a curfew and a private school was invoked. The girl retired sullenly to her room. The next day she went off to class as usual, but that evening she didn't return. The parents conducted their search privately for forty-eight hours and then turned anxiously to police.

Weeks later, through friends, they learned she was living in San Francisco's Haight-Ashbury. They went there hopefully and found her in a cramped walkup with five or six boys and girls her own age. The mother looked around the squalid flat in disbelief. It was so dirty she couldn't get up the courage to touch anything. The toilet facilities were primitive, the place reeked with the peculiarly pungent aroma of pot, perspiration and urine.

Her daughter regarded her coldly. "I'm not going home, and I'll only run away again." She thrust out a determined chin. "I belong here."

The mother compared this veritable pigsty with her own comfortable house. It just didn't make sense. There was a catch in her voice as she said, "We love you so much."

The girl stared back coldly. "My friends understand me; I'm staying." If they harassed her further, she threatened to get completely lost.

I wondered why the father hadn't talked to her, or brought in authorities.

My friend, the hotel woman, shook her head. "What good would that have done? She was tuned out."

It seemed to me that the people involved were more to blame than the drug. "What makes you so sure pot did all this?" I asked.

"Before turning on," my friend replied, "she was as gay and bright a girl as you would find anywhere."

The deteriorating process had begun simultaneously with her taking marijuana, so why look for some hidden cause when the obvious one presented itself.

"You know," the hotel woman said wryly, "these intellectual types even introduce pot to straights who don't want it."

This seemed a bit of a contradiction.

"They put it in their food," she said almost angrily. A columnist friend on a San Francisco paper had taken dinner with a couple in Berkeley one night. The cuisine had been casual, spaghetti and meat balls, a favorite dish, and he had partaken liberally, stowing it down. With a special feeling of well-being he had then gotten into his car and started back for San Francisco. He was halfway across the bridge, when his head began to reel, and a feeling of panic hit him. His hands trembled on the wheel, and he felt un-bearably warm. All he could see was a blur of headlights, and he had no idea of how fast they were moving, or of the speed of his own car. By an effort of will, he kept control, clinging in-stinctively to the wheel and riding the brake. To this day, he doesn't know how he made it home.

The next morning, a bit logy, he was puzzling over the ex-perience when the phone rang. It was his host of the previous night.

"How did it go?" he asked.

The newspaperman described his harrowing ride.

The other laughed, and then, blithely disclosed that his wife had ground up some "grass" and put it in the spaghetti.

"We thought you were old enough to know what's going on," he said.

The columnist quietly hung up.

Despite its hazards many were ecstatic in praise of grass or else felt it harmless because it had no immediate effect.

"There was another reporter not long ago who thought pot harmless," the hotel woman said grimly.

The reporter had represented a big daily back East, and his assignment had been Haight-Ashbury. Ingratiating himself with his hippie subjects, he had tried pot a couple of times, without any apparent effect.

Having done more than his reportorial duty, he relinquished all personal involvement in marijuana. However, subsequently at a pot party of prominent adult molders of opinion, he sensed the disdain marijuana smokers reserve for those without the spunk to emulate them. And so he reached for a cigarette, contemplating another desultory experience in the line of duty. He was halfway along, simulating the deep breathing of those around him, when an unaccountable malaise came over him and he started to shake. He felt a dull pain in his teeth and acute nausea. Cold sweating and panic followed. Frantic, he fled the party. That night, suffering an attack of the dry heaves, he made the startling discovery that marijuana could be more malignant than alcohol. "At least," he said, "I always knew how many drinks I could take."

When he wrote his newspaper story, he carefully left out his own experience. It might have done something to his image.

However, the hotel woman did have friends who were taking a stand from experience against the "harmless" psychedelics. They were a young couple, Winifred and David Kershaw, both twenty-four, who were part of a small but dedicated company conducting a vigorous educational campaign against LSD, pot and "speed." Kershaw, and others at the University of California, where he was taking graduate work, used their own special insight to alert the innocent. Their Committee for Psychedelic Drug Information, formed in 1966, was expressly launched to "make public their reasons for taking and then abandoning drugs." They had had a bird's-eye view of the drug scene in Cambridge, when young Kershaw was at Harvard, and his wife at Radcliffe, and they felt young America was tragically toying with its future. "Their hope," the hotel woman said, "was that other young people could benefit from their own experiences, and avoid the pitfalls they had skimmed over."

They had seen enough to turn themselves off forever. And despite their missionary zeal, they were anything, I found, but dreary reformers, "To think," Winifred Kershaw said with faint irony, "that after I had first taken LSD, I went back to my old high school in Contra Costa, California, and recommended that all students take it as a soul-revealing experience. I certainly have a lot to work off."

In their ventures into the current scene, the Kershaws were amused by the characteristic reaction of "acidheads" who got instant enlightenment with LSD, and yet couldn't make the simplest decisions. "Acid-heads," laughed David Kershaw, "have the answers to world problems, but can't begin to solve their own." A friend at Berkeley, a brilliant student of economics, had turned to pot and LSD. "Now after many trips, he goes around whispering that he could explode the economy of the country by presenting an entirely new economic concept of his own."

And why didn't he do it?

He didn't want anybody to have his secret.

LSD or not, my curiosity was piqued.

But the Kershaws hadn't learned the secret. "He's been even more secretive since he left the institution," Winifred sighed.

He had crashed, unpredictably, and been put away. The unreality of his experience had become reality in his whirling mind with resulting delusions of grandeur. Alternately, thinking himself the devil and God, he put on his old Army uniform and carried a gun to class, threatening ordinary mortals who didn't do him homage.

I had understood that many "trippers" had deep and abiding religious experiences.

Winifred nodded brightly. "So they say, but theologian Huston Smith has pointed out that they have religious experiences without ever becoming religious. The only reality, it often develops, is the harm the acid is doing."

She mentioned on acquaintance, a brilliant student of no small promise. "He had so many religious experiences, that he's now catatonic, sitting like a zombie in his father's home in Sacramento. He doesn't even think he's Christ anymore, but just sits there motionless, waiting for a train."

In some ways she felt pot was just as risky as LSD. "The

day of reckoning will arrive for chronic potheads too late," she said with a thin smile.

But was it really physiologically addicting?

She shrugged. "It certainly leaves its mark on the mind, where addiction must begin. Marijuana draws in bad thought forms, in time constituting part of the users' thinking—which is why they so outrageously defend something as outrageous as marijuana. Even the most enthusiastic acknowledge a discordant bombardment of thoughts, just as time and space are in themselves distorted in the experience. The distortion on one level inevitably reflects itself on all levels."

She thought a moment, frowning.

"Tim Leary told us when we visited his experimental center at Millbrook to put our wills in abeyance, and flow along with whatever came through, not resisting, putting the self in a suggestible, hypnotic state, while sitting there like a mushroom through it all."

They had seen this form of hypnosis carried to dangerous extremes. "Remember our friend at Columbia?" Winifred said, turning to her husband.

"The philosophy student?"

"Yes," she said, "the boy who was so inhibited."

He laughed mirthlessly. "Oh, yes, the pot fraternity at Columbia said pot would relax him and get rid of his inhibitions."

"What kind of inhibitions?"

"Girls—he was afraid of girls." Kershaw shook his head. "And so he smoked his pot, like every nice little college boy should, and started strolling around Morningside Heights, just off the campus, accosting every girl he ran into."

"He attacked them?"

"Oh, no, just approached them, the pot wasn't that strong, it was ordinary home-grown grass, an inferior variety of indifferent potency. Who knows what might have happened with hashish?"

"And then what?"

"Well, he wasn't very attractive, which is why he had inhibitions in the first place, and the girls didn't give him a tumble."

He kept smoking more and more, getting a little more disorganized mentally, and then under pot he got a clear-cut vision of how he would gain the attention he needed.

David Kershaw smiled ironically.

"He took off all his clothes and paraded around the Heights in the nude after dark."

It was a rather dramatic way of making friends. Drawn by female screams, the police collared the unclad student as he was hazily picking his way up the moonlit street. Thinking he may have suffered a mental breakdown they took him home instead of making an arrest. "They recognized," Kershaw said, "that he had blown his mind."

Why did pot so drastically affect some and not others?

Winifred Kershaw frowned. "Anybody's turn can come at any time. The intellectuals praising pot have no idea of what it may eventually do to them. Often pot will trigger an old LSD experience, or it may act alone with similar effect."

One of the Kershaws' Berkeley associates, a young divorcée, had been so impressed by a Timothy Leary lecture that she made a pilgrimage to Millbrook for her first hallucinogenic experience. It had not had much effect at the time, but six months later while visiting in New York, she tried pot in her hotel. It was instant nightmare. She walked out of her midtown hotel and was rolling up the street on a cushion of air when she felt a pair of hands pushing her into the path of a passing car. She took fright, and fled wildly down the street to escape certain destruction.

It was no wonder she had joined the LSD rescue squad— for there were no hands, except in her mind.

Winifred's conversion was at least as drastic. "Looking back," she smiled deprecatingly, "it all seems so stupid."

Her husband regarded her fondly. "Well, we all want to know

where we're at, and Leary and Alpert made it so simple. All you did was take a drug, and, presto, the universe was yours."

Their Millbrook adventure recalled my own visit there. What had struck me at the time was the unspeakable squalor of the place and the filthy mattresses lying side by side on the floor. The general untidiness, characteristically, was passed off as a quite justifiable rejection of the materialistic world.

The Kershaws laughed reminiscently. "Actually," Winifred said, "they had a very efficient maid, but they couldn't resist the impulse to turn her on, and she wound up thinking she was a queen, and wouldn't do any more housework."

A combination of events had opened Winifred's eyes—a bad trip, when least expected; disillusionment with the spiritual awakening promised by Leary, and the pragmatic realization that bad trips were a terrible price for an enlightenment as transitory as the wind.

They had been more impressed by the crashes than by the intellectual awakenings.

"Tell him," David said, "about the film-maker."

Winifred shook her head ruefully. "That poor man. He had had a number of trips before, but this time he had come up from a yoga ashram some sixty miles below Millbrook, leaving his wife and child there, while he popped in for a solo flight. This was the ultimate achievement, having the LSD experience by yourself." Unexpectedly, sitting alone in his room, he developed symptoms of paranoia and notified Leary, who cheerfully reassured him over the phone that sweating it out was therapeutic. There were more distress calls, all receiving the same response.

"He was up so tight," David put in, "that he went eleven days and nights without sleep." He reported a mission to save the world by committing suicide, and was told this vision, too, was therapeutic. He was obviously purging himself of ego.

Unable to sit by himself the subject took to the road. A visiting psychiatrist, approaching the center, reported at Millbrook that he had seen the film-maker running frantically down the highway. Nobody seemed more than dimly interested.

The psychiatrist, more concerned, drove back over the highway, locating the film-maker, who was still running furiously in the direction of New York City.

"Where are you going?" he asked.

Without breaking his pace, the man replied, "Philadelphia."

The psychiatrist couldn't get him to stop, and reluctantly turned back, thinking the runner would eventually tire himself out.

But it didn't happen quite that way. "He was in such a state of agitation," Winifred said, "that his excess of nervous energy carried him all the way to the ashram sixty miles away."

In some way, too, the original suicidal impulse had been strangely inverted, and the film-maker now felt that he could only save the world by killing his wife and child. Entering the ashram, he threw himself at his wife, and was subdued by others only after a violent struggle.

Still reacting wildly, he proceeded to New York City—by car— and shortly after his arrival there attempted suicide.

"I suppose," David said wryly, "they would have called it therapeutic suicide."

LSD pundit Timothy Leary was no stranger. I had spoken to him several times besides visiting his research center, and witnessed a party to morally support him in resisting marijuana charges. He was a man of some charm with a ruddy face and silver hair. He baited the Establishment good-naturedly, and seemed to have no trouble converting impressionable, revolt-conscious students to his League for Spiritual Discovery (LSD). I had first talked to him when, with another psychologist, Richard Alpert, he was thrown out of Harvard, marking the first time in a century Harvard had dismissed an instructor for "grave misconduct and neglect of duty." Experimenting with mind-altering drugs in Harvard's Center for Research in Personality, the pair had given 3500 doses of psilocybin, a less potent hallucinogen than LSD, to some four hundred subjects: graduate students in psychology and theology, M.D.s, artists, prison inmates. Meanwhile, they kept taking it as they gave it. According to David G. McClelland, head of Harvard's department of social relations, the more drugs the professors took the less interested they were in science. Leary disagreed. "This is more important than Harvard," he said. "Our research has almost limitless possibilities for the expansion of the human mind."

Subsequently, the expelled scholars set up an LSD utopia in Mexico, presented as a community for transcendental living. The over-all plan, Leary announced, was to train doctors and psychologists in administering LSD and other drugs in a special joy and happiness center in the United States. The rates for the Mexican paradise were thoughtfully worked out, two hundred dollars a month for room and board, plus six dollars for each hallucinatory experience.

Mexican officials, as had Harvard, asked Leary and Alpert to leave. Leary was nothing daunted. "If anybody shows us a better road to happiness," he said, "we'll drop our research, but we don't think they will."

He always seemed to be in and out of hot water. He was once arrested with his teen-age daughter, accused of bringing marijuana into the country from Mexico, and then at the 2500-acre LSD center at Millbrook, he was arrested with his teen-age son on still another marijuana charge.

His reaction to the second arrest was characteristically good-natured. The most distressing thing about the whole business, he said, was the police cutting his son's long hair. The hair, police announced, was clipped for sanitary reasons.

As he made the rounds of college campuses, urging students to "turn-off, turn-on, and tune-in," Leary began to emerge as a leader of a new cult, which equated LSD with a spiritual experience. "You should never take LSD unless you are in a state of grace," he said solemnly.

With his immersion in the new cause, his appearance had begun to change. His hair was now worn long, his dress was unconventional, and he had adopted what seemed a set, perpetual smile.

With a friend, I had visited him in Millbrook shortly after his return from a global honeymoon. To inquiries about his bride, whom he had married three months before, his lips parted in a thin smile. "I left with a wife and came back with a cheetah," he said.

He spoke eloquently at this time of LSD, and said that its function was completely misunderstood. "Nobody," he said, "can begin to understand what clear insight it gives into the self without taking it himself."

I had heard, even then, that some people reacted badly with it, and some had been institutionalized.

He shook his head. "I know of no such reactions under competent supervision."

I recalled that a brilliant scientist, a mutual acquaintance, who had taken LSD with the Leary group in Mexico, had suddenly gone berserk and been committed to a mental ward.

Leary's interest perked up briefly. "Oh, you know him," he said, "a wonderful chap."

I again questioned his unfortunate experience.

"Oh, that had nothing to do with it," Leary said easily. "He was all right at the time."

With typical graciousness, he invited us to tour the place. "Make yourself at home," he said.

My companion, a wealthy socialite, had been impressed by certain articles on LSD by Leary, and had toyed with the idea of perhaps getting to know herself—and the universe—better with one of the mind-expanding drugs. However, she was now less than enthusiastic. "I don't see where he has any special insights," she sniffed.

"Perhaps," I said, "it's easier to turn on mind-expanders than the mind."

On our tour, we had reached the main house, cut through the kitchen, where a young couple, sloppily attired, was preparing a late breakfast. They greeted us dully, with the briefest of nods, and went on with their preparations. In the building, we had picked up a guide, a young man who introduced himself as a critic of a book I had done on homosexuality. His reading, however, appeared to have joined rather than separated us, for he chose to look on me as an old friend, errant, to be sure, but reasonably trustworthy.

My companion was following gingerly behind, careful not to touch anything. "My," she said, with an expression of disgust, "why must everything be so filthy?"

Our guide seemed startled. "This is a revolt from the materiality of the crass commercial world," he said seriously.

She was not so easily mollified. "Well, do they have to revolt against soap and water?" Her nose was turned up and she appeared to be making an effort not to breathe the air around her. "There's no excuse for all this dirt," she insisted.

The guide shrugged carelessly. "It's all how you look at it; for some people, it has meaning."

"Yes," she said, "an excuse to be slovenly."

"Were they this way before they came up here?" I asked. He reflected a moment. "No, it's part of their development."

"Could it have resulted from LSD or pot?" I asked.

He nodded. "That may have given them some insight into what was important."

My companion grimaced. "Well, it certainly wasn't Procter & Gamble."

As Dr. Miras had suggested, I wondered whether LSD or marijuana in themselves might induce a slothful attitude, and consequent lack of ambition.

He laughed. "Of course, we don't acknowledge that it's slothful —but introspective. Don't think so much about how you look to others, as where you look in yourself."

We had now come to the group's sleeping quarters. Several bedrolls were sprawled out on the floor, flung about untidily in pairs next to each other.

"Very cozy," said my socialite friend, with an expression of distaste. "I suppose," she said, "this is some sort of love-in." She shuddered. "How can they sleep together in all this dirt?"

Our guide laughed cheerfully. "It's all part of emphasizing what's important—the exalted feeling itself or the physical locale."

She shivered. "How could there possibly be any feeling in this atmosphere?"

We were back in the kitchen now, and the conversation had turned to LSD specifically.

"Have you taken it yet?" I asked our guide.

He shook his head. "Not yet."

My friend pursed her lips. "No wonder he's so uniquely clean."

I considered the guide a moment. "I understand from Dr. Leary that nobody has had a bad LSD experience here."

He smiled enigmatically. "Did he tell you that?"

"He said it was no problem under supervision." I turned to my friend. "Wasn't that about it?"

She nodded. "He was rather emphatic on that score."

The guide frowned, contemplating me speculatively for a moment. The self-importance of imposing a startling confidence appeared to outweigh natural prudence.

In almost a whisper he turned to me, ignoring my friend. "Did you hear about last night?"

I shook my head.

His thin little chest puffed up, reminding one of a pouter pigeon. "If it hadn't been for me, we might have had a tragedy here," he said. His eyes traveled around the kitchen. "And right in this room."

"What happened?" I asked.

"What happened? Why, all hell broke loose." His voice fell to an intimate whisper. "This one fellow took an average dose of LSD—it was his first trip—and suddenly, without warning, he went stark raving mad."

Our guide walked over to a kitchen drawer and pulled out a large breadknife. "He grabbed this knife, and started after a couple in the kitchen. They were completely unprepared, and so was I." He smiled with pride. "But I quickly sized up the situation and took him from the back, getting a grip on his arm, until the others could jump in and disarm him."

After being subdued, the subject collapsed and went off to sleep. He appeared to be all right in the morning.

Our guide shook his head. "But it was pretty sticky for a while."

"Did Dr. Leary know of the incident?" I asked.

He smiled blandly. "He was told about it."

My friend and I exchanged glances.

"Let us be going," she said tartly, "before we catch something."

We climbed into our car, without anymore ado. Her face was frozen into an expression of disgust. "All I want," she said, "is to go home and take a bath."

And so that was my experience at Millbrook, where the Kershaws had been drawn by Leary's profession of a new religion based on spiritual awakening through drugs.

Winifred Kershaw was thoroughly disillusioned with Leary, and herself. "My instant enlightenment actually came when I saw for the first time what drugs were doing to him."

Her own drug experience was by no means unique. At first, she was convinced LSD had opened a brand new world of infinite possibilities. In her own intellectual enchantment she began seeking converts, taking to the platform to urge the young to emulate her experience.

Even though her last experience was frightening, she was grateful for it being bad enough to make it the last. "I was suddenly squeezed into a little box, with what seemed great physical pain." With each flare of pain, she had the gruesome feeling that she was dying. She broke down, sobbing hysterically, and was sure she was passing from this mortal coil. "It was horrible," she said, "an infinite variety of loathesome things were crawling over me, infesting my body and mind."

She had come close to crashing; and now shuddered thinking about it.

Her husband drew his arm around her, comfortingly. His own experience had not been as drastic, nor as searching. "I've always been rather solid," he said, "so LSD didn't bring me up tight. However, it does often open you up in a way you're not prepared for, dredging up what you're not prepared to look at." In his own experience, he had become steeped in his relationship with his wife. "There is a tendency to be absorbed in one hangup."

Kershaw cited one very common reason for so many different people taking LSD and pot—boredom.

"They try it out of emotional flatness, hoping for something that will lift them out of their doldrums."

Even with Winifred's bad trip, and their firsthand observations, they might still not have become anti-drug missionaries had it not been for their introduction to a "true" religious experience. Through a San Francisco socialite, familiar with the occult, they had become aware of the Indian master, Meher Baba, who transmitted his wisdom only through the written word. "If God can be found through the medium of any drug, God is not worthy of being God," Meher Baba had written.

Like many Christian teachers, Meher Baba taught that God was everywhere, and that only in finding a oneness with this universal God could man attain more than fleeting happiness. "As for possible use of the drug LSD by an enlightened society for spiritual purposes—an enlightened society would never dream of using it."

Meher Baba saw the importance of ego release for illuminating insights into the nature of things, but said LSD produced only the illusory and transient. "God can only be realized by loving Him with all the love at one's command—pure, simple and unadulterated love. It is absolutely essential for a spiritual aspirant who genuinely longs for union with God—the Reality—to shun experiments with the effects of certain drugs. These things do not uplift the aspirant nor draw him out of the rut of illusion. Experiences born of these practices wear off as soon as the aspirant withdraws from or is thrown out of the orbit of the effect produced by the technique employed."

Meher Baba's warning about LSD approximated Dr. Miras' on pot. "If the student world continues to indulge in the use of LSD, the best of its intellectual potential will be lost to the nation. Use of LSD produces hallucinations, and prolonged use of this drug will lead to mental derangement."

Unlike the Fearless Correspondent, the Indian holy man recognized that reactions to drugs vary. "There is some indication that one should regard the action of LSD as specific to the individual. One individual may be harmed more by using it one time than another individual who uses it thirty times. It must then be concluded that it is not safe nor advantageous to plan to use LSD two or three times for the experience it produces." And the same was true for pot.

In meditation, in prayer, in disciplining the mind, there was some preparation for constructive learning. But how did one prepare for a drug whose very impact was unpredictable, and which contributed nothing to one's philosophic development? At best LSD was often a chemical maze without beginning or end. "LSD apparently stimulates certain centers of the brain which are usually activated only as a by-product of the development of the spiritual seeker," Meher Baba found. "Activation is a normal process, and the seeker has then developed the capability to exercise safeguards. If these centers are artificially stimulated, the result is something like the forcing of a locked door. Then one is not certain that the door can be properly closed again."

For the Kershaws, who had seen it from both sides, Meher Baba made sense. Winifred realized that LSD and marijuana, while perhaps opening gates to paradise, seemed to close the door on common sense. "How articulately people would talk under these drugs and how ineffectually they would perform."

She had once appeared before a community of five hundred

drug cultists, who were distressed because their spiritual leader, arrested on marijuana charges, was jailed in lieu of five hundred dollars bail pending a hearing.

"They kept wondering what they could do to help him," Winifred recalled, "and I suggested that since there were five hundred of them, it would be a relatively simple manner for each of them to contribute a dollar—hardly a day's supply of pot—and bail him out."

All immediately saw the merit of the plan, elaborately discussed the pros and cons, over pot and LSD, until the beloved leader unhappily came to trial. "It was just too much of a decision for anybody to make," Winifred recalled with a sigh, "all they wanted to do was talk about it. You soon find this out about potheads, great talkers, small doers."

Winifred and David seemed so happy with each other, and themselves, it was difficult to conceive why they had ever tried drugs in the first place.

"There was no stigma to LSD, or pot, when we first turned to them," Winifred explained. "In Mexico and some areas of this country Indians took mescaline and marijuana in their religious practice. And in this framework of personal and universal exploration most younger people approached the drugs, almost as though it was an adjunct to their education."

David had listened, frowning. "People are always asking how my generation differs from earlier generations in their attitudes," he now observed. "Everything is interpersonal with us. Whereas my father looked on the grand scene, and wanted things done socially and politically without personal involvement—the Great Society, the Anti-Poverty Programs, and all that—my generation is aware that our national and world problems are essentially personal, and have to be settled in a personal way." He regarded me with a smile. "And taking a drug, a psychedelic, is an extremely personal thing—and so is the reaction."

He thought a moment. "It was difficult for my father to understand my own discontent with a world of tradition. Labels have no meaning with our generation anymore, unless whatever it is they represent has meaning in itself."

God, country, wife, all had to have special personal significance; otherwise they were hollow, meaningless symbols of what seemed at times a meaningless society. "We can't assume something works, automatically, when it hasn't worked for millions of other people," he said. "Actually, we are not revolting or rejecting so much as we are reappraising."

In this sweeping appraisal, it was interesting to note the hippie-swayed attitude toward the Negro. He was not a cause to be promoted, a pawn to be fawned over, an issue to be exploited, but a very personal individual. His own merit, or demerit, influenced acceptance or rejection, as with any other race, creed or color. There was no patronizing attitude, no question of tolerance, no implication of superiority—or guilt. "Everybody has his own bag," as one activist hippie pointed out, "and the Negro is no different. He makes it on his own or he doesn't. In each man is the measure of his own success."

Other labels were uniquely personified. Young Kershaw respected his father without being impressed by either his wisdom or years, except as they were truly expressive. After David became immersed in the God world of Meher Baba, his father with pleasurable surprise noted certain positive changes in him and commented favorably. David explained the changes were due to his exposure to the teachings of an Indian spiritual leader.

The father laughed. "Nonsense, your marriage must be doing it."

The son smiled now, recalling the incident. "Could I tell him that seeing God in everything, including my wife, had actually helped my marriage?"

What exactly had touched off this youthful trend to equating drugs with the interpersonal?

David regarded me solemnly. "The kids have seen that the traditional way of handling human problems won't work. And so they were looking for new ways, and when people of some distinction, with all kinds of prestigious degrees, came along and said that drugs were the way, there was some security in turning on."

"You must remember," Winifred cut in, "we are only beginning to check out what LSD can do to mind and body, and in time, similar reports will be in about marijuana."

"Actually," David said, "most of the bored college kids are interested in drugs as a means to greater understanding, and they soon find out drugs aren't the answer. People on pot always seem to need a party, and they keep all the hangups. They dump on the cops, the System, their parents—it never seems to get back to them. Whereas with Meher Baba, that's where it's at all the time, with you and the people around you, and your concept of the universe."

His most important interpersonal relationship was obviously his wife. He looked over fondly at her now. "What helps us individually, helps our marriage. People can keep one another upright, without leaning against each other all the time."

Singly and together, they were relating—interpersonally. "In my own case," Winifred said, "I'm trying to make up for any proselyting I did while I thought I had the word."

Ironically, her student audiences were as skeptical as she had been of moralizing, particularly when she warned of marijuana.

Her reference to marijuana reminded me of the couple who had prankishly slipped grass in their columnist friend's food.

Kershaw laughed. "That tells you about their judgment. They thought it was funny, and he almost went off the bridge." He frowned a moment. "The thinking of people on pot becomes so distorted after a while they don't see the distortions. They're the last people qualified to judge their own experience. It never occurs to them to question what they do under pot. Does everybody turn on records and play them backwards? Does everybody babble and giggle, and think they are getting it straight from the Koran? Does everybody float through the air and think anything possible, until they float back to earth?"

At Berkeley, the alienated turned out regularly to heckle the young missionaries crusading against drugs.

"We don't bug you about your bag," they said, "why bug us?"

Winifred had an answer for them. "If I see a blind man headed for a cliff, I must do something to stop him."

David laughed as he recalled some of the exchanges.

"Or they would sometimes ask, if God is in everything, as you say, and if God is truth, why isn't he in acid?"

Winifred had an answer for this, too.

"I generally tell them the story about the elephant," she smiled. Told by an Indian holy man that God was in everything, a man in the path of a stampeding elephant refused to budge as the animal bore down on him, ignoring the shouted warnings of the Mahout on the elephant's back.

The elephant's charge hurled him high into the air, shattering bones as well as faith.

On crutches, with his arm in a sling, he reproachfully confronted the holy man. "Why did you tell me God was in everything?"

"God is in everything," the holy man replied firmly. "Didn't the Mahout tell you to get out of the way? God was in him, too."

14

FINDERS—SEEKERS?

Jane was a bright-eyed slip of a girl, with a pretty, angular face. Her brown eyes reflected a quick, native intelligence. She was only eighteen, and yet had already lived a lifetime. She had begun drugs at fifteen—LSD, marijuana, "speed"—and psychoanalysis at sixteen. At seventeen, she was living with a young man in the Hollywood hills.

Jaded on marijuana, not having heard from the "experts" that Mary Jane didn't lead to heroin, she had already arranged for her first experience with Horse—Big H—when her addict lover, enamored of somebody else, threw her out.

While some may have thought her a poor little girl, she was hardly underprivileged. She was a runaway from a wealthy home, from parents who professed their love and concern, even as they sent her off to private schools and psychiatrists.

Oddly enough, I had met the girl through her parents at

Synanon, the drug rehabilitation center at Santa Monica, California, which regards drug use, marijuana as well as heroin, as a symptom of social stupidity. "What we are treating here," observed Synanon's guiding light, reformed alcoholic Chuck Dederich, "is simple, ordinary stupidity, for anybody who lets drugs direct his life has to be stupid."

In the worst days of heroin, the crashees had not been as strung out and helpless as the habitual users of LSD and pot. These were thoroughly bummed out, in a stupor lasting long after the usual three-day withdrawal of H-addicts.

Physically, and mentally, Jane had been at the end of her rope when she arrived at Synanon a year before. Not only was she debilitated but corroded with a rancorous mistrust of a world she thought of as hardly worth saving.

"How can you believe anybody out there?" she said indignantly. "Johnson says he isn't sending troops to Vietnam, and the next thing they're on the way. My parents say one thing, and do another—and the hippies, they're phony, too, kidding themselves they're something special, when all they are is gutless, heartless and brainless, because they aren't doing anything about the world they live in."

How had Jane—like many others of her class—become alienated from a home where she was so manifestly its center.

Jane had mulled it over herself, discussed it at Synanon, where the truth of her own attitudes were examined in a probing exchange with other addicts.

"At Synanon," Jane said, "I faced myself, and saw the truth, not only my parents' truth, but my truth. Here, there was honesty, with nobody having anything to gain through dishonesty." For the first time she was able to figure out what had happened. Her family had wanted one thing for her, and she another. "They saw me, selfishly, as an extension of their own aspirations." She could have anything she wanted, anything parental doting could provide, so long as her actions suited her parents. "How could I want what they wanted," she said, "when I didn't respect their goals for themselves. All my father was interested in was making money, planning holidays in Europe and talking about the Hollywood stars he knew, and my mother was right there with him. They gave me freedom, freedom to do the things they approved. I could go out anywhere, so long as it was with some nice Jewish boy, even though I often felt closer to other kids who thought like I did. I had freedom to think, so long as I got grades in subjects that required no thinking, and thought like they did."

All that was past now. In the framework of Synanon, where she would live for perhaps the next two years, Jane had been uneasily reconciled to her parents. They were no longer a strong influence, but in the daughter's reformation the parents finally saw their own faults, and were now providing a support they had never given before.

But Jane's was an uphill fight at best. As she knew from her own experiences with pot and LSD, there was no instant enlightenment. Nothing good developed externally without a corresponding development inside. There was no substitute for the optimism that came from faith in one's self, a faith built on the fearless expression of one's own aspirations. For the most of what drugs took from the young was their God-given right to test themselves on the trying scales of life. So what of the future for Jane, and others like her, devoid of faith, disbelieving in marriage, education or country? And what of a country, or world, with no business or family structure, no school or political body, no marriage, no family responsibility? What kind of a society would it be where anyone did what he pleased when he pleased, took drugs as he pleased, obeyed what laws he liked, and disobeyed those he didn't.

"Who," I asked Jane, "will collect the garbage?"

She smiled appreciatively. "The foundations of society will always be pretty much the same, otherwise we'd have nothing but chaos, but the hippies, even with their pretentiousness, have underlined the validity of the protest against a culture in which people have no real concern for one another."

In a brave new world, Jane saw a primitive personal society eventually emerging out of the bare need for survival. "Wars, jealousy, crime are motivated by fear, and only in a society living the Golden Rule will there be lasting peace." She laughed. "The hippies talk about the Eastern religions—zen, Buddhism, yoga, transcendental meditation—but it was all stated very well two thousand years ago, and never was it needed more than today."

There was a certain primitiveness in the rugged honesty with which the drug user denuded himself of all illusions. The Synanon game was the crux of the Synanon attack on the blight of "stupidity," with participants falling back on "gut-level insights," as Dederich put it, to strip a neophyte down to his bare bones. A verbal assault, with a "third-degree" intensity, often centered on one person. The very remoteness of an individual was a special challenge, as it often showed a special need. Virginia, tall, slim, blonde, better educated, more aloof than most, had been on morphine, Demerol, heroin. She was a hard-core addict, for whom Synanon was a final port of call, and her defenses were obviously up as the small group of rehabilitating addicts sat down to play the Synanon game.

"You think you're better than we are," was the opening blast.

The barrage continued, "You're always trying to impress everybody with your superiority."

"Yes, you're a complete phony."

As she reeled under these blows, trying to compose an answer, Virginia was charged with feeling superior to another girl because that girl was a prostitute.

"Not really," she finally shot back, "what I did to myself was even worse."

"You don't really believe that," the attack went on, "we've all been prostitutes, pimps, thieves, and you're right in there. So stop feeling so damn superior."

"I don't," she cried. "I'm really being honest."

The attack shifted. Where it had been a pounding assault, brutally mounted, it now expressed itself obliquely.

"All right," an ex-gangster said reasonably, "so you've been a dope fiend, right, or you wouldn't be here?"

Virginia gulped a few times.

"You got your drugs from the doctor, right?"

She nodded silently.

"So he was your old man?"

She puzzled over this jargon for a prostitute's protector.

"Oh, come on, don't be so blasted superior, we know what you are. We know you tried to kill your mother with a bottle, and how you let down your two husbands and two kids. What's so wonderful about you?"

She shrank back into her seat.

But the attack grew even more intense.

"You play the lady beautifully, but that act doesn't fool anybody. Now own up, drop the pose, admit you were no better than a prostitute. You were being kept by the doctor?"

She shielded her face. "Oh, no, no," she cried.

"Oh, yes, yes, my fine lady."

Convulsively almost she shook her head.

"Admit it, you were selling your body for the stuff. Admit it, you were a whore."

She looked up for a long moment, and her body went limp. "Yes," she sighed, "yes, yes."

The resistance to the hateful truth had gone out of her.

She was now looking at herself openly as she had once secretly, hating herself for being what she couldn't consciously admit she had been. But the emotion was no longer suppressed. Now, as she looked around, and saw suddenly the smiling faces, not full of the rejection she had feared, but beaming approval at her progress toward honesty, she felt a surge of hope, of acceptance, her first such feeling in years. She was on her way to understanding herself—and her drug habit.

Out of eye-opening, soul-searching experiences such as this, out of her own torment, and with the feeling of belonging at Synanon, Jane, too, had begun to look at herself and the world around her with new clarity. "You don't find out where it's at with drugs," she said, "and anybody who tells you different is kidding himself. The only thing pot ever did was get me on to more pot, and it would have been heroin next, because I was running out of kicks. It's all an escape, whether for a day or a week, but eventually you pay, and the price is a hard one."

Jane, at most, had only a glimpse of life's truths. Other clues, filling in the picture, came from enlightened sources of protest. The underground newspaper, The Oracle, analyzing the generation gap, stressed that the human revolution was part of an elemental struggle between "haves" and "have-nots."

"The malaise between the young and the old, which I do not believe to be of a similar type of quality with that of the past," commented Robert Theobald, "is due to the fact that the young perceive this break between our stated profession and our real actions, and they are no longer willing to live in this form of society without protesting. But they perceive far from clearly how protest can be organized."

He examined the validity of the youthful assault on "cookie cutter" education, under attack as an instrument of a stale, tasteless status quo. "The young are asking that the educational process deal with real life, and that it help them to understand real life, and that the education process does not, in general, do so. That, in effect, we are still teaching about the industrial age; and that our very pattern of teaching reinforces the industrial age values and prohibits their questioning.

"Now if it be true that we are constrained by our system, and if it be true that we are not challenging it in education, which is where one would expect it, it is quite clear that we are not going to succeed in getting the necessary changes." But in the very dynamics of revolution there was endless prospect of radical changes from any and every quarter. "The world is shifting from a stable conflict between the communist and the capitalist powers to a highly unstable conflict between the rich and the poor parts of the world, which means by extension and definition—a conflict between the White and non-White parts of the world.

"And when you consider that in this country immense lines of stress are developing between the poor and the rich, which again means predominantly between the White and the non-White powers, we really seem to have major immediate crises on our hands."

There were other issues, even more fundamental perhaps. "We also have long-run crises, in terms of pesticides, in terms of fertilizers, both in unbalancing the ecology and the environment, in terms of air and water pollution, and in the terms of the problem of finding good ways for us to live."

The Oracle, reflecting the thought-waves of so many of the young, was hopeful that emphasis on the personal, instead of the social, would condition the world in the same natural way that fertility and growth flowed out of rain, sun and air. "Along with renewed sense of the personal will come its counterpart, an increasing feeling of social oneness and universality. We will learn to live in continuous and deep involvement with each other, and this open and transparent sense of self will lead naturally to an open environment, transparent and interactive, where self-disclosure and acceptance are assumed as the basis of human growth."

Out of the new movement, with or without drugs, had come an attack on old labels, particularly those of race, creed or class, which in any way restricted the mounting drive for human identity. Anonymity was the anathema of the human revolutionaries, and while their efforts to replace it were often disastrous, they never lost sight of the goal. Even at random social get-togethers, seldom was anyone introduced except by name—usually first name—minimizing the importance of such constricting labels as writer, clerk, engineer, artist, or secretary. The emphasis was on rugged—albeit ragged—individualism.

Those who came through the drug experience safely, unharmed, while usually not the better for it, had often profited by the very open-mindedness which led to their experience, a sort of self-imposed prelude of self-analysis, or "nail soup," as Dr. Pinckney might well have put it.

However, the preoccupation with marijuana, LSD, amphetamines and other "soft drugs" was a threat to the very involvement restless youth was so valiantly groping for. For pot, like LSD, eventually addled the brain, weakened the resolve, and produced, ironically, the very limiting type of life style that the exponents of limitless horizons were decrying out of the other corner of their mouth.

Unlike the martini, marijuana was not an aphrodisiac. For while it released the inhibitions that retarded sex, it only accentuated that which the individual desired, seldom if ever sparking that for which there was no desire.

The Generation Gap was a very real thing. There were signs of it in nearly every circumstance of drug abuse. In the middle-class, the chief culprits were often the indulgent mother or the demanding father, the self-made man who wanted his son to follow in his footsteps, because he was blind to all other footsteps. He could not understand the adolescent, cast in his image, who was not busy at a job or getting his schooling, and he had no patience for any time-consuming soul-searching, which he considered a mark of indolence and shiftlessness. His son had to be up and doing, taking advantage of all the advantages the father's enterprises had gained for him. Otherwise, he was no son of *his*.

In the adult struggle for success, there was little time for considering the feelings or interests of others. And so, in their alienation, in their flight to freedom, the revolting young reacted rebelliously not only in not-achieving but in sharing. They shared what money they had, clothing, shelter, even the last morsel of food—or marijuana—and their generosity, their feeling for one another, was constantly evidenced in their sharing their cars on the roads and highways. Invariably (with the exception of an inquiring reporter), the motorists picking up the vagabonding young were no older than their passengers. And they did it with joy, found in the pleasure of sharing.

Nobody could say for sure how far and how deeply the youth revolution would fan out. In some areas, it seemed caught up in aimless violence, bordering on anarchy; in others, it was thoughtful and productive, rooted in reason and determination. As an off-shoot of the electronic revolution, the protest songs of the new minstrel singers, the Beatles, Dylan, Joan Baez, had the effect almost of the Marseillaise on another revolution in another generation.

The hippies, dirty, disdained, pathetic were still an obviously strong factor in dramatizing the need for a sweeping reappraisal of old values. Mingling with hippies, Professor Fred Davis of the University of California Medical Center, saw signs of the hippie subculture sufficiently modifying the attitudes of enough adolescents to produce a lasting impact on society. Many among the young, the broad middle-group, rejected the drug-ridden aimlessness of the hippie cause, while accepting the validity of their protest.

"Hippies," observed youthful activist Olie Westheimer, "felt defeated before they started. On the other hand, we saw some of the same things that the hippies hated in the System, and we hated them too. Sure, there was hypocrisy, sham, inequities, but we felt we could combat all of this while remaining within. We could carve our own lives in society, a life different from most of the people around us, but still in it. We could find jobs we enjoyed and wanted to work at, we could have all the freedom we wanted and all the rest—without drugs or indifference to personal values."

As an activist, Olie could not stomach able-bodied people her own age carefully going through the process of applying for public welfare, while sniggering at the System giving them this largesse. "What I found hateful and childish," she commented, "was the seemingly oblivious way hippies managed to uphold their own philosophy, which preached a life outside society, while begging off that society." She had examined their use—and abuse—of drugs, and found that after a while experimentation had dwindled to pure escape.

"Drugs," said Olie, taking a long, hard look at her peers, "were an easy out, creating a false sense of achievement. If one took them, saw the opportunities life offered, the capacity for understanding within oneself, and then *stopped,* I suppose that might be helpful—especially if the person never before realized his own possibilities. But this hadn't happened in very many cases. As a rule, kids started taking drugs and kept on. Now they're cutting out on LSD, because it's finally gotten through that it does all sorts of things to the human system, genetic breaks, madness, sudden death. But they go on with something like pot, without any idea of what it's doing to them."

We had obviously become a drug culture, and the younger generation's predisposition for illegal drugs was but an extension of an adult inclination. "Student drug users," Dr. Duke Fisher of UCLA pointed out, "are not at all impressed by adults and parents preaching to them about LSD being a 'terrible thing,' at the same time that adults continue to use alcohol, nicotine and massive doses of tranquilizers." On the other hand, the Learys and Alperts, having seen the Gates of Paradise psychedelically flung open, seemed almost driven to convert others to their folly. "We have found," psychiatrist Fisher reported, "that many missionaries of LSD try to convince and exploit the young person by maintaining that the only way to really find oneself is to use LSD . . . It is unfortunate that LSD seems to arouse a very definite missionary quality in the people who use the drug, since so many LSD users who are in positions that enable them to be close to young people find it difficult to be objective when discussing LSD with the potential user."

LSD was the great escape, but all too often it was an irreversible trip. For young people, struggling with vaguely formed problems, LSD and pot induced a distorted condition that—like heroin or other narcotics—permitted the user to avoid dealing with these rankling issues, depriving him of perhaps the greatest of all human satisfactions—the pleasure of meeting on his own the challenges of everyday living.

The drugs created new problems without solving the old. "LSD," Fisher found, "not only robs the young person of a chance to deal realistically with his feelings of aggression and sexuality but it also seems to create a tendency for withdrawal and a real 'dropping out from life.'" Hopefully, concerted campaigns had formed, not only among crashees, but by authorities such as Dr. Fisher and UCLA associate, Dr. J. Thomas Ungerleider, to point up the dangers of LSD. "Those of us who want to be of service to students and young people," Fisher said, "must stop cursing LSD and look toward providing information and assistance to the young people so attracted to it."

Marijuana, too, praised by some, was under attack by others. In February of 1968, setting a positive pattern, the New York *Daily News* staged a series of student forums dramatically outlining the significance of pot in the addicting process. Florrie Fisher, a heroin addict for twenty-five years, told adolescent audiences:

"You're not hearing this from the horse's mouth, I am the horse! It is true what the doctors say that marijuana is not physically addictive, but I know it is psychologically addictive. The hell with statistics—I am unto myself a statistic."

Her introduction to pot was familiar in today's context. "I wanted to identify with the boy I thought was gorgeous—a zoot suiter [the hippie of her generation], the whole bit, peg pants, the key chain. He smoked pot, so I did."

She soon discovered she was an addictive personality, as she went from one kick to a greater. "I don't *think* marijuana leads to heroin and cocaine," she said, "I *know* it. I know a thousand junkies, and they all started with pot, like me."

She enjoyed her kicks, before they made a slave of her. "I'm not going to lie to you," she told the youngsters, "I won't tell you that shooting dope didn't make me feel great. At gut level, I liked that feeling. But, intellectually, I know now that I cannot take one smoke of pot, one snort of Horse, one needle of heroin. I *am* an addict, not *was,* but *am.* I *am* an addict who hasn't used anything for years."

The strength of the pro-marijuana propaganda was reflected by the doubts of listening pot smokers, who had been told pot was no worse than tobacco or booze.

"I don't know why," one girl sniffed, "anybody on pot would need anymore psychiatric help than a cigarette smoker."

Florrie knew it wasn't enough to say that pot leads to something worse; she had already said that. Marijuana, as she had observed, could drastically alter the life style. "I know people who never graduated from marijuana," she said, "and on marijuana they committed crimes of passion and were electrocuted. They didn't have time to graduate to heroin."

The turn to drugs obviously reflected not only a need for young people to find a place for themselves in a confused and confusing world, but an abject loss in the faith of their fathers. The Maharishi Maheshi Yogi, the Eastern guru who attracted many Western seekers, including the Beatles and actress Mia Farrow, pertinently observed that the age of faith was gone, replaced by the era of experimentation. "The modern mind," he pontificated, "finds control restricting."

With one aspect of the Maharishi's philosophy, almost any seeker could readily agree: that the world's problems stemmed from the combined unhappiness of many individuals, and that racial strife and wars were the result of a great "peacelessness."

Had this "peacelessness," so clearly manifested in adolescent drug use, crystallized into an unparalleled revolt and rejection? Perhaps, as some suggested, our cities had grown too big, too fast, our technology made communication too intense, too rapidly, and in the giant sprawl that had risen about him, so chaotically and frighteningly impersonal, man had to search unprecedentedly to find anything of himself in his changing universe. The search through drugs for a personal self was readily apparent. In his revealing study of college level LSD users, Professor Robert Schwieder, the enterprising California sociologist, attempted to equate the growing drug problem to a growing revolt against monolithic conformity and the faceless anonymity it produced.

Nowhere was this conformity more rigidly stereotyped than in suburbia. "Considerable effort was made to create an environment that isolated the youngsters from the rest of the world." Schwieder explained, "Great effort was made to control the reading material of the growing youngsters. Only 'wholesome,' noncontroversial books were permitted. On the whole, the system was safe, only one set of ideas was presented to the child."

Suburbia was a tight, middle-class society. "Children were told they needed a college education to get the kind of jobs they would desire. In junior high school, they were told the grades needed to get into college. Any search for ideas that might result in a conflict [with the norm] was beaten down with the threat, 'This will not get you into college. Keep your grades up and conform.'" And the pot of gold at the end of the rainbow was tantalizingly dangled: "Conform now, so you can become free in the future."

Out of this stress on conformity came the "cookie cutter" education that so many dropouts and turn-ons so bitterly described, with its almost total dehumanization of teacher-student relationship. "The college class today may contain one hundred and fifty or more students. The professor does discuss the great men and their great ideas in a comprehensive way, but he cannot test student comprehensions of these ideas by lengthy essay tests. The only thing left are multiple choice or true or false questions. To pass these tests, the student had no need to understand ideas, but only definitions or fact that fit into a machine grading system. His higher education, instead of being the personal thing of a generation ago, had become part of the machine age."

The dropout didn't necessarily drop out of college, physically, but psychologically was no longer committed to the large society's value system. "He says to hell with a system that destroys individuals by reducing them to non-feeling computers," Schwieder found. "And he has, meanwhile, lost faith in anyone's ability to actually change the system so that a student could be human and get an education. Everywhere he looks, he sees the system becoming more powerful and the individual being swallowed up by desire for both tranquillity and the goodies of society."

The dropouts, dropping out bodily, had a corresponding contempt for the system they flatly rejected, and consequently looked to one another for justification and comfort. "These dropouts say that society, by declaring them outside the system, has only served to drive them closer to each other, thereby creating an atmosphere where they could interact at a deeply felt, highly personal level."

In the move to slip the shackles, the drug scene was a rather logical development. "These young men and women were raised in a society that instilled inhibitions on feelings as well as sheltering them from feelings. Any felt recognition of sexuality at even a verbal level was disrupting. Many youngsters who tried to interact with another human being in a deeply felt way, found they were prevented from doing so because of their own inhibitions. When they tried to discover their feelings, their lifetime of feeling-control, and their ego defense systems, prevented them from feeling much of anything."

In his group of middle-class LSD users, Schwieder had discovered the same stifling value system in the field of ideas. "They found little or nothing in the formal educational background to stimulate them. When they attempted to use their life experiences, they said the experiences were gutless and meaningless to the point of being absurd."

And so they kept seeking. "They turned to other devices that ranged through folk songs that do examine meaningful issues to bombarding themselves with eardrum damaging music or blinding light shows. Anything that will permit them to feel. Not necessarily to feel pleasure—they were quite willing even to feel kinds of pain, because pain is new and considered valuable."

Drugs were an easy way of breaking down inhibitions that got in the way of feeling. "Their need to feel," Schwieder emphasized, "found an outlet in highs—marijuana, barbiturates, amphetamines. They discovered combinations (chemical) which produced various kinds of feelings, each with its own kind of 'high.' A majority seemed to find through these drugs that they could begin to relate to other human beings! Others reacted differently. Some discovered that the amphetamines, barbiturates and marijuana removed their felt need to relate to others. For them, these drugs acted like the traditional narcotic—the drug experience became an end in itself."

Even knowing the dangers of brain and genetic damage, they had still taken LSD. And for Schwieder, there was the glimmering of a reason. "Most of the young," he observed, "have heard about the dangers—brain damage, even chromosome damage—but they know of the 'non-feeling' damage as well!"

Still, with the LSD casualty list swiftly building up, there was a trend to other drugs, mistakenly considered less dangerous, marijuana and the amphetamines. The need hadn't changed. "The revolt back to the feeling level," as Schwieder saw it, "was here to stay." And those closed off emotionally, would try ever new techniques permitting them to feel. The young, like their elders, had the alternative of finding stimulation within themselves, in faith, in God and the universe of which they were a part, or of continuing on a destructive course with drugs. "In the final analysis," sociologist Schwieder reasoned, "man perhaps is faced with an impossible problem—if he does not become more rational, he will destroy himself. On the other hand, if he does become more rational at the expense of his feelings, he has destroyed himself."

In the cycle of evolution was it significant that the unprecedented young people's revolution was occurring at this special juncture in human affairs? How much was due to the instant communication through the electronic revolution, heartening young revolutionaries all over the world with the certain knowledge they were not alone in their struggle? How much was attributable to a totally destructive H-bomb and an endless succession of wars, culminating in the senseless war in Vietnam, which in its very senselessness, disillusioned not only the youth of this country, but of the world, with the war-making Establishment.

"Man has long had within his grasp the means to transform his will, his goals and his character," said the magazine *Pace,* an instrument of moral rearmament, "not only to tame the forces of nature but to harness his own primitive hates, fears and greeds. He is endowed with the fascinating ability to think beyond his horizons and also to care for people beyond his acquaintance."

And *Pace* asked, as so many had:

"Why hasn't he done these things before?"

And it answered, as others had:

"Perhaps the horrible consequences of not changing did not threaten his survival as they do now."

Just as the Kershaws spoke optimistically of a growth in purpose through personal involvement, so, too, did *Pace,* reflecting a current that ran hopefully through the youth movement:

"Today, man is at the edge of a breakthrough in living, in character expansion. A new optimism has come in his thinking, an enthusiasm to see things improved and changed."

As youth saw it, the change would be sweeping, not through putting a few patches on the seat of the Establishment's pants, but through the evolution of a new outlook, which would as inevitably produce needed change as the dark clouds produced rain. In the activism of the New Breed lay the prospect of ultimately implementing the Great Teacher's lessons of two thousand years ago. It had little to do with science or savants. "The power to do this," *Pace* pointed out, "springs not out of the mouth of test tubes, the eyepiece of a microscope, the pages of a book, the pronouncements from pulpit, podium or political platform, but out of the lives of people who boldly put aside the cynical past and take up the challenge to live as sons and daughters of God—to replace hate with concern, indifference with love, materialism with faith, to become, in fact, the kind of people required for the twenty-first century."

And that, discounting certain of youth's misadventures with drugs, seemed to be where it was all at.

30710

HV
5825
S7

Stearn, Jess.

The seekers

DATE DUE			
DEC 15 1986			
NOV 29 1993			
DEC 18 1994			
OCT 5 1995			

Villa Julie College Library
Stevenson, MD 21153

DATE DUE

DEC 0 8 2003		

GAYLORD   #3523PI   Printed in USA